THIS BOOK WAS
PRESENTED TO THE
LIBRARY
BY THE AUTHOR

D0296073

THE BLIGHT OF BLAIRISM

F. A. R. Bennion

Lester Publishing
OXFORD

Published by

Lester Publishing
29 PEGASUS ROAD, OXFORD OX4 6DS
brianleste@aol.com

© F. A. R. BENNION
www.francisbennion.com

The moral rights of the author have been asserted.

First published 2002

ISBN 0 9542855 0 6

PORTSMOUTH CITY COUNCIL LIBRARY SERVICE	
320· 941	0954285506
	C800214712

Printed in Great Britain by Biddles Ltd, Surrey.
www.biddles.co.uk

To Gerald Howarth MP

Other books by Francis Bennion

Ethics

The Sex Code: Morals for Moderns
Professional Ethics: The Consultant Professions
  and their Code

Law

Statute Law
Statutory Interpretation
Understanding Common Law Legislation
Halsbury's Laws of England (title Statutes)
Tangling with the Law: Reforms in Legal Process
Consumer Credit Control
The Consumer Credit Act Manual
Constitutional Law of Ghana

Fiction

Victorian Railway Days

Poetry

Poemotions: Bennion Undraped

Contents

1   Pandering to the populace   7
2   Reforming the House of Lords   19
3   Integrity and disability   26
4   End of another old song   29
5   The Queen's Speech: a British institution   32
6   Fur and the mayor   35
7   Electronic communications   38
8   Too big for some of us to grasp   41
9   Fighting for the jury   44
10 Elections and referendums   50
11 Section 28 and the homophobes   56
12 A curious measure – the Disqualifications Bill   62
13 Prime Minister's Questions   66
14 Lord Chancellor's Questions   69
15 Rewriting history in the Court of Appeal   72
16 The *Marchioness* and fancy dancing   78
17 Henry VIII is alive and kicking   81
18 Mr Shaun Woodward's lecture on decent behaviour .   84
19 CRAPS dropped   88
20 Mr Baldry MP and the Indian Moneylender   91
21 Education gimmickry   95
22 Red Ken and hunting pink   98
23 The Human Rights Act   101
24 Corporate homicide   104
25 The sad case of Mrs Loizidou   108
26 A professional body for teachers   111
27 The House of Lords inspects itself   114
28 Prohibiting fur farming   117
29 The Whitsun adjournment – and multiculturalism . .   120
30 Inspecting the Crown Prosecution Service   129
31 Laura Spence and the Hallowed Halls of Academe . .   135
32 More feet on the beat in London?   138
33 The right to roam   141
34 Pub names: true Courage and good Manners   144
35 Madam Speaker and the Sultan of Spin   147
36 Rising for the summer recess   150
37 The Religion (Relief from Trivialisation) Bill   153
38 Open letter to an Asian would-be MP   159

39 Word hijacking – discrimination again 164
40 Jimmy Hood and the fuel crisis 168
41 Misgivings on the International Criminal Court. . . . 174
42 In honour of Mrs Dunwoody 177
43 Lord Donaldson of Lymington and
    the Parliament Acts 180
44 Rooted in dishonour? 183
45 Jokes and the Queen's Speech 187
46 Finding Britain's place in an enlarged Europe 190
47 Gazumping, gazundering, daisy chains etc 193
48 Improving our tax law: a brave try 196
49 Why this conspiracy of silence? 199
50 On the morning after the night before. 204
51 When religion mattered 207
52 When shall we join the euro?. 212
53 What shall we do about Derry? 215
54 Opening the doors of libraries 218
55 Ageism and beardism 221
56 A candid friend of Viscount Tonypandy 224
57 A Filkin filleting or Vazectomy 227
58 The Commons at its best 230
59 Foot and mouth 237
60 Does your credit need repairing? 240
61 Our Armed Forces and the modern world 243
62 Ulster the endless problem. 247
63 Women-only short lists 257
64 The problem with voting 260
65 Mrs Dunwoody triumphs 263
66 More word hijacking – this time it's 'investment'. . . 266
67 Jo Moore the merrier 269
68 Blair's Nemisis: Daft Mo 282
69 Blairism buried 288
70 What is Blairism? 304
    Index 311

1

Pandering to the Populace

I come to expose the horrible blight of Blairism, for it is
indeed a horrible, treacherous, wicked doctrine. For the
true English it stinks to high heaven. Negating and
contradicting all that old England stands for, Blair –
himself privileged to be a highly-educated product of old
England (public school and Oxford) – should we think drop
on his knees, abase himself, kiss the English ground, and
confess his shame at the vile things he has done, is doing,
and is determined in the future to do to degrade still
further, and more and more, until it sinks into the mud, our
noble old country England. That abasement, one knows,
will not happen. Shame is not in the Blair vocabulary, at
least when applied to himself. So he needs to be exposed.
Obviously he has to be exposed. He must be exposed. It is
very high time he was exposed. Someone has to do it. If no
one else will do it, I will. Quaffing my Somerset cider, lying
at ease in a tavern near Taunton, by God I will take up pen
and do it! So here goes.

During each of the eighty years of my life I have agonised
at the insidious year by year undermining of my wonderful
country England, once seen as best in all the world. As a
schoolboy I celebrated, with the others, Empire Day. We
British had shouldered the White Man's burden and taught
Africa proper values (which they then promptly forgot). We
had brought enlightenment to India, and taught its people
valuable lessons (which they still appreciatively retain). We
had presented our high values to other parts of the world. It
all deserved, and deserves, to be celebrated, but where is
Empire Day now? Where indeed is the Empire? Where even
is the Commonwealth? Sunk, one would have to say, in a
dismal morass – and about to disappear out of sight. Blair
looked the other way while all this was happening, and sent
his best wishes to Mr Mugabe.

This book is a late, late, perhaps too late, probably far too
late, clarion call in defence of my old England against
wicked Blairism. The Englishman Tony Blair, privileged to

be our present Prime Minister, panders to the populace only at one level – the lowest. What England means at higher levels passes him by in public (though I'm sure not in private). In his heart of hearts this Blair is really and truly an élitist, but for reasons of political ambition masquerades as an egalitarian. Nothing is more pathetic than the clever man dressing down to please the boorish populace, and with them the all-important boorish media. Blair is shameless in that regard. Swallowing another gulp of Somerset cider I say: watch out. As G K Chesterton once wrote, we are the people of England that never have spoken yet.

We are talking here about the Right Honourable Tony Blair, a highly ambitious élitist barrister who became Prime Minister of the United Kingdom when new Labour won the general election of 1997 and was continued in that office when new Labour won the following general election in 2001. Blair accomplished this difficult double feat by pandering to the populace in a very clever Fettes-and-Oxford way. His expensive, exclusive, education had taught him what was required to gain and retain power in a democracy. Being ambitious, he went on to profit from that. He enthusiastically pandered to the populace, still does so pander, and will go on doing so until he is stopped.

My cherished edition of the *Encyclopedia Britannica* is the eleventh, published in 1911. It is regarded by those who know about these things as the best ever edition of that work, since it was the last to be produced by Cambridge University. (At that point they sold it to the Americans, renouncing élitism in favour of hard cash.) What that 1911 edition says about Blair's public school is –

> Fettes College, an imposing structure in a semi-Gothic style, designed by David Bryce and called after its founder Sir William Fettes (1750-1836), is organized on the model of the great English public schools.

So the Scots, as so often, copied England. If the great English public schools were not élitist what were they? What indeed are they, down to today? The same goes for Oxford University, my own alma mater and Blair's: England's oldest university. It was established in the Isis water meadows, not so far from Magna Carta's Runneymede, in the long-ago twelfth century when the Norman King Henry II was on the throne of England. After 1066 the Norman-French invaders settled down to mould the Anglo-Saxons into the England we know today. Our country remained much the same for a thousand years, shaping a distinct populace and a homogenous people. At the end of that period, soon after World War Two, came the massive incursions from outside. They were calculated to destroy England as a nation, but astonishingly many English people did not care about that. A good few (or should I say a bad few?) even welcomed it. They did not care about England. Let 'em all come they said. Either these people did not realise that to let everyone in would destroy England (in which case they were stupid) or they positively rejoiced in the destruction of England (in which case they were traitors). Take your choice. The result is the same, either way.

What did all that English history matter to ambitious Tony Blair when towards the end of the 1990s there were votes to be won from not being élitist, indeed dumping on élitism: votes that would put his little self in power? It was time, little Blair thought, to deny his English origins and don a politic disguise. This was startlingly successful, and bred a virus we now know as Blairism. The slimy microbes proliferated, and now threaten to bring down our famous constitution. Indeed they may already have done so, though I hope not. There may still be a time for rescue, if readers heed this warning. But you will all have to wake up from your long doze. One defect of the English is that they are very good at dozing. When you warn them of a future danger they open one eye and say: let's wait till it's here; it may never come. I would say, as the Americans in our former colony say, let's kick some ass!

Blairism, a British political phenomenon of the twenty-first century (though it began late in the twentieth), may be seen as the ultimate manifestation of the intellectual shame and degradation known as Democracy. This form of government panders to the ignorant populace, instead of doing what intelligence and art tells us ought to be done to achieve humanity's highest aims. Winston Churchill caught the essence when he described Democracy as the worst possible form of government – except all the others

9

that have been tried. That is the nub. The other forms of government depend on the honesty, ability and sincerity of individual autocratic rulers. Thinking of Mr Mugabe and others, we realise that cannot be guaranteed; is indeed unlikely. So in the end of our civilisation we were landed *faute de mieux* with the dreaded and defeated system of government known as Democracy, imposing on us all the lowest of the low when it came to standards. It happened because there was no practical alternative. The élitist, highly educated, Mr Blair knew and understood all that – and decided to profit from it. There were spoils to be won, and he fancied grabbing them.

The system known as Democracy places rule ultimately in the hands of the ignorant populace. It is assumed, without much evidence, that these ill-bred uneducated people can be trusted, in their own interest, to do what is right for the community as a whole. When assisted by an active and honest civil service (such as obtains on the whole in England, *pace* Mr Stephen Byers), this system may seem to work up to a point. Yet it can still be crass and abortive, as Blairism demonstrates.

Blair has decided that English children should be taught citizenship. His syllabuses for doing this do it is true contain some obvious good sense, for example that pupils should be taught the elements of our criminal justice system and how central and local government works in England. I am not so sure about phrases like these (taken from Key stages 3 and 4 in the official Blair programme of study for 'citizenship'): 'the diversity of national, regional, religious and ethnic identities', 'the world as a global community', and 'the wider issues and challenges of global interdependence and responsibility'. On the contrary I think our children should be instructed first and foremost in their heritage of English values. Later on, as they grow near adulthood, they may take their own decisions about whether or not to investigate wider horizons. That is a matter of free choice for them. We believe it is a grave mistake to confuse young children with such wider issues before they have secured a firm grasp on their own inherited culture and values. Otherwise they possess no secure touchstone against which to contrast and measure alien concepts, and so may be led into confusion.

The concept of English citizenship (like many other such concepts) involves a number of compartments of knowledge and thought, which need to be fitted together. They are not static, for nothing human stays still. But a society like England needs to be careful how it permits them to develop and change. We English need to remember that such evolution is always within our control, and in that regard we must exert our power as a nation. This is a question of values, and naturally we want our English values to prevail in our own country England, just as say Muslims want their values to prevail in *their* own countries, which are very many throughout the world. (Muslims make very sure that this is in fact what happens.) We want our values to be at all times the best. Yet they must remain *English* values, shared and propagated by our adults and handed down by us to our children through the medium of our schools system. (Yes, teachers are meant to *teach!*)

One aspect of our history concerns class. John Major famously said that he looked forward to making ours a classless society, in which he is not thought to have succeeded. Margaret Thatcher said that class is a communist concept, grouping people in bundles and setting them against one another. This contains an element of truth. People are indeed grouped in bundles, though this has not anything to do with communism. In England the bundles are formed of like-minded people. A person may find himself or herself in a number of different bundles. If you are an Arsenal supporter, you are in a bundle composed of Arsenal supporters. If you are also a barrister, you are in a bundle composed of barristers. If you are a barrister specialising in company law you are in a smaller bundle composed of company law barristers. And so on. Most of us find ourselves in a large number of different bundles. Some of these may have class connotations; others not.

Many people have written about this topic of class. One of the most helpful is David Cannadine in his *Class in Britain* (1998). In that book he says that there are many ways in which people envision the social order. 'Thus regarded, the history of all hitherto existing society is no longer the history of class struggles: rather, it is the history of a limitless number of individual self-categorisations and subjective social descriptions – of which class is only one among a multitude of competing and frequently changing vocabularies'. My point is that English children and adults should concentrate on the vocabularies that properly belong to their own country, though that does not of course preclude reasonable participation in wider international matters. However such participation by an English person should reflect his or her cultural identity.

I mentioned above the various social bundles into which people find themselves strapped. Where does class come in here? In particular is it still relevant and helpful to talk of the upper class, the middle class and the lower or working class? In 1976 Patrick Hutber, then city editor of the *Sunday Telegraph*, wrote an excellent book entitled *The decline and fall of the Middle Class and how it can fight back*. This book was based on the proposition that there was such a thing in England as the middle class, and that it should fight its corner against such onslaughts as the taxation horrors of the Chancellor of the Exchequer Denis Healey (now Lord Healey) in his three 1974 budgets. This essentially middle class product of Bradford Grammar School and Balliol had as his main aim a wholesale redistribution of wealth and income in England, a reminder that much political and other agitation has nothing to do with ethnic or cultural questions.

In truth such labels as upper class, middle class and so on are too crude and broad to be helpful in most contexts. Class has a more subtle meaning in many areas. A particular person may indeed find himself or herself strapped into many different bundles, but most of them will have a common dimension. If an Oxford professor is within bundles labelled 'opera lover', 'student of politics', 'expert in old silver' and 'Chelsea supporter' we can see that three at least of these are homogenous. If we hesitate to apply to him a label such as upper middle class, because it is too inexact, we would still wish to attach to him some label, such as highly-educated aesthete. Obviously many such labels could be devised, and when meticulously allocated they would have a great deal of social significance. In our minds (often silently) we do allocate them.

They correspond to the bunch of people with whom we feel most at home and comfortable, and that surely is what class means today. Blair's favoured concept of the 'inclusive society' contradicts that, and is false to human nature. Cannadine says of Tony Blair 'he is primarily interested in talking about community, consensus and conciliation, and class gets in the way of such talk'. That may be true, but then Tony is a politician, always with his eye on gathering votes and being re-elected. The rest of us perceive that culturally class, if properly defined, is still an important concept in our lives.

All right, Blair is ambitious – but so are most politicians. What distinguishes Blair is that his ambition knows no bounds. His style has been called presidential. This is because Blair senses that in the United Kingdom of the twenty-first century the appeal to the populace of Her Majesty the Queen is lessening. A growing number of Her Majesty's supposedly loyal subjects are calling for a Republic to replace what they see as the outdated Monarchy. In the opinion of the Blairite faction, no one could more suitably be found to head the expected, anticipated, new Republic of the United Kingdom than the said Tony Blair. We must be on our guard against this man. His ambition is overweening.

That is not all. The European Union is heading for its ultimate personification as the United States of Europe. Such a tremendous, echoing body must also soon require a president for its head. Who would be more suitable, when the time at last arrives, than the revered Tony Blair, presumed to be currently, at that future time, already President of the United Kingdom of Great Britain and (possibly) Northern Ireland? (I say 'possibly' because Blair has done his utmost to detach us from that mostly loyal body of British citizens.)

Still further down the line into the future there is persuasive talk of a World Government, possibly happening within the lifetime of the young among us. There too a President will be needed. Modestly, Tony Blair acknowledges that he bears that possibility in mind also. He is working towards that end. All it needs is a little nudging, and that might quite possibly happen. . . Blair admits he is not worthy of such honour, but that might not stop him attaining it. Perhaps we British should be grateful that one of our own might be so crowned. But the decent ones among us feel it should not have been so obviously sought.

The horrible blight of Blairism functions in the following way. You must offer the ignorant populace what they think they want. If you are a clever Fettes and Oxford barrister you know very well that what the populace think they want is often not going to be good for them, and so not what they ought to want. To tell them this would smack of paternalism, and so not be politically correct. It would seem patronising, and so again would not be politically correct. Blair loves to be politically correct. Therefore (says Blair to himself, prompted by his equally-clever wife Cherie) you must appear to shun it, and tack along another way. It may be dishonest not to come clean on the product of your educated thoughts about such essential matters, but never mind all that. Blairism requires suppression of such qualms. It has not got very much to do with honesty.

So if you are a Blairite considering Nye Bevan's flawed masterpiece the National Health Service you close your eyes to the fact that it is ridiculous that patients who can afford to do so should not be required to pay for their vital healthcare just because they don't want to. You pander to the populace and let them escape such just payments, so that they can afford to jet off to the Costa Brava and elsewhere for their usual year round holidays. That is the treachery of Blairism.

If you are a Blairite observing the plight of our kith and kin at the infamous hands of the vicious dictator Mugabe in what used to be called Southern Rhodesia you look the other way, leave them to their fate, and fly off to chat to immaculate democrats such as Mr Putin of Russia or the current replacement for the despotic Emperor of China.

If you are a Blairite wondering what to do about the hectic problems of Northern Ireland you forget all about what used to be called treason. You ignore the fact that County Down is just as much a part of the United Kingdom as the county of Surrey, and collude with its traitorous enemies. You look the other way when the British subject Gerry Adams refers to his very own Prime Minister (Mr

Blair) as 'the British Prime Minister'. You grant Adams lavish allowances and a handsome office suite in the Palace of Westminster, where he has no business to be since he will not take the required oath or affirmation of allegiance to the British head of state (not, as yet, Mr Blair). That once more is Blairism.

Another feature of Blairism is that you must constantly change the familiar features in our nation's landscape. Blair cleverly calls it modernizing, and is indifferent to the well-worn plea that if it ain't broke you don't fix it. That takes me back to my schooldays. He is part of your English heritage, so study Shakespeare, said Field Marshal Viscount Allenby. We callow youths in the Harrow School Speech Room sniggered. To us boys at that time, Shakespeare was a byword for tedium. And Field Marshal Viscount Allenby was if anything worse. So of course we let off a few stink bombs. We sniped and sniggered, stupid snots that we were. In our extreme youth, even though from good homes, we did not know any better. But Blair does know better.

I too have learnt better since. Today not many people bother to read word for word the texts of Shakespeare's plays. This is not surprising, because to the mostly uneducated folk of our time, known as the populace, they are impenetrable. Yet to try to glean is worth the effort: you come out feeling amazed. These plays, we are told, were written for the London groundlings of the sixteenth century at the Globe Theatre on the south bank of the Thames. How could these ignorant illiterate peasants have understood the elaborate sophisticated wordplay Shakespeare deploys in his wonderful plays? Where did he learn that advanced language? I do not know, and nor does anyone else – but we still revere the plays. They have much to tell the people of today (who include Mr Blair, as well as the populace). Take Lear 1.iv. The duke of Albany says: 'Striving to better, oft we mar what's well'. How concise the language! How neatly it fits Tony Blair's senseless desire for everlasting change under the tiresome catchword modernization! How well Shakespeare deserves his place at the head of our literary canon! But Blairites reject the idea of a literary canon, to be handed down to future generations. To them Bob Dylan is as worthy a poet as Dylan Thomas.

Another sinister aspect of Blairism is the rejection of we English people who are white (still the vast majority). We are the old inhabitants. We were born white, and we will die white. Blair himself is white. Nearly all English people are white. Blair's (white) appointment as executive head of the BBC, Greg Dyke, infamously complained that its staff were 'hideously white'. Blair's (white) appointment as chairman of the BBC governors, Gavyn Davies, infamously complained that the whites take more than their fair share of the BBC output and prefers to favour Asian youths on the streets of Leicester.

Nowadays, under Blairism, to be white is to be somehow regarded as third class. To be Asian fawn is better. To be Afro-Caribbean black is best. Today that's how you get the top jobs – especially within the British Broadcasting Corporation or BBC, whose Reithian motto is 'Nation shall speak peace unto Nation'. Surely we can speak peace without renouncing our nature. I am grateful to be white (and I bet Tony Blair is too). I celebrate it, rather in the manner of F W Rolfe in the following poem. It was written in 1890, a sensible time when boys and men bathed naked in public.

Deep blue water as blue can be,
Rocks rising high where the red clouds flare,
Boys of the colour of ivory,
Breasting the wavelets, and diving there,
White boys, ruddy, and tanned and bare,
With lights and shadows of rose and grey,
And the sea like pearls in their shining hair,
The boys who bathe in St Andrews bay.

A summer night, and a sapphire sea,
A setting sun, and a golden glare:
Hurled from the height where the wild rocks be,
Wondrous limbs in the luminous air,
Fresh as white flame, flushed and fair,
Strong young arms in the salt sea spray,
And the sea seems alive with them everywhere,
The boys who bathe in St Andrews Bay.

So I say to hell with rejecting us because we are white –
especially when the one who rejects is white himself.

There is much much more that is wrong with Blairism,
and indeed with Democracy. The best things in our lives
derive not from Democracy but Aristocracy, though I
hardly dare venture to say that. Whispering and cowering,
I faintly suggest, seconds before I am clobbered, that we are
still battening on the fruits of a system we have lately
rushed, under Blair's leadership, to despise and throw
overboard. Where would our tourism industry be without
the magnificent castles and mansions built by British
aristocrats of the past (and the same goes for Ireland's
tourism industry)? Blair has the cheek to call all this our
'heritage', while basely rejecting the forces that brought it
into being and ejecting its representatives from the second
house of our Parliament which is named after them, the
House of Lords. He prefers to stuff it with the gang who
have gained the title Tony's cronies.

What sort of culture would we enjoy if we relied entirely
on what goes on today? The only answer is a council house
culture, and who in their senses wants that? If anyone
doubts what I am saying let them listen to a performance of
that haunting song, which has captivated us all for the past
seventy years, *A Nightingale Sang in Berkeley Square*.
Under Blairism it could never have been produced because
Berkeley Square would never have been produced. That
trite popular song harks back to a past essentially based on
élitism. The word is anathema to the Blairites, yet it holds
the key to the true culture we still rush to worship. The
hypocrite Blair is in the forefront of that rush.

There are many more incidents in the lamentable
chronicle of the rise and cheap success of Blairism, but I
will not go on just now. Instead what I propose to do is
present some snapshots of what so far has actually
happened under Blair as Prime Minister of our beloved
land. Concrete example is more effective than generalized
hand-wringing. The following chapters of this book give
some examples of what I have observed, pretty closely at
that, of what can happen to us under the clammy populist
regime of Mr Blair. They give chapter and verse, because I
am a man brought up to be careful and scholarly, and cite

his sources. I am used to doing that, though in this polemical squib I eschew those aids detested by dumbed-down Blairites, namely footnotes.

At the end of the book I offer some reflections on the ghastly fate that, if we are not very careful, may await us all at the hands of this man Blair and his horrible cohorts. The final word is: England arise and gird up your loins! Wake up to the blight of Blairism before it is all too late and England is lost for ever.

2

Reforming the House of Lords

Towards the end of 1999, just after having been asked to write the weekly political series on which this book is largely based, I went downstairs to watch Prime Minister's questions on the Parliament Channel. The spectacle seemed safe and ordinary, even dull. Speaker Betty Boothroyd, well-upholstered and comfortable, kept the MPs in order like Matron in the rowdy dorm of a boys' prep school under the old wholesome dispensation. The Leader of the Opposition, William Hague, fired awkward questions at the Prime Minister. In reply, Mr Blair did every clever thing but answer the question. He shot back little teasers at Mr Hague, which that gentleman likewise side-stepped. It was familiar, predictable and cosy. There was much laughing and good-natured mickey-taking. Gordon Brown, Chancellor of the Exchequer, grinned at his opposite number – whoever that was. Had I perhaps taken on a boring task?

I soon got my answer. Watching the TV news later that evening I learnt that gunmen had invaded the Armenian Parliament and shot dead the Prime Minister and the Speaker. That is not likely to happen at Westminster, even in the dire 21st century. I felt that we British need to value the privileges we enjoy, and opened my notebook.

In the Lords on 26 October 1999 the Earl of Burford leapt on the Woolsack in protest while his noble colleagues were debating the House of Lords Bill. This was designed to end the right of hereditary peers to sit and vote in our second chamber. There would soon be an interim House of Lords composed of 550 life peers and 92 hereditary survivors. How will it behave? Perhaps the members will feel more free to challenge the Government, since the new House will have greater democratic legitimacy than the old largely hereditary House of Lords. We shall see how it all works out.

What composition and powers will the permanent second chamber have? That remains shrouded. The Royal

Commission considering the matter was required to report by the end of 1999. In evidence to it I made various suggestions, some of which I will go on to mention for what they are worth. I believe the new second chamber should not have power to reject a Government Bill, and any amendments it makes to such a Bill should be solely for the purpose of improving the working of the resulting Act. They should not be wrecking amendments. There needs to be a provision corresponding to the Parliament Acts 1911 and 1949 to ensure that the Government of the day retains control of its legislation.

Wisely, the Royal Commission was required by its terms of reference to have regard to the need to maintain the position of the House of Commons as the pre-eminent chamber of Parliament. For this reason I believe that members of the second chamber should not be elected by any form of universal suffrage. Such election is the sovereign badge of democratic legitimacy. The nation should not have one lot of elected members (the House of Commons) ranged against a second chamber any of whose members could claim a like or similar democratic backing. It does not take a terrier dog to grasp the bickering that arrangement would produce.

As members of the second chamber (let us call them Senators) we need aware people of individual independence, with a record of competence and experience in relevant areas of the national life. By 'aware' I mean people with some idea of what parliamentary processes involve. Here intelligence is required, as well as experience and knowledge. Even under 21st century democracy the sullen lumpen proletariat must submit to being ruled by their betters (for they do have betters). That is so even though the scheme does reluctantly accept hated élitism. In my view élitism should not merely be accepted but hailed by the populace as their salvation. We do not want the blind leading the blind. We need the cleverest and best to lead us.

Regrettably, the new Senators would not be the landed or aristocratic betters of olden days. Rather they would be the more mundane so-called betters who can show they know something of the present world. When it comes to amending and passing Bills the Senators also need to have at least a rudimentary knowledge of how legislation works, which is not a skill that is common. None of these Senators should be regarded as the delegate of any outside organisation such as a professional body (e.g. the General Medical Council or the Law Society) or a representative body (e.g. the Trades Union Council or the Local Government Association).

In addition there should be a fairly large number of ex officio appointments to the second chamber, (which I am now calling the Senate). The disadvantage is that some office holders may be thought unsuitable for parliamentary service. The advantage is that the invidiousness of personal selection, with its accompanying risk of canvassing, favouritism and prejudice, is avoided by automatic ex officio appointment. Furthermore many worthy people do not wish to submit their names for this kind of selective process and might otherwise regrettably be lost to the nation's counsels.

So I suggest that willing retired holders of state offices such as the following, if not currently MPs in the House of Commons, should automatically be members of the second chamber or Senate (subject to an age limit): cabinet minister, permanent secretary in the Civil Service, senior armed forces officer, law lord, senior ambassador, British EU Commissioner, Bank of England Governor, Regius professor and so forth. All these would be persons who had been appointed to their posts officially (usually by or on the advice of the Prime Minister). Office holders not appointed officially should not rank for ex officio appointment, because it is not right that membership of a basic element in the constitution should depend to any extent on private patronage.

There has been talk of appointment of other members being made by an Appointments Commission. That cannot be the answer. Who is to appoint the anonymous helots of the Appointments Commission? This can only be Mr Blair, so he would be appointing members of the second chamber or Senate at one remove. It is better to grasp the nettle and accept that the Prime Minister should appoint directly. An alternative, if we must have this system, would be to let the Cabinet appoint. Now let me give you a letter from

Viscount Davidson published in *The Times* on 18 January 2001.

> It is clearer by the day that the reform of the House of Lords has become not only a dog's breakfast but a farce. In that spirit might I in all seriousness suggest that the Government repeal the Life Peerages Act, abolish all life peers, bring back all the hereditaries, and start all over again?

This echoed what I had been thinking for some time. For the British it is not for many reasons satisfactory either to elect or appoint members of the second or revising chamber. The hereditary principle is retained for the Monarchy, an institution which meets with much acclaim. If we were sensible we would now go back to supporting the hereditary Monarchy with its former support, an hereditary Peerage.

I offer one simple reason for doing this. In former days an hereditary peer was created by the Monarch, on the advice of the Prime Minister, because the person in question was of supreme worth (I am speaking of the period before the infamous days of Lloyd George and Maundy Gregory, when peerages were openly bought and sold). Science now tells us that the genes of such a peer of first creation were likely to have been superior to those of most other people. In his or her heirs those genes were likely also to produce, down the line, superior offspring, well capable of governing. I know that too often the aristocracy did not live up to these high notions, but perhaps that was because they were not expected to.

But Mr Blair is determined on an Appointments Commission, in other words a Quango. Queen Quango, whom I shall revisit, is much loved by both the Conservative Party and the Labour Party. Why is that objectionable? Because this unregal Queen, not answerable to anyone, performs state functions which in this country in the 21st century should instead be carried out by a Government answerable to the electorate.

Particularly obnoxious is the emerging Quango called the Appointments Commission. This monstrous beast was foreshadowed in the Government white paper *Modernising*

Parliament Reforming the House of Lords, published on 20 January 1999. It was taken up in the Wakeham report on the future of the House of Lords. Under Wakeham the Government of the day, answerable to the people, would lose its exclusive right to determine who shall be a new member of the second Chamber, and will indeed have no such right at all. This is because, said Wakeham, the present immemorial right of appointment, exercised by recommendation to the Monarch, 'puts too much power in the hands of the Prime Minister'. The question is whether the suggested alternative does not put too much power in the hands of this faceless Quango the Appointments Commission.

The way membership of the Appointments Commission is arrived at is vital. The Wakeham report says it should consist of a mere eight people. Three should be nominees of the main political parties, and one a nominee of the Convenor of the Cross Benchers. The remaining four should be independents selected according to what are known as the Nolan principles. A minority of Appointments Commissioners should be existing members of the second Chamber. None should be an MP.

It would be outrageous to award such impressive constitutional powers to such a small body of undistinguished citizens. They are powers to appoint our law makers, who in themselves (never mind their appointors) ought to possess enormous prestige. Nevertheless both Labour and Conservatives enthusiastically embraced this horribly unsound proposal. The Conservatives went so far as to introduce into the Lords (for what reason I know not) a Bill to carry the proposal out, the Life Peerages (Appointments Commission) Bill 2000. It did not pass. Mr Blair, deciding against any such Bill, determined to slit his own throat (that is introduce the Appointments Commission) by stealth (that is by using the Royal Prerogative). The news was broken by a press notice on 4 May 2000, followed by a parliamentary question on 23 May.

Mr Gordon Prentice (Pendle): How often has the Appointments Commission met?

The Parliamentary Secretary, Privy Council Office (Mr Paddy Tipping): The Appointments Commission is an independent body, appointed on 4 May. I understand that it has not yet met, but that it will do so soon.

This new Quango will select only the non-political members of the House of Lords, that is the cross-benchers. It also takes over the functions of the Political Honours Scrutiny Committee. In the press notice Mr Blair said that he would determine the number of nominations he will invite from the Commission. He undertook to recommend their nominations to Her Majesty for the conferment of nobility 'except in the most exceptional circumstances, such as those endangering the security of the realm'. The seven members of the new Commission, chosen for some unfathomable reason with the aid of a private firm of accountants calling itself PriceWaterhouseCoopers, included three nominated by the main political parties (Lords Hurd and Dholakia, with Baroness (Brenda) Dean) and four who are relatively unknown. The doughty Mr Prentice, a Labour back-bencher, asked: 'Are we not getting ourselves in a terrible pickle over this Appointments Commission, which will be advised by a firm of chartered accountants as to the persons who are suitable for membership of the second Chamber? Will it be open to the Appointments Commission, under its terms of reference, to appoint people to the upper Chamber by random selection, in the way that juries are appointed? Is that a bizarre suggestion?

Mr. Tipping: Yes.

Sir George Young, sixth baronet (Eton and Christ Church) and former Conservative minister, showed his failure to grasp the essentials by asking whether the Government's prerogative-derived Appointments Commission was not 'but a pale shadow of the independent statutory Appointments Commission that we really need, so as to remove the enormous patronage that remains in the hands of the Prime Minister?'

Mr Tipping, dodging the question, said the Government wanted to build on the Wakeham report. He added: 'The independent Appointments Commission is an important first step. If we could arrive at a consensus on the way forward, I hope that we should quickly move to the Wakeham recommendations'.

This particular Quango is not yet securely seated on the Quango throne. However if a sleepy nation does not speedily wake up there will be no shifting her.

I return to this topic of House of Lords reform in chapter 4.

3

Integrity and Disability

The House of Commons, which Edmund Burke called the highest tribunal of the nation, is a peculiar institution. For more than half a century I watched its workings at first hand and can testify, as many others have done, that it has a character exclusively its own and retains this come what may. Despite themselves, and even against their will, it stamps those privileged to become its members with a unique impress of integrity. This was witnessed over the Blair Government's Welfare Reform and Pensions Bill, introduced in 1999.

A great point of principle was thought to be at stake with this Bill. Its opponents said that by it the Blair Government was trying to renege on the obligation to honour a nationwide contract, initiated half a century earlier by Sir William Beveridge and confirmed by Parliament. Put simply, the contract is that if you obediently pay your National Insurance contributions throughout your working life you will be entitled to your benefits in due course. Old and tired, you can retire in comfort and with honour. No one can take that right away from you. It is yours by Act of Parliament, that unshakeable guarantee (as it used to be thought). The benefits become payable when you reach retirement age, or earlier become unfit for work. They become payable even though you have through other means (for example a works pension) more than enough to live on in your old age. All that is immaterial.

For Blairite politicians it is irksome to think that under this highfalutin Beveridge scheme the state becomes obliged to make payments to people who are really quite well off (a few of them very well off). These politicians itch to tinker with Beveridge so as to withdraw the right to receive the payments from such unmeritorious folk, even though they have paid their contributions throughout their working life. Benefits, Blairites think, should be reserved for the deserving poor, or even the undeserving poor. All that really matters is that the recipients of these benefits should be 'poor'. It is obscene that any of the rich (deserving or undeserving) should get their hands on them.

Skilful politicians (and the Blairites are very skilful) know how to go about achieving such ends. You do not start with a frontal assault, withdrawing from rich *older* people (it is politically incorrect to speak of *old* people) their right to a pension. No, you begin by attacking a smaller target, say the disabled. If they succumb you have gained ground, and can later advance to attack the old (sorry, older) age pensioners. These are the tactics its opponents accused Blair's Government of deploying with the Welfare Reform and Pensions Bill.

On 4 November 1999 the Times reported that, in a fraught debate in the Commons the previous night, Labour rebels had denounced Blair's welfare reforms as a betrayal of all the party stood for. Trying to stem the onslaught, Mr Sam Galbraith MP (Labour) said: 'It is time to stop thinking of National Insurance contributions as inviolate'. Weasel words indeed. Try switching them to private insurance policies. 'It is time to stop thinking the Prudential should honour their policies and pay up as and when the small print requires'. Sickening and disgusting is all one can say – but that's Blairism.

More weasel words followed from Mr Blair: 'We actually have extended means-testing to other forms of contributory benefit. In the end it comes down to a simple question of how we spend the amount of money we are going to spend on disability'. Never mind what the disability contract says. We as a nation are justified in rejigging it provided the aggregate we spend on the disabled does not go down. And anyway, we have got away with it before. Shabby or what?

The Government made concessions worth £150 million to sweeten the pill, but still many Labour MPs voted against. That's how Commons integrity affects people. The Times reported (5 November 1999) that if peers did not toe the line when the bill returned to the Lords the partial reprieve granted by the Government to hereditary peers in the interim arrangements could be at risk. Might that be called blackmail? I rather think it might.

Not all the old traditions are being jettisoned, despite Mr Blair's onslaught on 'conservatives' (with a small c) at the 1999 Labour Party conference. On 1 November 1999 the Commons defeated by a majority of 68 a Government move to end the practice of printing two definitive copies of every Act of Parliament on vellum, a fine kind of parchment prepared from the skins of calves, lambs or kids. This would have meant a saving of £30,000 a year, but the House was unmoved by this statistic. Dr Nick Palmer, a Labour member of the Commons Administration Select Committee, which put forward the change, argued that 'Parliament should not be using animal products where it is not necessary'.

Voting as usual with their feet (clad in animal products) even his own MPs rejected this plea.

4

End of Another Old Song

Tony Blair summarily ejected from the ancient and honourable House of Lords all save a rump of the hereditary peerage. Even that rump was not intended to be preserved for very long. This recalls the Act of Union in 1706. The abolition by that measure of the old Scottish Parliament was characterised by James Ogilvy, first Earl of Seafield, as the end of an old song.

Yet the present sad removal need never have happened. As Bret Harte's truthful James said, of all the words of tongue and pen, the saddest are these: 'It might have been'. If those concerned with preserving our ancient second chamber had proved more alert it might have been that it could have continued as before. The debating and revising functions it constitutionally has do not require members of the House of Lords to be democratically elected. Members sitting by right of heredity have numerous advantages to the public weal. They are independent. Their genes, as I have suggested, are likely to give them the high qualities for which the original title-holder was ennobled. There is no fuss about selecting them, and no question of prime ministerial patronage or Quangos.

So it might have been a very good thing if hereditary peers had survived as members of the House of Lords. How might that have been achieved? Long ago I showed the way, but it was ignored. In a letter published in the Times on 5 August 1980 I pointed out that if the next Labour Government abolished the House of Lords it would be because the House had failed to reform *itself*, 'which it could do tomorrow by a simple resolution'. I said in that letter –

What is needed is the minimum alteration required to rectify the only serious defect in our second chamber, its inbuilt Conservative majority. . . 431 peers take the Conservative whip, while 162 take the Labour whip. . . The abuse lies in the voting power of this permanent

29

majority, rather than its right to take part in a debate. Here is how the House could effect its own cure.

The House passes a resolution confining the right to vote to peers who correspond in number and party allegiance to the balance of parties in the Commons. On request, the Speaker in the Commons tells the Lord Chancellor [the Speaker of the House of Lords] how many MPs take the whip of each party. (There is a precedent for this in section 2 of the Ministerial and Other Salaries Act 1975.) The party leaders (or the peers themselves) then nominate peers [whose] numbers correspond to the proportions notified by the Speaker. Substantial changes in the Commons (as after a general election) are immediately reflected by corresponding changes in the Lords.

There are precedents for such self-denying ordinances by the peers. In theory any peer without legal qualifications can attend and vote when the House sits in its judicial capacity. But the last time this happened was in 1883, when the vote of the lay peer in question was ignored. A more recent precedent is the convention (invariably obeyed) that peers given leave of absence do not vote.

This voting reform, if carried with the whole-hearted approval of the peers as a permanent change, would remove any pretext for abolishing the House of Lords. It would not damage the character and traditions of that House (as an influx of elected peers might do). . . We would not be tinkering with our constitution more than is necessary. The British are wise to be cautious here, for constitutional practice which has grown up over centuries has contended with and adapted to many forms of crisis. It therefore contains within itself the mechanism for dealing with similar crises if and when they occur (as the proposal in this letter illustrates).

No notice whatever was taken of this sublime suggestion, which bears an uncanny resemblance to the mechanism now included in the House of Lords Act 1999. A few years ago (on 19 March 1996) I tried again. I wrote to the publicist Lord Rees-Mogg as follows. 'In view of what is said in your Times article of yesterday about House of Lords reform I would refer you to my letter in the Times of

5 August 1980, which for convenience I enclose. My suggestion has the great advantage that it could be achieved by the House of Lords acting entirely on its own initiative. This would be much more dignified than waiting for Mr Blair!'

Lord Rees-Mogg condescended to send me a one-line reply dismissing this suggestion out of hand. His condescension did not bow to including even one reason why my suggestion was unsuitable. Yet if the Lords had reformed themselves all those years ago in the way I suggested is it likely that any head of steam would have built up in the 1990s for ejection of the hereditaries? Not even Blair could have won on that one. It all goes back to what I said in chapter 1 about the way the British ignore danger until its hot breath is felt on their neck – by which time it is usually too late.

I now refer back to the letter from Viscount Davidson mentioned in chapter 2. By hindsight we can see that it was a very great mistake to pass the Life Peerages Act of 1958. The Monarchy continues to be based on the hereditary principle. We now see that that principle should have continued to be applied to the second House of Parliament. The reason is like the reason that justifies democracy: bad as it is, there is no better system possible. Appointment by Mr Blair reeks of cronyism. Election would threaten the role of the House of Commons. Descendants of those doughty warriors appointed as peers by Edward I or Henry VIII, or on the recommendation of the Earl of Chatham, Mr Gladstone or Mr Attlee, are likely to possess the right genes to rule us.

It seems we need them.

5

The Queen's Speech: a British Institution

I am writing this the day after the delivery by Her Majesty of the 1999 Queen's speech at the opening of Parliament. The first thing I note is that the speech is full of references to 'modernising'. It begins by saying Mr Blair's Government seeks to modernize the country and its institutions. The reason given for this is to 'meet the challenges of the new millennium'. In fact there is no challenge facing Blair's Government that is produced by the fact that each of our years will in future start with a 2 instead of a 1. How long will it be before we can leave behind this monotonous insistence on what is no more than a calendar quirk?

There was not much evidence of modernising our institutions when I watched the ceremony of opening the new Session. The Parliament building designed by Barry and Pugin early in Queen Victoria's reign consciously echoes the splendid colours and designs of the Middle Ages. It was medieval pageantry that inspired those eminent Victorians who worked out the ceremonial we still see today, despite Mr Blair's professed desire to 'modernize' everything. This self-important play-acting was perhaps suited to the great Victorian Empire. Every bit of it has significance for the historians of our constitution. It is grand as a museum piece. But for a working legislature suited to the vaunted 'new millennium'? I wonder.

Trial by jury is one ancient relic Mr Blair *would* like to consign to a museum. 'A Bill will be introduced to give the courts themselves the power to decide whether certain defendants should be tried by jury or by magistrates.'

The jury is a British institution too deeply entrenched in the national psyche even for the parvenu Blair to dislodge. The judge who conducted the trial of Daniel O'Connell in 1844, Thomas Denham, said that trial by a jury of one's peers is a security to persons who are accused. In America Judge Learned Hand elaborated this by remarking that the institution of jury trial is favoured by the public because jurors are anonymous and the individual can forfeit his liberty only at the hands of those who, unlike any official, are not accountable for what they do. A third reason he gave, perhaps the most important, is that no one is likely to suffer of whose conduct the jurors do not morally disapprove, and this 'introduces a slack into the enforcement of law, tempering its rigor by the mollifying influence of current ethical conventions'. One constitutional element against which the jury gives protection is the judge, yet under Mr Blair's proposals 'the courts themselves' would have had power to withdraw jury trial from those accused of crime. Obviously that stinks. Fortunately for our wellbeing Blair's base proposals did not pass. Jury trial remains as it was, no thanks to Mr Blair. More about this in chapter 9.

What would Labour do about the terrorists? We asked ourselves that question in those innocent days before 11 September. 'A Bill will be introduced to modernize [of course] and make permanent the powers available to respond to all forms of terrorism.' Yet was it not Labour who previously, year after year, opposed annual renewal of the statutory powers against terrorists?

The voting system is to be 'modernized'. 'My Government will. . . bring forward a Bill to reform our electoral procedures to make it easier for people to participate in elections.' Under this there will be polling booths in supermarkets. Perhaps an internet facility will be offered, as with on-line banking. Voters will be enabled to enjoy the enviable (if anonymous) facilities afforded by call centres. Does all this cheapen the hard-won democratic right of universal suffrage? A move the other way would be to copy the Australians and make failing to cast one's vote a criminal offence. But Blair would consider this 'judgmental'.

The gracious Speech gave an airing to two reforms proposed in the First Special Report of the Select Committee on Modernisation [that word again!] of the House of Commons, Session 1998-99. The Committee recommended (1) the carry over from one Session to another by agreement of certain Bills and (2) more pre-legislative scrutiny of draft Bills.

Carrying over a Bill scraps the salutary rule that you start a clean Session of Parliament with a clean sheet. Parliamentary Counsel (who draft Government legislation) consider it a great nuisance to have to publish a *draft* Bill because it is one that obviously is not yet ready to see the light of day. On (1), the Financial Services Bill introduced last Session 'will be carried over to this'. On (2), 'My Government will continue to provide greater openness by publishing legislation in draft for public scrutiny.' A start on this will be made with Bills enabling the UK to ratify the International Criminal Court, promoting more efficient water use and leasehold reform as well as commonhold for flat owners. It all made me dizzy. I sympathised with my former colleagues in the Parliamentary Counsel Office.

By way of tailpiece I offer a nice oxymoron. 'A Bill will be introduced to give people greater access to the countryside and to improve protection for wildlife.'

6

Fur and the Mayor

How long will it be before Blair introduces a Government Bill to ban the rearing of animals for providing food for humans? The sequence might go like this. We start with the Fur Farming (Prohibition) Bill, which was introduced into the House of Commons on 22 November 1999, and later became law. The only type of activity currently within its range is mink farming. A person is guilty of an offence if in England or Wales he or she keeps animals solely or primarily for slaughter for the value of their fur, or for breeding progeny for such slaughter. The maximum penalty is a fine of £20,000. The so-called Countryside Minister Mr Elliott Morley MP said in the Commons on 23 November 1999 that the Bill was justified on public morality grounds. This overlooks Genesis iii 21: 'Unto Adam also and to his wife did the Lord God make coats of skins, and clothed them'. (I return to that topic in chapter 28.)

Next we will get a Bill banning the keeping of animals solely or primarily for slaughter for the value of their hide. If it offends public morality to keep animals for their fur it must be equally wrong to keep them for their skin. For both the object is that people shall wear the product, whether as fur coats or hats or as leather footwear (I make no mention of ladies' handbags or the carpenter's useful apron).

A supporter of Blair's minister Mr Morley might say people do not need to wear fur in England or Wales because the climate is not cold enough. That is absurd. It can get very cold in north Wales, and on parts of the east coast of England. A government would not try this nonsense in any really cold country such as Finland or Russia: the people would not stand for it. There they know that animal fur is and has always been essential outdoor wear. Can Blair's morality vary with temperature?

If it is immoral to rear animals for clothing (which of course it is not) it must be equally immoral to rear them to eat. We all know there are alternatives to roast meat, such as titivated soya beans. I give it ten years before a

Government anti-livestock rearing Bill comes along proclaimed as the vegetarians' charter. Meanwhile back to fur.

What would the new London Mayor, Ken Livingstone, do about the fur Bill when it became law? He and his extensive entourage will be bound to feel inhibited from dressing in sable like their antique opposite numbers at the City of London's Mansion House, though there is no express prohibition of that in the measure that sets up the new and unnecessary Mayor of London, the Greater London Authority Act 1999. I have been glancing through this Act, which received royal assent on 11 November 1999. It runs to 425 sections and 34 Schedules, so there will not be space to say much about it here. After the fun and games with the prospective candidates Ken Livingstone and Jeffrey Archer, one's first thought was to look at the functions of the new-fangled Mayor of London. As you would expect, it is not easy to decipher these.

The story starts with the Greater London Authority, which consists of the Mayor and the Assembly of 25 members. Elections are to be held on the first Thursday in May every four years, beginning in 2000. The functions of the Mayor and the Assembly are more or less interchangeable, though some are only exercisable by the two acting jointly. There are three principal purposes, to promote (1) economic development and wealth creation, (2) 'social development' (whatever that may be), and (3) the improvement of the environment. Simple administration is not mentioned. The Secretary of State for the Environment, Transport and the Regions has power to issue guidelines, so Government control will be maintained. If, as may well happen sometimes, the Mayor and Assembly are of one political persuasion and the Secretary of State is of another, sparks will inevitably fly. That is not provided for.

The Mayor is required to develop and implement policies for the promotion and encouragement of safe, integrated, efficient and economic transport facilities and services. To further this he must prepare and publish a document to be known as his transport strategy. He must also pursue various other strategies, such as a spatial development strategy, a biodiversity action plan, an ambient noise strategy, and (of course) a culture strategy. In relation to the last, the Mayor will be assisted by a Culture Strategy Group. Here 'culture' (where is Herr Goering?) includes the arts, tourism, sport, ancient monuments, and treasure and antiquities of a movable nature. It also includes broadcasting, film production and the media generally. Clearly Londoners are in for an interesting time culturally. I could find no provision disturbing the alternative (and much earlier) Lord Mayor in his ancient Mansion House.

Mention of that august building reminds me that a leader of my own legal profession, Lord Bingham of Cornhill, recently told a Mansion House audience that most people find repellent the habits of thought, speech and bearing which characterise professional lawyers. Evidently his Lordship, who has done very well out of his ancient profession, forgot a hoary proverb. It's an ill bird that fouls its own nest.

7

Electronic Communications

That we live in a new parliamentary age is evidenced in various ways by the Electronic Communications Bill, given a second reading in the Commons on 29 November 1999 and passed into law as the Electronic Communications Act 2000. Opening the second reading debate Patricia Hewitt, Blair's Minister for Small Business and E-Commerce (I kid you not), said that when her grandmother left Britain nearly 100 years ago, it took her months to reach Australia, and months after that for her first letter to reach home. 'These days', she continued, 'a letter takes less than a week, but an e-mail takes less than a minute, just one small example of how our world is being transformed by electronic networks'.

This rang a bell with me. My own octogenarian great-great-aunt boarded ship to emigrate to Australia in the 1880s. After two months' sailing she died on the voyage without reaching her destination, so her anxious relatives in Lancashire never got that first letter home. She was buried at sea.

Ms Hewitt went on to tell us that electronic networks – the convergence of communications and computing – are changing everything. They destroy old jobs and create new ones at terrifying speed. They have transformed global trade, creating financial markets in which billions of dollars (what about pounds sterling?) are moved around the world daily. They are transforming manufacturing, allowing teams of engineers to work around the world, around the clock, designing new products and testing them in simulation before the prototype is even built. They are transforming education, she added, and they will certainly transform politics. She congratulated the honourable Member for Rutland and Melton, Mr Duncan, on achieving a parliamentary first – an electronic petition to the ancient but still modern House of Commons.

I mentioned in chapter 5 the experiment of publishing Bills in draft. The Electronic Communications Bill is an example of this. A draft of it was published on 23 July 1999 as part of an elaborate consultation process begun under the previous Conservative government. The Trade and Industry Select Committee of the House of Commons published a special report on the draft bill.

The First Parliamentary Counsel recently explained another parliamentary innovation. As a result of a recommendation made by the House of Commons Select Committee on Modernisation, and adopted by both Houses of Parliament, explanatory notes are being published for all Government Bills. The note for the Electronic Communications Bill, available on the Internet, runs to seven pages and is very helpful. It tells us that the Blair Government's policy is to facilitate electronic commerce. It has also set itself targets for making Government services available electronically: 25% by 2002, 50% by 2005 and 100% by 2008.

The Commons were told that when enacted the Electronic Communications Bill would facilitate the modernising process. Its main purpose was to help build confidence in electronic commerce and the technology underlying it by providing for (1) an approvals scheme for businesses and other organisations providing electronic signature and other services; (2) the legal recognition of electronic signatures; and (3) the removal of obstacles in other legislation to the use of electronic communication and storage in place of paper.

On object (1), an electronic signature is defined as anything in electronic form which (a) is incorporated into or otherwise logically associated with any electronic communication or electronic data; and (b) purports to be so incorporated or associated for the purpose of being used in establishing the authenticity or integrity of the communication or data. Thus it is a thing associated with an electronic document that performs similar functions to a manual signature on a conventional document. It can be used to give the recipient confirmation that the communication comes from whom it purports to come from ('authenticity') and that it has not been tampered with ('integrity'). The approvals scheme will provide for a register of providers of such services.

On object (2), the Bill provided for the admissibility of electronic signatures and related certificates in legal proceedings. On object (3) it gave the appropriate minister power by order to remove legislative restrictions which prevent the use of electronic communications or storage in place of paper. A large number of provisions in statutes on many different topics currently require the use of paper. Many involve communication with Government departments by businesses or individuals – including submitting information or applying for licences or permits. Other cases concern communications between businesses and individuals.

An example of legislation that needs amending in this way is the Companies Act 1985. The department of Trade and Industry has consulted about whether the Act should be amended to enable companies to use electronic means to deliver company communications, to receive shareholder proxy and voting instructions and to incorporate themselves.

We shall see about all that. Having myself been for more than twenty years a daily user of computers and all things electronic, I suspect that here for once Blair has got it about right.

8

Too Big for Some of Us to Grasp

Television news constantly shows unfortunates in places like Florida and the Caribbean who are overwhelmed by gales and floods proceeding from hurricanes with bizarre names. On a psychic rather than physical plane, I suffer in much the same way from the effluvium issuing from human rights enthusiasts, of whom the exemplar is the egregious Lord Lester of Herne Hill. Do these people realise the significance of what they are about? I refer not merely to Algerian terrorists and other threats to public safety, who thereby sleep more easily. As Janet Jones says in her book *Labour of Love*, these sea-changes can be too big for some of us to grasp. Ms Jones is the wife of the extinct Labour volcano Lord (Ivor) Richard, who was leader of the House of Lords until Tony Blair sacked him for not being on message. Janet's book is her diary of events behind the scenes of the youthful Blair Government.

Nowadays every Government Bill has a statutory mantra headed EUROPEAN CONVENTION ON HUMAN RIGHTS. This is followed by –

> Mr Secretary Blank has made the following statement under section 19(1)(a) of the Human Rights Act 1998: In my view the provisions of the So-and-So Bill are compatible with the Convention rights.

The vagueness of the Convention articles means this is more pious aspiration than firm conviction. Much rests on 'In my view'.

Through four editions and fifteen years the opening sentence of my 1,000 page textbook *Statutory Interpretation* has announced that the search is for order. That search is being made increasingly difficult. Formerly we had single-level law, where for a particular case there is one text (say an Act of Parliament) or a series of same-type texts which need to be conflated (say a group of Acts of Parliament on the same topic). That was difficult enough to construe, but now we have other levels also. Typically, the provisions of the Act or Acts of Parliament have first to be tentatively construed as they stand, perhaps with difficulty. Then under the new regime the (provisional) result has to be tested against an 'upper' text such as a European Community directive or an article of the European Convention on Human Rights. The position is even more difficult in devolved territories like Scotland, where one must also juggle with a lower level of *vires* (powers). Whatever values are served by this, order is not one of them. Legal certainty, and ability to find out what the law is, inevitably suffer. If starting from scratch, who would design such a crazy system? Order, coupled of course with justice, is the prime object of law. That is what citizens require. They want to know, when the need arises, just what the law says their rights and duties are in a particular area. That becomes increasingly difficult to find out, and Mr Blair is not helping.

The English Bar is increasingly given over to human rights cavortings. A recent issue of its house journal *Counsel* revels in the new dispensation. One would think the holy grail had been discovered. Sir Lancelot is played by the aforesaid Lord Lester of Herne Hill. For some reason he here disguises himself under his pre-honorific name of Anthony Lester. Is this mock modesty, or something more sinister? One cannot tell. I look back to the time when as a Home Office adviser this man plagued me throughout while I was drafting the Sex Discrimination Act 1975, and afterwards roundly and unsoundly criticised the product. A more private objection is that for his title he stole the name of a place in south London of which I have youthful memories. It was in lodgings in Herne Hill that I got the result of my Bar finals. Dashing across the road to buy *The Daily Telegraph*, I learnt that I had come fourteenth in the country. It might have been better, but it might also have been a lot worse.

This Lord Lester of my cherished Herne Hill attempted to refute the argument of Michael Gove in *The Times* that the new human rights dispensation gives too much power to the judges. Finding his refutation unconvincing, I explained why in a letter the Times published on 26 November 1999. I pointed out that his Lordship gave the game away by saying that these judicial powers are needed in case Parliament acts oppressively. In England what is oppressive is often a matter of opinion. In future it will be judicial, not parliamentary, opinion that prevails. Is that democratic? Where is the input of the people? Blame Mr Blair.

Lord Lester correctly says that under the Human Rights Act courts must construe our statutes compatibly with the Convention only where this is 'possible'. Again that is deceptive as a safeguard. European courts frequently stretch the meaning of statutes to give a 'creative' result. Lord Chancellor Derry Irvine recently stated that under the Human Rights Act our courts are likely to follow these expansive European methods. He added that 'the strong interpretative techniques' that can be expected to be applied by our courts to British statutes in Convention cases include 'straining the meaning of words or reading in words which are not there'. We have been warned.

Back to Janet Jones, who is a teacher. I have reached 4 May 1997 in her triumphant diary recording the arrival of Blairism as a force in our country. Of the Mayday general election result which brought Blair to office in that year she writes: 'New Labour have a majority of 254 over the Conservatives. If New Labour lose 100 seats in the election of 2002 they will have a majority of 154 to take them to 2007'.

I only hope she doesn't teach arithmetic.

9

Fighting for the Jury

When I hear the word 'culture', Herr Goering is supposed to have said, I reach for my gun (actually it was Hanns Johst). English people, bred on Magna Carta, have the same gut reaction at any threat to jury trial. Such a threat was posed by the Criminal Justice (Mode of Trial) Bill, given a second reading in the Lords on 2 December 1999 and still not passed into law. The effect of the Bill was to take away the right of the accused to choose between summary trial and trial on indictment (that is before a jury) in the many cases of offences triable either way. Instead the court would in future decide the mode of trial, in other words whether the accused will have a jury to decide his or her fate. We might here remember the ancient charge to the prisoner. It was: How will you be tried? The old answer was: By God and my country. That is significant. The 'country' referred to was made up of fellow citizens.

Historically a jury was defined as a body of laymen summoned and sworn (*jurati*) to ascertain, under the guidance of a judge, the truth as to questions of fact. The basic question has always been, and indeed still is, how to discover the truth. Ordeal by water or fire, based on Christian belief or superstition, was used as the test until its banning by the Fourth Lateran Council in 1215. In that same year Magna Carta pointed the future way with its reference to *judicium parium* or trial by one's peers. Here peers means equals not lords. As we are all equal nowadays that denotes anyone at all (and anyone at all, from the age of eighteen upwards, is what one may expect to find in a current English jury box).

Why does Blair want to make this change? There are suggestions that it is to save money or speed up the processes of justice and reduce delay. There is also the matter of prosecutorial pique. Too many unmeritorious defendants are playing the system in the hope of getting out of well-merited punishment. Often they have previous convictions, and are therefore damned from the start in some eyes. The hard-bitten authorities who manage our criminal justice system have no belief at all in the notion that an old lag might turn over a new leaf. Hence the following curious statement by the Attorney General, Lord Williams of Mostyn, on moving the second reading of the Bill: 'Is it right that someone, let us say, who has ten previous convictions for shoplifting a jelly or a banana from Tesco is automatically entitled to the right to trial by jury?' No one seriously believes that is the key question. For a start, previous convictions are not allowed to be revealed to the jury (though even that salutary rule is threatened with abolition under Blair).

Lord Williams introduced an even lighter note, derived from his days as a barrister on the Wales and Chester circuit. 'A number of us', he said, 'have spent many happy hours at the Bar defending people – they always seemed to be farmers – who were charged with breathalyser offences'. On that circuit, he added, provided your client was not an English speaker it was quite normal to secure an acquittal. Drawing in the LibDems, Lord Williams said 'I am glad to see that my noble friend Lord Carlile nods and smiles at these memories'. No doubt he was recalling Milton in *L'Allegro* –

> Haste thee Nymph, and bring with thee
> Jest and youthful jollity,
> Quips and cranks, and wanton wiles,
> Nods, and becks, and wreathéd smiles.

On behalf of the Conservatives, some shrewd points were made by Lord Cope of Berkeley, who as plain John Cope interviewed me long ago when I was being put on the party's list of approved parliamentary candidates. He said that financial savings will be illusory in view of the appeal process proposed. 'The other thing which is likely to prove illusory is the idea that the Bill will speed up the process of justice. When the proposal for magistrates alone to decide the trial venue was put forward in 1993 by the Royal Commission, and again in the Narey report on delays in the system in early 1997, the present Home Secretary said he thought the reduction in delay would prove illusory.' Now he was in office Mr Jack Straw, who held a tutorial for their Lordships immediately before the second reading, had conveniently changed his mind.

The LibDem view, expressed in the second reading debate by Lord Thomas of Gresford, was against 'the wonderful new reform which is now being put forward'. Slightly more interesting than this puny salvo was the glimpse of his youth vouchsafed by this Lord Thomas, who has been a Crown Court recorder for 25 years.

> My father was a policeman. I was born in a police house. I spent the first five years of my life living in a police station, after which it became a magistrates' court... In my teenage years I used to leave school at one o'clock and go to the police station to eat my dinner in the police canteen. So I imbibed the "canteen culture" of the police force with my sausage and mash.

To which one can only add 'Ah! Happy days!'.

*   *   *

Half a century ago, when I used to sit day after day in the uncomfortable cramped official box in the House of Commons chamber, I came to respect many of the highly–competent backbench MPs of those times – none more so than the doughty Leslie Hale. For more than twenty years this excellent man served as Labour MP for Oldham West. Oldham is a modest town in Lancashire, where as a girl in the nineteenth century my maternal Grandmother worked her guts out as a cotton mill hand. Now to my horror Oldham features in the newspapers for fights between the new Asian community there and the aboriginal whites. This would have made no sense to my dear lamented long-dead Grandmother. In her day Oldham was for Lancashire folk, and by that I mean people who looked back for generations on life in what is still entitled to be known as the County Palatine. To understand all that you need to study some English history, which not many do. Mr Blair prefers English pupils to study the history of distant foreign lands, all in the name of 'multiculturism'. More about that later.

The stout shade of Leslie Hale was raised in the debate (7 March 2000) when the Commons gave a second reading to the Criminal Justice (Mode of Trial) (No. 2) Bill, the first version (mentioned above) having foundered when the House of Lords thankfully wrecked it. Now, against opposition from all sides, Blair's Government was having a second try to get the Bill enacted. It was the promoter, Home Secretary Straw, who mentioned the late Mr Hale, or rather Lord Hale (for near the end of his life he was deservedly ennobled). Straw did this not to praise him; rather the reverse. He said-

> I draw some comfort from the fact that at almost every point that a Home Secretary has sought sensibly to modernize our system of jury trials, he has been met with similarly vocal opposition. . . In 1967, Roy Jenkins proposed to change the requirement of a unanimous verdict to that which the European Union now likes to call a qualified majority. The proposal was met with howls from all sides. I give the House a flavour of the reaction by quoting the then Labour Member for Oldham West, Mr. Leslie Hale, who said of the proposal . . . "never before in the history of Parliament has there been a provision undermining the constitution of the nation, the liberties of the people and a system of justice that, with all its faults, is the envy of the world, on less evidence, with less consideration, and with a more complete absence of reasoning in its support".

You note that Mr Hale said then that England had a system of justice that, with all its faults, was the envy of the world. Would any Labour MP of today say that? I will tell you what the supposedly patriotic Englishman Mr Jack Straw MP said in the debate. He said that in enacting this Bill we bring ourselves into line with the better practice of almost all comparable jurisdictions, and come closer to the practice in Scotland. He added: 'Often Scotland is, rightly, held out to be a nation with a more effective criminal justice system than ours'.

So that is what has become of English pride in Magna Carta and trial by jury. It has been traitorously struck down by a man who in the reference books continues to proclaim himself a Bencher of the Inner Temple, that high sanctum of English law. Shame on this pathetic man of Straw.

Why should anybody worry about Straw's determined attempt to emasculate the jury? Let me give some more reasons. The jury, said Sir Robert Megarry (former Vice-Chancellor in the High Court of Chancery), plays a large part in liberty. He added that it is for the Bench to protect the jury. Are the Bench of today doing this? The answer is no. Mr Straw said of his anti-jury Bill: 'In 1993, it received the unanimous backing of the royal commission on criminal justice. Today, it enjoys the active endorsement of the Lord Chief Justice, Lord Bingham, and of the vast majority of the High Court Bench of nearly 100 senior judges; of the Magistrates Association, representing 30,000 justices of the peace; and of all three police associations, representing more than 125,000 police officers. . .'

If this is really so, why does the niggling doubt remain? Mr Straw himself gave the answer in February 1997, when he was in opposition: 'If. . . a Member of Parliament or even a Secretary of State were charged with an offence of dishonesty, would they not insist on being tried by a jury? If that is the case, why should others be denied that right of election?'

Mr Straw says he has changed his mind since then. Others have not. For the Conservatives, Sir Nicholas Lyell, a former Attorney General, put his finger on the truth by pointing out that the (defective) logic of the Home Secretary's argument was that, because magistrates generally provide a fair trial, the right to trial by jury can be largely dispensed with.

Mr Straw's revised Bill was even worse than the earlier one, which allowed a respectable accused's reputation to be taken into account in deciding mode of trial. Then political correctness struck. Giving credit for a good reputation was criticised as discriminating against ethnic minorities and the unemployed, so it was omitted from the No. 2 Bill. Mr Straw's plea, hotly disputed by the Bill's opponents, was that the Bill would save £120 million a year. Twenty-nine Labour MPs voted against the second reading, which was nevertheless agreed. Would the Lords again save us from this English Bill that kow-tows to Scotland and rejects respected English jurisprudence? It turned out that yes they would, and did. At the time of writing, the argument continues.

I would point out that those who say we should be deprived of the ancient protection of jury trial when the offence is 'minor' should think again and use some sense. They say, for example, that to be charged with theft of a small amount is a minor matter not warranting jury trial. If they themselves were charged with theft, even of a small amount, they would not think it minor. The prestigious Professor C E M Joad of 1950s Brains Trust fame died in disgrace because he was caught trying to cheat the railways of a shilling or two. Lady Barnett of equal wireless repute died in disgrace because she was convicted of shoplifting. Mr Blair needs to remember Shakespeare: 'The purest treasure mortal times afford is spotless reputation'.

10

Elections and Referendums

An important stage in the comprehensive facelift Blair's first Government sought to give our constitution arrived with the Political Parties Elections and Referendums Bill, which had a second reading in the Commons on 10 January 2000. It was a major Bill, consisting of 147 clauses and 21 Schedules. It aimed to break the code which our ancient British constitution has established after many vicissitudes. Would it succeed? Yes indeed it would. Blair saw to that. It was passed into law as the Political Parties Elections and Referendums Act 2000.

Blair's code-breaking Bill was divided into ten parts, the first nine of which deal respectively with the setting up of a new Electoral Commission, the registration of political parties, accounting requirements for registered parties, the control of donations to parties and their members, the control of campaign expenditure, controls relating to third party national election campaigns, conduct of 'referendums' (which spelling looks awkward compared to the more correct 'referenda'), control of election campaigns, and control of political donations and expenditure by companies. The final part contained miscellaneous and general provisions.

The essence overall was *control*. Being admittedly a control freak, Blair seeks to control us all in every way; but many of us do not think that is the essence of democratic government. Fighting on, we true democrats require our government to let us lead our lives, merely providing the defences. The megalomaniac Blair is not happy with that simple idea. He wants to rule as an emperor, not merely facilitate (anyone could do that). Moreover he wants to change. Everything in sight must be constantly changed, which is most unsettling. On any view that ambition is obstreperous, and clearly well beyond the remit of an elected politician. Blair thinks nothing of that, feeding on his vainglory.

To be fair, Blair's Bill drew comprehensively on the

work of the Committee on Standards in Public Life, chaired first by Lord Nolan and later by Lord Neill of Bladen. It was the first time that the way political parties conduct themselves had been the subject of statutory regulation, even though such political groupings have been a feature of our parliamentary system of government for more than 300 years. History has not much place with Blair, nor has true democracy.

The general functions of Blair's new-fangled electoral commission will include reporting on particular elections and referendums; the review of electoral law; the provision of guidance in relation to party political broadcasts; and what the explanatory memorandum calls 'promoting understanding of electoral and political matters'. (Does this sound like attempted brainwashing of the electorate?). There are also transferred to the commission the existing functions of the four Parliamentary Boundary Commissions and the two Local Government Commissions (one for England and the other for Wales).

The Home Secretary, Mr Jack Straw, moving the second reading of this Bill, said that while political parties are vital to the effective functioning of any representative democracy, the parties of today do not simply sustain a particular set of political leaders in office. As in any mature democracy, political parties also provide both a crucial link between the citizen and the elected Government of the day and some of the key processes by which that Government is held to account. Parties must, Straw relentlessly went on, be capable of discharging effectively those onerous responsibilities, and that necessarily re- quires money. Parties might secure funding from one of two basic sources: subventions from the state or contribu- tions from their own supporters. The Neill committee recommended against the first, and the Government concurred. Rather than underpinning representative de- mocracy, over-reliance on state funding could in the end undermine it.

Democracy, Mr Straw added, does not come cheap. Those who are able should be ready to dip into their pockets to help to sustain it. 'We have reduced the pressure on political parties by more than doubling the taxpayers' funds available to Opposition parties. Such is the generous spirit that we have brought to government that the subvention of state aid to the Liberal Democrats has increased by a factor of three and the Conservatives now receive more than £3 million of state funding to help them to make their opposition effective.'

The Neill committee recognised that, in order to restore public confidence in the political process, it was important to put an end to what they termed the 'arms race' in election spending. Campaign spending at a national level by the two main parties has increased from an average of £5m in 1983 to £27m in 1997. The perceived need to match, if not exceed, spending by the other side has put a tremendous burden on the parties, which the Government feel it is necessary to reduce. That was one purpose of the Bill.

For the first time, the Bill introduced controls on election spending at a national as well as local level. Our Victorian forebears, when faced with growing electoral abuse, introduced the Secret Ballot Act 1872. They then introduced the Corrupt Practices Act 1883 to stamp out the buying and selling of votes, something that was done brazenly at that time. It helps to put current levels of campaign spending into perspective, said Mr Straw, to note that, at the 1880 general election, after controls were introduced, candidates spent the equivalent of £106m at 1997 prices. However they spent it at a local, not a national, level. National politics scarcely existed.

For the Conservatives, Sir George Young basely said his party accepted the Neill recommendations and would not obstruct their passage into law. He added that it is common ground that 'politics should be cleaned up'. David Winnick (Labour) urged the Government to reconsider the proposed £5,000 threshold above which donations to political parties will have to be declared. He would have been happier with a lower figure, say £2,000, but the Government stood firm on this.

The Blair Government's determination to plough on regardless, and force through a huge wodge of constitutional legislation while they still have the chance, led in the autumn of 2000 to the House of Lords being recalled a month earlier than the Commons. Important Bills are introduced first in the Commons, so their later stages have to be carried through in the Lords. Towards the end of a Session business therefore piles up in the Lords, so its members lose a large slice of their summer vacation. This is a great pity. Busy people should continue to have a tranche of sunny summer and harvest time to recharge their batteries. The fools, particularly in the education field, who think that workwise the year should now be divided into five equal orderly segments know nothing of history, the seasons or human needs. During the year's round, a sizeable spell of oblivion is obligatory at some point. Or else we shall all suffer.

The Political Parties, Elections and Referendums Bill was one among many reasons why their Lordships were called upon to assemble untimely in mellow autumn and talk away in face of a darkened, vacant Commons chamber. The committee stage came up on 12 October 2000 and I shall tell you a little of what happened.

For political parties, especially small ones, this might be called the Gravy Train Bill. There is taxpayers' loot on offer. Ecstasy on this point is tempered by the fact that much of the said loot will be needed to pay the costs of new hurdles to democracy erected by the Bill itself. Margaret McDonagh, General Secretary of the Labour Party, thought it might require them to hire ten more clerks just to deal with the accountancy procedures required to verify that donors do not overstep the mark. Oh Ecclestone, what tribulations shall we suffer in thy name! (Those who prefer may substitute, Sainsbury, Robinson, Mittal or other munificent Labour benefactors at will.)

The Bill provides for the taxpayer to meet start-up costs initially incurred by small political parties. Lord Beaumont of Whitley (Eton and Christ Church) moved to delete 'initially'. He thought there would be a need, 'not only for a one-off start-up grant, but for continuing grants that should run for at least a while afterwards'. No doubt there will be such a need. We would all very much like taxpayers' money to help us profitably to go on with what we have started. But is this Liberal Democrat peer justified in demanding it? The Government spokesman Lord Bassam of Brighton did not think so.

This Lord Bassam of Brighton intrigues me. He is not to be confused with the late Alfred Bossom MP, a property man who managed to get himself made a baronet in 1953 and a peer in 1960. He was of old Anglo-Saxon stock, proudly named after King Alfred the Great like his father before him – if Lord Parekh (cheekily of Runnymede) will allow me to mention such a thing. It was Bossom of whom Winston Churchill remarked that his name was neither one thing nor the other.

For the Conservatives Lord Mackay of Ardbrecknish accused Lord Bassam of admitting that the Bill was 'cumbersome and bureaucratic'. He added that as a result of it the three main political parties will each incur additional annual costs running into at least six figures. Yet, said Lord Mackay, 'the last thing we would want to see as a result of the Bill is the stifling or even bankrupting of political parties, in particular the smaller ones which are not represented here'.

Viscount Cranborne implored Lord Bassam to cast his mind back into the dim recesses of history and think about how the Labour Party was brought into being. He said it came to be transmogrified from a small sectarian group of people into the principal opposition party to the Conservatives because of the extremely ill defined rules governing party regulation. He added that one of the great difficulties in the constitutional arrangements of our country is that there is an ill defined relationship between political parties (which are an essential part of our system) and the more carefully defined constitutional elements. 'One of the effects of the Bill is that. . . the flexibility which allowed the Labour Party to come into being. . . will become a thing of the past. In a curious way, the Labour Party, having taken advantage of that flexibility, is pulling the ladder up behind it'.

Later events cast a stern cold light on this Bill, which as I have said passed into law as the Political Parties Elections and Referendums Act 2000. Thereafter it soon became apparent that Mr Blair, even though Prime Minister, would stop at nothing to raise funds for his

Party, now known as New Labour. A series of political scandals followed, culminating in the affair of Mr Mittal in 2002. The name of Mittal lines up along with other suspect Asian names, such as Hinduja and Vaz. We are witnessing the incursion into our chaste country of the values of another culture.

11

Section 28 and the Homophobes

Several features of our parliamentary processes as revised, indeed transformed, by the modernist Mr Blair, were displayed on 6 December 1999 when the Lords debated the Local Government Bill (later passed into law as the Local Government Act 2000). Moving the second reading of this questionable Bill, the environment minister Lord Whitty said, in the usual grandiloquent display of a 'modern' Blairite politician, that the Bill would revitalise local democracy and change the way local communities govern themselves and how they shape their future. What cheek! This Blairite creature Whitty produced no evidence that local communities want or need to be thus revitalised – but then such evidence is not now considered necessary. We must get what Mr Blair thinks good for us, and be grateful. He decides. How awful that is, I think to myself as I cravenly slink to my quarters after the debate.

The Bill gives new powers to local authorities, powers which are said to be there to promote the economic, social and environmental wellbeing of their communities. It creates new executive arrangements for councils, involving separate executive and scrutiny structures with powerful roles for all councils. It introduces a new ethical framework for councillors and council officers. It provides for more frequent local elections to improve the accountability of councils to their electorates. It enables local authorities to fund support services for vulnerable groups via a new single budget. Finally it repeals the inflammatory anti-homosexual provision known as section 28 (of which more anon).

The 'modernized' parliamentary procedure is exemplified by the fact that in the summer of 1999 Parts II and III of the Bill were scrutinised in draft by a Joint Committee of both Houses. The draft Bill had been published, as part of the Government's policy document *Local Leadership, Local Choice*, for debate and discussion by local authorities and local communities. The Government later published their formal response to the Joint Committee's report, accepting some of its recommendations. Lord Whitty explained that by the committee stage the Government would bring forward amendments to the Bill in response to recommendations by the Joint Committee and also 'to better reflect the policy set out in *Local Leadership, Local Choice*'. In other words the vaunted modernized procedure meant that the House was called on to give a second reading to a text which did not remotely represent the Government's final thoughts on what should be included in this very important Bill, which sets the longstanding basis of our country's local government on its head. Their Lordships displayed the confusion one would expect from this Alice in Wonderland procedure, so reminiscent of 'sentence first, verdict afterwards'. It has otherwise long been known as putting the cart before the horse.

Tagged on to the general provisions of the Bill was clause 68. By itself this occupied half the time of the House in the second reading debate, so I shall occupy the remaining half of this chapter with it. As Baroness Seccombe sardonically remarked, in the new-fangled explanatory memorandum the controversial clause 68 'commanded all of three lines'. It read as follows –

> Clause 68 repeals section 2A of the Local Government Act 1986 (inserted by section 28 of the Local Government Act 1988), which prohibits local authorities from intentionally promoting homosexuality, or from promoting the teaching in their schools of the acceptability of homosexuality as a 'pretended family relationship'.

The section 28 issue is like the foxhunting issue: either you think one way or you think the opposite way, and you are not likely to be converted by opponents. This sort of dispute presents great problems for democracy, for it is not necessarily right that the opinion which at the crucial moment is held by the Commons majority should in the end prevail and subjugate the minority. Minorities also have rights. The pro-section 28 argument was put forcibly by the Duke of Norfolk –

> I am against homosexuality because, in the first place, it is unnatural. One must go into frank details in this

matter. The male body is made to go with a female body, not to go with another male body. That is how the male body has evolved.

Simple really.

As usual, the Bishop of Oxford, Richard Harries, sat on the fence and faced both ways. The church, he said, 'looks to marriage as the proper context for full sexual intimacy'. At the same time, he also said, 'it needs to be recognised that in any class there are likely to be one or more pupils who feel attracted to members of their own sex'. That of course is true, so why cavil? It can only be because we demand clearcut positions, which may not always be possible of attainment. But why cannot the Bishop of Oxford come out of his hutch and boldly say this? That is what we expect of him, as a Prelate of the Church.

Lord Whitty disagreed strongly with the Duke of Norfolk. Section 28, he said, is a pernicious piece of legislation. 'The number of assaults, self-inflicted wounds and suicide attempts among young gay people bears witness to that'. Oh yes? Where is the evidence? None was produced. But we have to admit it may be there.

What no one in the debate pointed out was that in its judicial capacity the House of Lords has already disowned section 28. In Fitzpatrick v Sterling Housing Association Ltd [1999] 4 All ER 705 Lord Clyde cited a New York judge who ruled that the word 'family' includes 'two adult [homosexual] lifetime partners whose relationship is long term and characterised by an emotional and financial commitment and interdependence'. On that basis, said Lord Clyde, 'the concept of "family" is now to be regarded as extending to a homosexual partnership'. In the Appellate Committee of the House of Lords this view prevailed by three to two.

The committee stage of the Bill began with another row. This was on the novel procedure whereby a Government Bill is first published in draft. A former MP for Yeovil, Lord Peyton, opened for the Conservative Opposition by saying it was a rotten Bill, made worse by this new-fangled procedure. The Government had already put down no less than 284 amendments for committee stage, arising from consultations under the new procedure. More were threatened. In its second report (15 December 1999) the Delegated Powers and Deregulation Committee said 'We do not think it satisfactory to proceed in this way'.

Lord Elton asked the Government spokesman to explain how such an astonishing number of amendments had arisen in the department without the aid of any debate in the Commons. 'Normally when one receives an enormous raft of amendments it is as a result of debates in another place, where the Government have had matters drawn to their attention which, sensibly, they then seek to put right . . . why were these amendments not suggested before the Bill was printed and put before your Lordships' House?'

For the LibDems Baroness Hamwee added her voice to these critical comments, and twisted the knife. Why, when asked for a version of the Bill with the Government amendments written in, was the Minister's office forced to use old-fashioned physical cut-and-paste methods rather than modern technology? That sits ill with this Government's proclaimed devotion to 'modernisation' she added.

I mentioned above an article by the First Parliamentary Counsel explaining the new system of providing explanatory notes to Bills, including 'the full wording of provisions that are being textually amended by the Bill'. It is a historical curiosity that, although it has only recently been generally adopted, I myself first devised and used this sort of textual memorandum over a quarter of a century ago (see my *Statutory Interpretation*, 3rd edn, page 489). Computers have advanced amazingly since then, so why was Baroness Hamwee made to suffer in this primitive way? The House was not told.

She did not suffer alone. 'I had already mentioned to a number of interested outside organisations', she told the House, 'that the Minister had agreed to produce a revised version. Those organisations were pleased because their lives would have been made easier and they had expected to be able to see that version through electronic means . . . I am sure noble Lords will agree that such outside bodies often provide invaluable assistance with their comments on how proposed legislation may affect their areas. I am sad that in this case the Government were unable to make use of modern technology.'

Lord Dixon-Smith pointed out that there was also another document, 160 pages of it, which sets out, as part of the new-fangled consultation procedure, Consultative Drafts of Proposed Guidance and Regulations on New Constitutions for Councils. 'So not only are we dealing with a major Bill which is to be changed in a dramatic way; much of the detail, the body and the substance of what is going to affect local councils, is in another document which is not before us.'

The reply for the Government was given by Lord Whitty, better known in former days as Larry Whitty, general secretary of the Labour Party. He said he was not prepared to be abashed about the tabling of amendments. Many areas of the Bill had been subjected to 'a new and very important innovation in the way we approach legislation in this Parliament. . . Clearly, we are still on a learning curve in relation to pre-legislative scrutiny'.

Lord Peyton queried the fact that clause 1 gave a local authority power to 'do anything they consider likely to achieve' any of the new objects the Bill allots. He proposed an amendment to remove 'they consider', making the test objective rather than subjective. Lord Whitty retorted that the Bill was a very important turning point in broadening freedom of choice for local government, and putting back responsibility on to local councils for looking after the wellbeing of their communities. *Wednesbury* rules would apply, and that was sufficient safeguard. Lord Peyton's amendment would leave remote courts, and not aware local councils, to decide what activities could be under-taken. That was the opposite of what was desirable. The House agreed with Lord Whitty, defeating the Peyton amendment by 126 votes to 84.

What of the provision of the Bill repealing the notorious homophobic clause 28? It did not survive the homophobic attack on it in Parliament, and was transmogrified into section 104 of the final Act. What a meek turnaround! The official explanatory note on section 104 records that, rather than repealing section 28 as originally proposed by Mr Blair, it merely effects a slight modification to it 'by clarifying that it does not prevent head teachers, teachers or governors of maintained schools from taking steps to prevent any form of bullying'. Nobody ever seriously thought it did prevent such steps being taken. This was a little bit of sticking plaster applied to save Mr Blair's face. It was a very rare example of the fact that he does not invariably get his own way.

One feature of the Bill on which Blair did get his way later caused a great deal of trouble. This was the provision requiring humble parish councillors to register a great deal of private information about themselves. These local volunteers do yeoman service without pay. They could do without such intrusive red tape and bureaucracy. We may have to do without them if their anger and irritation causes them all to walk out (as many have done already). That would be a pity.

12

A curious measure:
the Disqualifications Bill

The main effect of the Disqualifications Bill (passed by Mr
Blair's subservient Parliament as the Disqualifications
Act 2000) was to amend existing legislation so as to allow
members of the Irish legislature (I kid you not!) to sit as
MPs (and draw their lavish allowances) in our proud,
august, democratic House of Commons, the high elected
assembly of the United Kingdom of Great Britain and
Northern Ireland. Why should a member of the Irish
legislature wish to sit in our House of Commons?
Conversely, why should a British constituency wish to
elect as its representative in the Westminster Parliament a
member of the Irish legislature? What was Mr Blair
playing at?

Some newspapers suggested that this was a complex plot
to further the interesting political career of the hated
bearded creep Mr Gerry Adams, of IRA fame (or infamy).
Such a quaint notion was never hinted at by the
Government spokespersons on the Bill. We know what
Mr Adams, elected to Westminster in the 2001 general
election, thinks about taking the oath or affirmation of
allegiance which is a necessary prelude to assuming his
seat. He refuses to do it, thus disenfranchising every one of
his constituents in West Belfast. Would not Mr Blair be
better engaged in presenting a Bill which dealt with that
gross anomaly, rather than creating a new one? It would be
an obvious provision to enact that if a person elected to a
Westminster seat declined to take the necessary oath or
affirmation he should be disqualified. In a letter *The Times*
published on 16 May 1997 I said –

> You report the Speaker's ruling that the two Sinn Fein
> MPs who decline to take the oath of allegiance, and so
> cannot assume their seats, must not after all use the
> facilities of the House of Commons. This does not wholly
> resolve the problem posed by MPs like Martin

McGuinness and Gerry Adams who, in the Speaker's words, choose not to take up their responsibility as Members. Such MPs deprive even those constituents who did not vote for them of effective parliamentary representation. It is nauseating for Mr Adams to say, as you report: 'I have a duty, as has Martin McGuinness, to represent my constituency'. It seems necessary to state the obvious and point out that the sole purpose of a parliamentary election is to procure the election of representatives who *will* 'take up their responsibility as Members'. I suggest that what is needed is an amendment to the duties of returning officers as laid down by the Representation of the People Acts. If a returning officer learns that a candidate has indicated that if elected he intends not to take the oath of allegiance the officer should have to require him to sign a statutory declaration of intention to take the oath if elected. Refusal to sign would disqualify the candidate from standing in the election. The voters who nominated him could then choose another candidate who better understood the nature of what he was about.

None of that was acknowledged by Mr Blair. In a mere two days (24 and 25 January 2000) the Bill was put through all its stages in the House of Commons, a haste usually reserved for dramatic emergencies. Where was the emergency here? It was not vouchsafed. Douglas Hogg for the Conservatives complained that the junior minister deputed by Mr Blair to rush it through had failed to give the motive behind the Bill. His questions carried a note of peevish incredulity. Why are we being asked to address this matter now? Where does the pressure come from? What is going on?

Answer came there none, though the junior minister did mention some factors which, he said, were *not* the reasons behind the measure. It was not part of the Good Friday agreement. There was no question of it being the means of achieving Irish unification by the back door. That was not its objective, nor would it be its consequence. The nearest the minister came to anything positive was the following.

We have now, as a result of the changes that have taken

place and the relationship that has developed over recent years, been able to put behind us, to some extent, some of the difficulties that had arisen between the Irish Republic and the United Kingdom. It is time to build a sounder basis to our institutional relationships and to provide a basis on which we can proceed, as two islands just off the mainland of Europe, with many common links, historical and otherwise, between the United Kingdom and the Irish Republic – a basis for ensuring that those closer links are given some institutional background. I believe that that explains this fairly modest Bill, and I hope that honourable Members will find it satisfactory.

Honourable Members did not find it satisfactory.

Mr Gerald Howarth (Aldershot): The Minister seeks to draw a parallel between the Republic of Ireland and Commonwealth countries, but Commonwealth countries have Her Majesty the Queen as their head of state. An honourable Member in this House is required to take the Oath of Allegiance. The Bill covers people who, being representatives of foreign countries, cannot take the Oath of Allegiance to the Queen. Moreover, the south of Ireland is a republic. Is not the Bill therefore creating a huge anomaly?

Mr. Ken Maginnis (Fermanagh and South Tyrone): Since [the minister] predicates his argument on the relationship between the Irish Government and this Government, I wonder whether he has had any representations from the Fianna Fail party, Fine Gael, the Irish Labour party or the Democratic Left, expressing an ambition to have a dual mandate? Or is this measure purely a concession to be enamelled on the side of the Good Friday agreement and to facilitate only and exclusively Sinn Fein-IRA?

Mr. Michael Mates (East Hampshire): There are only two sovereign institutions in these islands – the Parliament here and the Parliament in Dublin. The others are subordinate to one of those sovereign Parliaments. By changing that rule, the honourable

Gentleman is allowing people to join two different sovereign Parliaments with two different aims in mind, so there is a major conflict of loyalty.

The minister failed to deal with any of that. What he said in conclusion was –

Over many years, we have developed close working relationships with the Irish Government, but with agreement now in force between us on constitutional issues, the way is clear for the formalisation of that relationship. To some extent, the Bill provides some basis for that.

To some extent, the Commons debate on this Bill provides some basis for saying this is just another British Government fudge on Ireland.

To add insult to injury, the Speaker's ruling mentioned in my 1997 Times letter was reversed in 2002 when, under pressure from Prime Minister Blair, Adams and McGuiness were after all given offices in the Houses of Parliament. I had better not try to express my feelings about that. This book is not printed on sufficiently fireproof paper to withstand it.

13

Prime Minister's Questions

The cognoscenti around Westminster and Whitehall call Prime Minister's Questions PMQs. Every Wednesday afternoon, for half an hour, Mr Blair faces interrogation in the House of Commons. Before Mr Blair arrived on the scene it used to be every Tuesday and Thursday, for a quarter of an hour on each day. That did not suit Mr Blair's convenience so he altered it, without prior consultation with the Opposition, the Speaker or anyone else. We may judge how this weekly parliamentary institution works by considering the PMQs on 9 February 1999.

The highlight of PMQs is the setpiece challenge by the Leader of the Opposition, armed cap-À-pie in self-right-eousness. I will leave that till the end. A mini-highlight is the challenge by the leader of the LibDems Mr Charles Kennedy, clumsily armed in fustian Scottish righteous-ness. On this occasion he chose the plight of old age pensioners, of whom I happen to be one. Mr Kennedy was not so crass as to use the term 'old age pensioners'; he deferentially called us dotards 'pensioners'. This is in line with the modern practice of referring to 'older' people, rather than old people (which is what we are). 1999, believe it or not, was labelled the International Year of Older Persons. Ugh. Older than what, one might ask? A child of three is older than a child of two. Being 'older' means nothing of any importance. So why insinuate this liverish term into our national discourse? And so widely? It is all a nonsense of course. But do they see it? Most of them, it seems, do not.

In the debate Mr Kennedy had two points. (1) Why were we pensioners getting the measly rise of only 75p a week for the year 2000? (2) What will happen to rural post offices if the old age pension is increasingly paid to bank accounts, as the Government plan? Mr Blair retorted that we ancients were getting a lot more than 75p a week. What about the £100 fuel allowance? What about the minimum income guarantee? Moreover, 'pensioners over the age of 75 will get free television licences from autumn 2000. There are also, of course, free eye tests, the national concessionary bus fares scheme and the many other things that we have done for pensioners in this country'. So that's all right. Of course it is not 'we' (that is Mr Blair's Government) who have done it, but the taxpayers as a body. Mr Blair, our leader, only decides where the handouts shall be. It is the mass of citizens who pay, but Mr Blair is not interested in that. It is too close to the truth.

On the post offices Mr Blair played his usual modernisation card. It would, he said, be wrong to stop the switchover from paying benefits in cash to paying them into a bank account. 'It would be absolutely absurd to have the technology to do that, to have invested in it and then to waste that technology. In respect of the rural post offices, I also put forward a number of things that will help them to deal with the new situation. If the Liberal Democrats are really saying that, even if we have the technology to pay money direct into people's bank accounts, we should not do so, I disagree with them.'

A feature of PMQs since the general election in May 1997 has been the number of Blair babes and other Labour backbenchers who spoon-feed the Prime Minister with easy questions he will relish answering, having themselves been spoon-fed with those questions by the Labour whips. Here is one clever example from 9 February 1999.

Mr Nigel Griffiths (Edinburgh, South): Will my right honourable Friend confirm that the working families tax credit benefits 1.5 million families by an average of £24 a week? Does he agree that, when the Tories have mastered that simple arithmetic, he can tell Archie to tell Michael to tell William, and that we shall see another U-turn?

Thus spoon-fed, Mr Blair launched in reply a spirited attack on the Conservatives. It took up a few precious minutes of his half hour on the rack.

Modernisation let Mr Blair down when it came at last to his duel with the Leader of the Opposition, Mr Hague. In far-off Cardiff a confidence motion was about to be debated in Mr Blair's devolutionary baby the Welsh Assembly. The man he parachuted in as Labour leader, Alun Michael, expected to lose this vote so he resigned before that could happen. New Labour's electronic pagers did not inform Mr Blair of this dramatic event in time to stop him saying 'I believe that the Welsh First Secretary is doing an excellent job and so does the Labour party'. Tory pagers were working more efficiently. Primed by one, Mr Hague leapt in.

Mr William Hague (Richmond, Yorks): Will the Prime Minister comment on the fact that within moments of his expressing full confidence in the First Secretary in Wales. . . news came through to the House that the First Secretary had resigned, before the vote of confidence had taken place? [*Interruption.*] Will the Prime Minister confirm that that has happened, and if it has, will he confirm also that the next big test of devolution will be the choice of a new First Secretary without any interference whatever from the Prime Minister?

Mr Blair of course confirmed neither, limiting himself to an ill-humoured reference to 'fun and games down at the Assembly'. Next day it was announced that the Labour Party in Wales had elected as their new leader Mr Rhodri Morgan, the man they had wanted all along (but the Prime Minster didn't).

14

Lord Chancellor's Questions

I dealt in the previous chapter with questions to the Prime Minister. Now comes the turn of the Lord High Chancellor (that is his formal title). We are still in the Commons. For obvious reasons there cannot be questions in the Commons addressed to the Lord High Chancellor (or Lord Chancellor as he is now known). What happens instead is that there are questions to a humble Parliamentary Secretary in the Lord Chancellor's department, in this case Jane Kennedy MP. Known as one of the 1997 Blair babes, this young woman began her working life as a residential child care officer with Liverpool City Council, and then became an area organiser for NUPE. Although not a lawyer, she is a member of the Belgian Shepherd Dog Association. Does that give us confidence in her ability to answer questions directed to the Lord Chancellor? I rather think not, but that is the way British politics works in the 21st century. Jane's House of Commons grilling occurred on 22 February 2000.

The Conservative Dominic Grieve MP kicked off. He is a barrister who spent some years as a lay visitor to police stations before becoming an MP in 1997. He asked Ms Kennedy why he had gained the impression that representations by the Council of Circuit Judges on issues such as court layout, new court building and information technology were disregarded by Tony Blair's Lord High Chancellor, otherwise known as his former pupil master Derry Irvine. Derry's representative on earth (or at least in the Commons) tartly replied that she could not be held responsible for any impressions Mr Grieve might form.

Gerald Bermingham (Labour), another barrister, got a friendlier reception from Ms Kennedy for his request that the Lord Chancellor, bearing in mind the change in format and procedure arising from the incorporation of the European Convention on Human Rights into our law on 2 October 2000, should ensure that the judges sitting in the Crown Court will have been well tutored in the complex nature of these idealistic proposals and the various cases that have been decided in the European courts. The Blair babe said he had made a good point. She demurely added that great efforts were being made to ensure that the judiciary and those responsible for administering the Court Service were well briefed on all implications of the momentous Human Rights Act 1998.

A third barrister, the Conservative Nick Hawkins MP, was rather more directly rude to Lord Irvine of Lairg, the Lord High Chancellor (widely known as Derry). Did Ms Kennedy accept that it was a matter of profound concern if Derry gave the impression that he goes through the motions of receiving delegations from the judiciary, while the judiciary feels that its views are simply being ignored and that all that is happening is a face-saving exercise? Increasingly as one talks to people at all levels of the legal profession (complained Mr Hawkins), the impression left by this exalted Blairite figure is that he is contemptuous and dismissive of any representations that are made to him.

Ms Kennedy ignored this, and moved on. Obviously she had no answer. What answer could there be?

How many times, asked Mr Gordon Prentice (Labour), has the Lord Chancellor sat in a judicial capacity in the last twelve months? Four times, said Ms Kennedy. 'That is four times too many' retorted the sprightly Mr Prentice. Ms Kennedy begged to disagree. If the Lord Chancellor were not himself a judge, she said, he could not have the necessary close relationship with the senior judiciary. The relationship between the executive and the judiciary could therefore deteriorate, with damaging consequences and consequential risks to the judiciary's independence. Even to opponents, it sounded plausible.

Now came the turn of a solicitor, David Kidney (Labour). He wanted to know about the progress made by the Office for the Supervision of Solicitors in dealing with complaints against his brethren. Ms Kennedy told him there were fewer outstanding cases than before, and the last month had also seen an improvement in the turn-around of complaints. 'However', she went on, 'there are still areas of serious concern, particularly in relation to the quality of adjudication of complaints. My colleague as

Parliamentary Secretary, my honourable Friend the Member for Wyre Forest (Mr. Lock), will be visiting the OSS on 20 March 2000 to discuss these concerns. In the meantime, we will continue closely to monitor the progress made at the OSS'. Reminded of the reserve powers conferred by Blair's Access to Justice Act 1999, she said it would be better if the OSS itself met the targets set by the Government. If it did not, the Government would act. Bravo! Who could cavil at that? But it signified a betrayal of professionalism. Such betrayals are an everyday occurrence with Mr Blair.

Ian Bruce (Conservative), who is not a lawyer, then informed the House that one of his constituents is Mr Tony Walden-Biles, a leading light in the organisation which calls itself Complaints Against Solicitors – Action for Independent Adjudication (CASIA). 'I have on a number of occasions taken him to see two Conservative Ministers and now three lots of Labour Ministers. They all promised that as the supervision of solicitors was not really going according to plan and that as it was a last chance, the Government would probably start to impose supervision of solicitors from outside. Why do Ministers constantly say at the Dispatch Box that they are still not happy with the OSS while doing nothing about it? When my constituents have a serious complaint about solicitors, they are not satisfied with simply having their bills reduced and having a maximum compensation limit of £1,000.'

Ms Kennedy nodded but stalled on that one. The clock above the Speaker's head indicated that her ordeal was over. She had not done too badly, considering. But our constitutional legal system was left mangled.

15

Rewriting History in the Court of Appeal

The Times front page on 31 July 1998 carried the untruthful banner headline 'Bentley is innocent'. Its law report for that day spelt out how the Court of Appeal, headed by Lord Bingham of Cornhill CJ, had overturned not only the Derek Bentley murder conviction but also a fundamental principle of English law. This is expressed, as so often, in Latin maxims. Mr Blair's judges of today mostly dislike and reject Latin maxims (though there are notable exceptions). This is a sign that law, in the eyes of many, has ceased to be a scholarly profession. Such people do not realise what they owe to scholarship.

The principle to which I refer is cocooned in the maxim *res judicata pro veritate accipitur* (a thing adjudicated is to be received as true). Related maxims are *interest reipublicae res judicata non rescindi* (it is in the national interest that judgments be not rescinded) and *interest reipublicae ut sit finis litium* (it is in the national interest that legal proceedings be not protracted). These maxims indicate that, once normal appeal procedures have been exhausted, a case should not be reopened except for compelling reasons. Such compelling reasons exist where a convict is languishing in prison when new evidence suggests his conviction may be unsafe. That was not the position with Bentley. He was not languishing, but long dead.

Who nowadays cares about these dusty old legal maxims, especially when couched in the decent obscurity of a dead language? The then Chairman of the Bar Council, Anthony Scrivener QC, suggested that the courts should 'bar Latin once and for all' on the ground that 'the Romans and their civilisation have gone forever and that their language went with them' What a dismal abdication of the Bar's old position, adopted for the good of society!

Scrivener's suggestion about scrapping Latin might have carried more weight if in the same speech he had not used 'longevity' as meaning prolixity in apparent ignorance of its derivation from the Latin *longevus*, long life. More recently Lord Justice May said that 'the time has come to abandon all Latin tags'. In 1730 the use of Latin in court proceedings was forbidden by the statute 4 Geo 2 c 26, repealed as spent by the Civil Procedure Acts Repeal Act 1879. Perhaps it wasn't spent after all. Our legal system may now indeed be mature enough to dispense with the props furnished by Latin tags, though I dispute that. So can it also dispense with the principles these tags embody? That seems unlikely. So why not retain the tags to remind us of the principles?

The law publishers Sweet & Maxwell used to publish a handbook called *Latin for Lawyers*. I still have my student's copy of the second edition, dated 1937. It contains over a thousand Latin maxims, preceded by an exordium (apologies to Mr Scrivener *et al.* for the use of this Latin term, which means a statement made at the beginning of a discourse). From this I should like to quote.

> Law, like moral philosophy or politics, has its maxims which sum up in a pregnant sentence some leading principle or axiom of law. . . Like the rules of the common law, [they] derive their source and sanction from an immemorial antiquity, from frequent judicial recognition, and from the imprimatur (apologies as before) of the sages of our law. . . The merit of the maxim is twofold. It is a useful generalisation of law wherein every student who would become his gown may note, as Wingate says, how the same key opens many locks, or, to put it another way, how all cases are reducible to a few theses.
>
> The other merit of the maxim lies in its epigrammatic form. Like the proverb, it embodies "the wisdom of many and the wit of one". . . . Nowhere more than in its maxims does the robust good sense of the common law of England display itself; and does not one of those very maxims warn the critic that no one ought to be wiser than the laws?

Robust good sense was not apparent in the recent Bentley case. What was that expensive collection of highly trained lawyers doing, mulling at public expense over the trial of a long-executed youth? The short answer is that they were responding, as the law required, to a reference from the new Criminal Cases Review Commission. The full answer involves rather more than that.

The Court of Appeal held that Bentley's conviction of murdering PC Miles on the night of 2 November 1952 should be quashed as 'unsafe'. The sole grounds for this ruling were defects they fancied they found in the summing up by the late Lord Goddard CJ, whom even so Lord Bingham acknowledged to have been 'one of the out-standing criminal judges of the century'.

It is not my contention that the Court of Appeal were wrong in their finding that Bentley's conviction was unsafe. My assertion is that they had no business to be considering the matter at all, since Bentley was tried and convicted by the standards of his day. By those same standards his conviction was upheld on appeal. I well remember the heated public feeling at the time, and the anger aroused by the foul murder of PC Miles at the hands of Bentley's warehouse-breaking accomplice the 16-year old thug Christopher Craig. Bentley too was armed, with what his executioner Albert Pierrepoint called 'a knuckle-duster with a vicious spike upon it – in itself a lethal enough weapon'. But it's history now. What are we doing resurrecting it? What on earth are we doing rewriting it?

Here are some more questions.

The appeal was lodged 'on behalf of' the deceased Bentley by his niece Maria Bentley-Dingwall. Why should Bentley's niece have the right to put the law in motion in this way half a century later? How far are we to go back in reversing history? Suppose there had been no niece, nor any other surviving relative? It is a mere accident that in 1998 there are any known relatives of the long-dead Bentley. Jurisdiction should not hang on accidents, and we should let history rest. It is the height of presumption to think that in this generation we can reverse history. It is more than presumptuous: it is absurd. No previous generation would have been so stupid as to try it.

At the time, fifty years ago, the pathetic Bentley brought an appeal against his conviction in accordance with the law of that distant period. It was heard by the Court of Criminal Appeal (now abolished) and after due considera-tion dismissed. Bentley was then hanged, as the law of that time decreed. Under the long-standing policy of our law, outlined above, that should have been an end of it. Why does our generation think it has the right to overthrow that wise policy of our law and dig up and reverse this ancient history, at enormous public expense?

The Bentley jury sat in judgment in the days when qualifications were required for jury service. It was not, as now, open to every 18-year old school leaver with or without O levels. The Bentley jury sat in judgment in the days when a jury's verdict had to be unanimous. Nowadays dissent is allowed. So that jury of mature, qualified, citizens of those early post-war days sat in court, heard the evidence, assessed the demeanour of the witnesses, listened to the Lord Chief Justice directing them on points of law, and then *unanimously* found Bentley guilty. Half a century later the Court of Appeal, relying only on paper records and sitting in a different age, presumes to say their verdict is 'unsafe'. Why should this be?

It happened because today's Court of Appeal thinks it knows better. It thinks the experienced Lord Chief Justice Goddard did not instruct the jury adequately on the burden of proof resting on the prosecution, and the fact that they had to be satisfied of guilt beyond reasonable doubt. This despite the fact that Goddard's handling of the case was, long ago, upheld on appeal. Now the Times untruthfully proclaims 'Bentley is innocent'. Why was this untruthful? Because quashing a verdict of guilt as 'unsafe' is very far from saying that the accused was innocent. The over-whelming likelihood is that, despite any supposed deficiencies in the trial judge's direction, the 1952 jury came to a true and fair verdict on the evidence, as they were sworn to do. Bentley was not 'innocent'.

Awareness of the unreal nature of what he was about comes through in the judgment of Lord Bingham. He admits that in considering anything like the Bentley appeal the liability of a party to a joint enterprise has to be determined according to the common law as now understood, not as it was understood in 1952. The conduct of the trial and the direction of the jury have to be judged according to the standards which the court would now apply, and not according to 1952 standards. Worse, the safety of the conviction also has to be judged according to the standards which the court would now apply. Finally Lord Bingham said –

> Where between conviction and appeal there have been significant changes in the common law, as opposed to changes effected by statute, or in standards of fairness, the approach indicated requires the court to apply legal rules and procedural criteria which were not and could not reasonably have been applied at the time.

It is scarcely necessary to say more to indicate what a travesty this so-called appeal was, but one point may be added. The reasoning behind the appeal would have applied equally if the 1952 Home Secretary, Sir David Maxwell-Fyfe, had responded to some public pressure and reprieved Bentley. If that had happened Bentley would by now, like his accomplice Craig, have served his prison sentence and been long at liberty. Would it really be right that a man with his record should have his conviction retrospectively quashed nearly half a century later and thereafter rank as a victim of gross injustice entitled to massive compensation from today's taxpayers? What sensible person could think that? Yet that is what would have happened.

Should we excuse the Court of Appeal in the Bentley case because they were merely performing a function wished on them by statute? Again, I think not. There is nothing in Lord Bingham's judgment to show that he and his two colleagues found their task in any way objectionable. Our generation needs to be reminded of that pregnant saying of L P Hartley's in his novel *The Go-Between*: the past is a foreign country, they do things differently there. Or to put it even more succinctly: you can't change history, and you shouldn't even try.

Mr Blair is very fond of issuing so-called 'apologies' for things done before any of us were born. The tendency to do this is a sickening feature of modern life. An apology is worthless and meaningless unless issued by those who were actually guilty of the offence in question (if indeed it was an offence). It is a central indictment of Mr Blair, and his political philosophy Blairism, that even history is not safe from their revising clutches. The casualty is truth. Any regime that reverses or denies truth is condemned, because of its falsity, to obloquy.

16

The *Marchioness* and Fancy Dancing

'Another day, another inquiry, another publicly-funded examination into a tragic event.' I quote from the *Daily Express* of 17 February 2000. The reference is to the announcement in the House of Commons on 14 February by Mr John Prescott, Secretary of State for the Environment, Transport and the Regions, that under the Merchant Shipping Act 1995 s 268 a further judicial inquiry was to be held into the *Marchioness* disaster. This tragedy occurred on the River Thames in London on 20 August 1989. 132 people were enjoying an evening riverboat party when the dredger *Bowbelle* struck. Within minutes the Marchioness sank. 51 young people died, and many more were injured. Mr Prescott told us that Lord Justice Clarke would chair this new public inquiry.

Very properly, Mr Prescott referred to the grief of the families. He added that a new public inquiry could not bring their loved ones back 'but it can, I hope, bring some peace of mind to know that their case can be told and lessons can be learned for the future'. In the debate following, Joan Ruddock MP, shadow Minister of Transport at the time of the disaster, urged Mr Prescott 'to ensure that we are all safe on our great river at any time'. Of course that can never be ensured, as she must have known. (If she did not she was unfit for her office.)

Previous inquiries into the *Marchioness* disaster include: an investigation by the marine accidents investigation branch; two inquests, at the second of which the coroner's court held that the 51 had been unlawfully killed; an investigation by the police and Crown Prosecution Service followed by the prosecution of the master of the Bowbelle (the jury twice disagreed, resulting in his acquittal); and an inquiry chaired by John Hayes, secretary-general of the Law Society.

In 1992 Mr Prescott referred to all this as 'legal fancy dancing'; but it was not by any means over. 'On 18 August [1999],' he told the Commons on 14 February 2000, 'I announced a wide-ranging public inquiry. . . It was chaired by a senior judge, Lord Justice Clarke. It was an open public inquiry. Its scope was broad and its examination detailed. . . For the first time, all the relevant documentation was gathered in one place and everyone concerned could make their case. The inquiry reviewed current safety standards on the river and Lord Justice Clarke's report was published quickly, as I requested, on 2 December 1999. Lord Justice Clarke was also asked to advise 'whether there is a case for a further investigation or inquiry into the circumstances surrounding the Marchioness disaster and its causes'. His second report, dealing with that issue, is being published today. . .'

In his second report the overworked Lord Justice said there was indeed a case for yet another inquiry. Mr Prescott mercifully added: 'Lord Justice Clarke considers that the scope of the inquiry will be sufficient and that the public interest does not require a further inquiry into the police investigation, the two inquests or the failure to secure criminal convictions'. Thank goodness for that.

But Mr Prescott also said: 'The bereaved families have expressed forcefully their great distress at the removal of the hands from the victims for fingerprint identification purposes, without advising the next of kin. . . I have set up a non-statutory public inquiry into that specific matter under Lord Justice Clarke to run side by side with the judicial inquiry'.

In connection with these further inquiries Mr Prescott said he would look favourably on applications made by the relatives of the victims and the survivors for legal costs to be met from public funds. There has been a great deal of other public expense, and there will be more. Lord Justice Clarke has been withdrawn for a protracted period from the job for which he was appointed, the work of the over-burdened Court of Appeal. Even after ten years, this sorrowful matter is not to be allowed to rest.

Patrick McLoughlin MP, Parliamentary Under-Secretary of State at the time of the *Marchioness* disaster, said his [Conservative] Government did not hold a public inquiry because the marine accidents investigation branch had been set up, and it was better left to them. He added that the air accidents investigation branch has long been accepted as an authoritative body, and that there has not been a public inquiry into an air accident since 1976 although there have been serious incidents involving great loss of life.

Mr Blair's Government is prone to wringing its hands over the past and reopening long-dead events (remember Derek Bentley and Bloody Sunday). In conclusion I quote again from the writer in the *Daily Express* of 17 February 2000: 'I have serious doubts about whether inquiries ever really achieve anything at all other than to eat up a vast pot of public money to deliver recommendations that are little more than common sense'.

17

Henry VIII is alive and kicking

Our late revered Tudor monarch King Henry VIII liked chopping off people's heads. It was what he is best known for. Therefore, by some devious logic, his royal name has been attached to the modern constitutional device of giving Government Ministers power to repeal or amend Acts of Parliament by delegated legislation – in other words by orders they make themselves. They don't need to go to Parliament for approval; they can do it on their own. Democrats profess a dislike of this arbitrary procedure. Judges, being all good democrats, share this dislike. One judge, Lord Scarman, described a Henry VIII clause that came before him as 'startling'. Another senior judge, Lord Bridge, said that a power to modify the provisions of a statute 'should be narrowly and strictly construed'.

But still they try it on.

A recent example was in the Representation of the People Bill of 2000 (later passed into law as the Representation of the People Act 2000). This sought to change electoral procedures in relation to electoral registration and absent voting, and allowed for experiments involving innovative electoral practices. It also made changes in electoral law (1) to make it easier for the disabled to vote, and (2) to create an offence of supplying false particulars on a nomination form. In all this it gave effect to recommendations made by the Working Party on Electoral Procedures, a group chaired by the then Labour Home Office Minister, George Howarth MP, and containing representatives from the main political parties, local government and electoral administrators.

The Working Party recommended, among other things, that pilot schemes for innovative electoral procedures, such as weekend voting, electronic voting, early voting, and mobile polling stations, should be run by a local authority so that their effectiveness could be evaluated, and that the successful ones should be used (or as the official memorandum puts it in the modern jargon 'rolled out') more widely. This is where our old friend Henry VIII comes in.

Clause 10 of the Bill allowed the Secretary of State to make orders enabling local authorities in England and Wales to run pilot schemes of innovative electoral procedures at particular local government elections. A local authority running a pilot scheme was required to produce a report on the scheme, including an assessment of its success in facilitating voting and (if relevant) the counting process. The report must include a statement on whether, in the local authority's opinion:

* turnout was higher than it would otherwise have been,
* voters found the new arrangements easy to use,
* the new procedures led to any increase in personation or other electoral fraud, and
* the procedures led to an increase or saving in public expenditure.

Clause 11 (the Henry VIII clause) empowered the Secretary of State to make an order providing for an innovation which has been piloted successfully by a local authority to apply generally and permanently in the case of particular kinds of elections. *That includes parliamentary elections.* Uproar!

This particular Henry VIII clause had been sniped at all through the Bill's progress, first in the Commons and then in the Lords. It had also been condemned by the Select Committee on Delegated Powers and Deregulation. On 29 February 2000, at Report stage in the Lords, Lord Goodhart moved an amendment on behalf of the LibDems, supported by the Conservatives, to delete the reference to parliamentary elections. He said –

It is true that the mechanism of elections is not as important in the scale of things as is the franchise, but it is still a matter of considerable importance. Until now all issues, such as the question of the days on which elections are to be held and the time that polling stations are open on those days, have always been dealt with by primary legislation. What we will now have is power to roll out a pilot scheme across the country for all elections on the basis possibly of one trial in one local government area. We believe that to be quite inappropriate.'

The language was quiet, as befits the House of Lords, but their Lordships braced themselves for a tussle. Then the Minister, Lord Bassam of Brighton, rose. There was a hush. The Minister spoke. 'My Lords, it is not customary for a Minister to intervene at such an early stage in a debate, but it may help the House if I do so.' Expectation increased. The Minister continued –

> I can advise your Lordships that we shall be bringing forward Government amendments to Clause 11 at Third Reading. The effect of the amendments will be to limit the power to roll out successful innovations only to local government elections.

Sensation! Democracy had triumphed. Parliament had proved its worth. The try-on was called off. The constitutional need for a second chamber was yet again vindicated.

But why did it happen in the first place? Lord Bassam gave a clue –

> It was a power that was recommended by the Working Party on Electoral Procedures – and I can assure your Lordships, having made inquiries, that the working party meant the power to apply to all elections and not simply to local elections.

Which just goes to show that you cannot trust mere working parties to get things right on major constitutional issues.

Still people go on trying to prove that dear old Henry VIII was wrong, and shouldn't be followed today. Still they fail. The latest victims were the so-called metric martyrs in 2002. Instigated by their counsel Michael Shrimpton (who should have known better) they sought to persuade the Divisional Court that the power conferred by the European Communities Act 1972 to make, by delegated legislation, amendments in Acts of Parliament was invalid. The Divisional Court threw them out. Old Henry triumphed, as he has always done.

18

Mr Shaun Woodward's Lecture on Decent Behaviour

Being a turncoat MP is nothing new. The eighteenth century satirist Peter Pindar described William Windham MP as 'Turncoat Windham, to no party true'. There have been numerous shameless successors to Turncoat Windham. The latest of this changeable kidney is the likeable Mr Shaun Woodward.

At the general election in 1997 this agreeable man stood as a Conservative and was enthusiastically elected as such by the honest burghers of Witney, a market town near where at that time I lived in Oxfordshire. Then, to the grief and rage of the said worthy burghers, Mr Woodward suddenly declared that he was after all the *Labour* MP for Witney. His constituents, protesting that they were not consulted on this interesting transformation, were told by their elected representative, the said Mr Woodward, to like it or lump it. He was sitting pretty, bolstered by the wealth of the heiress he had been so fortunate as to court and marry. By that right he dwelt in a handsome mansion house, and the burghers of Witney could go hang. They couldn't touch him.

The turncoat Mr Woodward might have remembered some more worthy predecessors.

There was Bruce Douglas-Mann, elected in 1979 as Labour MP for Merton, Mitcham and Morden. By 1982 this man felt obliged to defect to a grouping of the time known as The Alliance. He thereupon resigned his House of Commons seat at the 3 Ms and offered himself to the voters all over again under his new insignia. At the resulting by-election they rejected him, but he had done the decent thing.

Again when Dick Taverne (now Lord Taverne), then Labour MP for Lincoln, left his party in 1972 he too resigned his seat and stood again in the resulting by-election. He was successful in being re-elected. Again, he had done the decent thing – and that time it paid off. But

Taverne could not be sure that it would. He did what in those days people thought one ought to do. It went without saying.

Mr Shaun Woodward of Witney did not do the decent thing. It was because nowadays under Blairism doing the decent thing does not go without saying. Under Mr Blair there has been a lurch in public standards of behaviour, though to be fair it started even before he took control. Dear little Shaun rejected requests that he should follow in the noble footsteps of Douglas-Mann and Taverne. Taking now the Labour whip, he still clung to his safe Tory seat, his parliamentary privileges, his comfortable salary, and his pension rights. He was unmoved by the predominant opinion in the little town of Witney, which was that he should at once apply to become Steward of the Chiltern Hundreds (an expedient whereby MPs are excused further attendance in the House of Commons and at the same time relieved of their emoluments).

Mr Woodward's first Commons speech as a defector to Labour was delivered on the second reading (9 March 2000) of the Race Relations (Amendment) Bill, brought from the Lords. The Bill's main purposes were to extend the Race Relations Act 1976 as respects public authorities and to make chief officers of police vicariously liable for racist acts by their officers. In his speech Mr Woodward delivered a lecture on decent behaviour, assuring us that 'the pursuit of decency is a moral quest'. In the course of this he attacked my old friend Gerald Howarth, the Conservative MP for Aldershot. He quoted with opprobrium what Mr Howarth had said in the Commons in March 1999, during a debate on the Stephen Lawrence inquiry: 'no Government have ever received a mandate to turn the United Kingdom into a multicultural society'. If he had cared he might have added that if any Government had sought such a mandate it would have been emphatically refused by the electorate.

By sleight of politics, our supposedly democratic society has been peaceably revolutionised by a change the majority of our populace were never asked to vote for, never in fact voted for, and never would have voted for. That this was not followed by revolution is a tribute to British phlegm – or a sign of British flabbiness and decadence. It was certainly a sign that under our present system democracy is allowed to prevail only when the liberal intelligentsia approve of its decisions.

When that soggy approval is not forthcoming, as with capital punishment, corporal punishment, parental disciplining of offspring, disgust at anal intercourse, and of course free-for-all immigration, democracy is denied without explanation. If an explanation were to be vouchsafed it would be on the lines that we really can't submit to democratic decision when the voters are so obviously bigoted and misinformed. But of course the argument never in terms gets as far as that. . .

The wealthy apostate Shaun Woodward criticised Gerald Howarth's statement regretting that some people from abroad are not content to learn and accept our native customs and traditions, but wish to assert their own. Here he might have cited Mr Justice Singer's statement in the KR abduction case on the law's need to protect ethnic youngsters from parents who, motivated by cultural or religious values deriving from overseas, seek to subject them to coercion by forced marriage or forced residence abroad. The judge warned parents of ethnic children to understand that they may face considerable difficulties if they hope on the one hand to bring them up in an English educational system and society, but at the same time to retain every aspect of their own traditions and expectations.

The Conservative MP Dr Julian Lewis countered Woodward's sentiments: 'Unlike the honourable Gentleman, I am a third generation descendant of an immigrant family. My family recognised that it was incumbent on us to adapt ourselves to some extent to the history and culture of the country to which we were coming. It is not unreasonable to ask that of people who have chosen to make their lives here'.

Then Woodward gave us all our orders. We must not, he said, fear multiculturalism: 'we have to desire it'. When his turn came to speak in the debate, Gerald Howarth rebuked Woodward, saying his speech was 'particularly nauseating. . . [h]e campaigned vigorously for the Conservative party, attacked this Government and then, overnight, switched and suddenly found that everything that the Conservatives had done was nauseating and anathema. . .'

So not everyone is prepared to take lectures on decency from the heiress-financed Shaun Woodward. The MPs taking part in that debate did not of course know that after the next general election in 2001 Mr Blair would arrange for Mr Woodward to be parachuted into the safe Labour seat of St Helens in Lancashire, where the bemused voters did not know what to make of him. He was not at all what they were used to, being straight-speaking northern folk.

19

CRAPS dropped

Recently the Home Office announced that our long established and highly respected Probation Service is to be renamed. This in line with Blairism, whose mad agenda is to change everything and throw all our history overboard. What the Home Office came up with as the new name was the Community Punishment and Rehabilitation Service, which hardly trips off the tongue. Few thought the change a good idea, especially when it was pointed out that the inevitable acronym would be CRAPS. There would also be everlasting doubt on the part of intelligent crappees about whether 'community' governed 'rehabilitation' as well as 'punishment'. This type of phrase is a source of ambiguity which is very well known – except apparently to some Home Office officials. (Actually it was meant to govern both concepts.)

Despite appearances, there was behind this rather obvious piece of Home Office silliness some good reasoning (or what Mr Blair's New Labour likes to call joined-up thinking). A consultation paper entitled 'Joining Forces to Protect the Public', issued in August 1998, began the process. The usual sort of ponderous official wit behind the title of this paper rose from the fact that it envisaged that certain forces, such as police forces and probation services (they are not 'forces', but never mind) might be joined together so as better to protect the long-suffering public from who knows what. The paper alleged that a series of Acts of Parliament have merely served to consolidate an outdated reflection [how do you consolidate a reflection?] of a service that has been engaged in change and modernisation for many years. Legislation, it went on, still directs probation officers to 'advise, assist and befriend' offenders. This phrase, it alleged, is completely out of line with modern reality. What a pity. I always thought 'advise, assist and befriend' was a good and generous phrase to describe what probation officers ought to do in relation to the hapless unfortunates committed to their care.

The consultation paper led to the Criminal Justice and Court Services Bill, introduced in the Commons on 15 March 2000 and later passed as the Criminal Justice and Court Services Act 2000. *Part I* created new probation and family services; *Part II* set up a system to prevent 'unsuitable' people from working with children (how common that useful adjective has become). *Part III* dealt with community orders, including greater use of electronic monitoring, and introduced new powers for the compulsory drug testing of alleged offenders; *Part IV* introduced a new power to allow the police access to Driver and Vehicle Licensing Agency (DVLA) driver records and increased the penalty for parents who fail to ensure that their children attend school regularly. I have space only for a few details of the probation arrangements.

The consultation paper proposed various ways in which the prison and probation services could work together to improve protection of the public and reduce reoffending. As a result of the consultation process the Home Secretary, Mr Jack Straw MP, decided that the two services should not combine, but should retain their separate identities while using complementary methods to achieve these common goals. No doubt he thought Parliament would confirm him in that and other relevant decisions (as it did), but the official explanatory memorandum on the Bill was constitutionally wrong to assume that. The House of Lords might have insisted on contrary views.

The Home Secretary thought existing arrangements under the Probation Service Act 1993, which provided for 54 separate probation services, were not working efficiently, and that the probation service's responsibility for Family Court work did not fit well with its core aim. Accordingly the Bill created a unified probation service for England and Wales, which will be directly accountable to the Home Secretary. It will have a structure based on 42 local areas, each with a board composed of representatives of the local community (who are presumed to understand the needs of their people). The boundaries of these areas will match those of police forces, a step towards the Government's aim of improving efficiency by creating common boundaries across all agencies in the criminal justice system. The Children And Family Court Advisory and Support Service (CAFCASS), also created by this Bill, will take over Family Court work, leaving the probation service to concentrate on working with offenders.

Two days before the Bill was introduced, a little interchange took place in the House of Commons. Mr. John Bercow (Conservative) asked the Home Secretary to make a statement on his plans to change the name of the Probation Service. The Minister of State at the Home Office (Mr. Paul Boateng) said he was grateful to the honourable Gentleman for the opportunity to announce that his Department had listened to the representations of those who thought CRAPS not a good idea. There had been a change of mind in the Home Office. 'We intend that the new unified service will be called the National Probation Service of England and Wales.'

Mr. Bercow: My joy at that reply is literally boundless . . . I warmly congratulate him – at the risk of inflicting the gravest possible damage on his future political career.

Mr. Boateng: I am delighted to have brought a little joy into the honourable Gentleman's life.

20

Mr Baldry MP and
the Indian Moneylender

Elizabeth Filkin, then Parliamentary Commissioner for Standards, raised the lid on that constantly bubbling and murky pot the Sovereign's Fount of Honour, so often in our history more accurately described as HM's Fount of *Dishonour*. In the nether world, Maundy Gregory rubs his greasy bloated hands while reading, printed on asbestos for the local inhabitants, the Eighth Report of the Select Committee on Standards and Privileges. This is mainly, though not exclusively, concerned with the financial and honorific affairs of Mr Tony Baldry, barrister MP for Banbury (Conservative). At the time in question Mr Baldry was a minister in John Major's Government, so for once this affair does not reflect on Tony Blair (though he might learn some lessons from it). As a barrister who once sought to become a Conservative MP, I cringe in shame at this tawdry tale. I wish Mr Baldry would do that too, but it is not likely he will. That is not the way things go, nowadays. Not nowadays, in the sickly world of Blairism (which infects more than itself).

Mr Blair tells us that we now enjoy open government. To prove it, and his zeal for the computer information revolution (known as IT), Mr Blair has made available to his subjects a website called *www.open.gov.uk*. So why, if government is now so open, do we not know more about another interesting matter mentioned in the aforesaid Eighth Report of the Select Committee on Standards and Privileges? I refer to the fact that the Lord Chancellor's Department now keeps a list, forwarded from time to time to higher authority and always kept up to date, setting out the names of Persons Deserving of an Honour.

I return to Mr Baldry. The Eighth Report of the Select Committee on Standards and Privileges endorses a memorandum by Ms Filkin relating to a complaint by Mr A Milne, a solicitor, levelled against Mr Tony Baldry MP. The report says: 'On 2 January 1997 Mr Baldry received the benefit of a loan of £5000 from Mr Sarosh Zaiwalla. On 14 January 1997 he wrote to the Lord Chancellor's Department recommending the inclusion of Mr Zaiwalla in the next Honours List. In that letter he made no mention of his financial relationship with Mr Zaiwalla'. Shame! Oh for shame! What have we sunk to? Mr Baldry, what do you think you are doing? What will the aspiring kids among your constituents think? Have you not let the side down? Should you not set an example?

Ms Filkin's careful and accurate report includes various documents throwing light on the Baldry affair. A letter from Mr Milne reveals that he was at one time a partner with Mr Zaiwalla in a firm of City solicitors. Mr Milne asks Ms Filkin to look into Mr Baldry's habit of booking breakfasts at the House of Commons 'in the name of a non-existent organisation, the Asian Business Breakfast, which is simply a marketing label of Zaiwalla & Co, in order to get round the rules for such bookings'. He asks 'whether it was proper for Mr Baldry to have given a reference for Mr Zaiwalla to receive a CBE, at a time when he hardly knew Mr Zaiwalla, as part of the price for the loan which he received, [or] to have used a ministerial car to attend the offices of Zaiwalla & Co to negotiate the loan'.

The report reveals that Mr Milne had written a letter about all this to the leader of the Conservative Party, Mr Hague, saying 'I believe that Mr Baldry approached Mr Zaiwalla because he desperately needed funds and Mr Zaiwalla had made other payments to politicians and had a reputation as a moneylender. I believe that Mr Zaiwalla's nickname within your party is "the Indian Moneylender" and I would question whether it was proper for Mr Baldry to use an official car to visit an Indian Moneylender'. The key findings by Ms Filkin, endorsed in the report, were these.

Mr Baldry was not required to register the loan from Mr Zaiwalla because the concession he received did not exceed the threshold of £215. Although clients of Zaiwalla & Co were from time to time invited to the breakfasts I have received no evidence that Mr Baldry booked the dining rooms 'to get round the rules for such bookings' or that the Club was 'simply a marketing label'. *Complaint not upheld.*

Mr Baldry should have registered Zaiwalla & Co as clients for the purpose of booking House of Commons dining rooms from June 1998. *Complaint upheld.*

Mr Baldry failed to uphold the Code of Conduct when he provided a recommendation to the Lord Chancellor's Department that Mr Zaiwalla be awarded an honour without being open and declaring the loan he had received twelve days previously. *Complaint upheld.*

For the latter sin, Mr Baldry was required to make a personal apology in the chamber of the House of Commons. He duly did this on 23 March 2000. Perhaps we should not be too hard on him. These things happen. Let him who is without sin cast the first stone, and so on and so forth. What really intrigues me is that list of prospective honorands kept by the Lord Chancellor's Department. You won't find any of that explained on www.open.gov.uk, and I wonder why not. Aren't we as citizens entitled to know? But then Blairism, truly analysed, is not about the rights of citizens. It is about supporting what Blair calls *The Project*, and carrying it forward for ever. If you are in you are in. Otherwise you are out.

Ms Filkin's report gives just a tantalising glimpse of what goes on in this Blairite world of ours. The prime mover in trying (unsuccessfully) to get Mr Zaiwalla's name on to the Lord Chancellor's list of Persons Deserving of an Honour was Lord Feldman, one time chairman of the National Union of Conservative and Unionist Associations and author of *Some Thoughts on Job Creation*. Why did the noble lord Lord Feldman do this? Was he acting in some quasi-official capacity for the commoner Mr Hague, then Leader of the Conservative Party? Shouldn't we be told more about the workings of this mysterious list? It is not after all just a party matter.

The answer is that of course we the electors should be told more, much more, but we know that is not going to happen. Keeping the voters in the dark is an aspect of modern democratic working that it seems cannot be escaped. It harks back to the autocratic past, which we are supposed to have escaped. But the powerful way powerful people operate is in truth an aspect not of autocracy or democracy but full-beefed humanity. That is simply the way we humans are built, so we had better learn to tolerate it. It is not going to go away. Blair enhances it, but underneath him it is there all along. . .

21

Education Gimmickry

I recently received a letter from the Sarah Bonnell School, an inner London secondary school at Stratford. It came from a person described in the letterhead as 'Ms Cauthar Maryam Latif Tooley, Headlearner/Headteacher'. Earlier I had queried Ms Tooley's use of the term Headlearner on the ground that it was a foolish gimmick. In the letter Ms Tooley denied this. She said she took very seriously her position as one who was learning along with the students. I stand by my description. For a school head publicly to describe herself as 'Headlearner' must confuse the ignorant children, themselves seeking to learn, and diminish their respect for teachers. The term panders to the fad of so-called child-centred learning, where the school staff do not presume to know any more about anything than the little children do. That silly pose is one of the many things wrong with modern education in England.

Other things that are wrong were displayed in the House of Commons on 5 July 2001. Mr Blair's new Education Secretary (the post is now renamed Secretary of State for Education and Skills – another gimmick) is Estelle Morris. A major piece of gimmickry displayed on 5 July 2001 was the new Labour concept of specialist schools. Grammar-school type selection of pupils to separate the sheep from the goats (to use that still useful biblical metaphor) is anathema to Blair's Government, yet parents tiresomely go on demanding it. So a way round has to be found, and specialist schools are the current answer. The Minister informed the House that from September 2001 there would be 684 specialist schools 'and we are working towards a target of 1,000 by September 2003'.

The fact that the Government's ultimate target of 1,500 specialist schools by September 2006 relates to almost half the secondary schools in England shows that something very peculiar is going on here. Are the nature and character of half the nation's secondary schools really going to be drastically altered, or is this just another piece of Blair Government window dressing? One Labour MP suspected the latter.

Mr. Gordon Prentice: If we are to have specialist schools, I am rather attracted by the Liberal Democrat policy, which is to make all schools specialist schools. We could then call them comprehensives.

More gimmickry was afoot.

Estelle Morris: It is our aim that all secondary schools develop their own ethos and mission. Some will find their voice in the specialist school movement and others will do so through training schools, beacon schools or church schools. That is the nature of diversity.

What rot! All schools inevitably develop a character of their own, whether good, bad or indifferent. Only a crass New Labour government could gild this truism into a glittering artefact with airy talk of 'ethos and mission'. What a beacon school is I know not. Perhaps it trains lighthouse keepers, though I thought the demand for these had dropped off in recent years.

Mr Prentice, Labour MP for Pendle, returned to the attack on specialist schools. He had read in a newspaper that there was a plan to put private companies in charge of departments within such schools.

Mr. Gordon Prentice: As a member of the Labour party's national policy forum, let me ask the Minister where that idea came from. It was never discussed in any of the Labour party's policy forums and, as the Minister will know, it was never discussed at the Labour party's annual conference last September. If we are going to have bizarre suggestions on a regular basis, the Government should at least honour us by telling us who was responsible for the idea in the first place.

The Minister vouchsafed no information whatever concerning this latest gimmick. Instead she took refuge in gobbledygook about 'outsourcing'.

Estelle Morris: There are no circumstances in which I or my Department would force a school to outsource one of its departments.

The inevitably selective nature of these new specialist schools worried a Liberal Democrat MP.

Mr Phil Willis (Harrogate and Knaresborough): Does the Secretary of State agree that her policy on specialist schools is akin to creating a giant McDonald's-like franchise within our school system? The difference is that anyone can go into a McDonald's, but specialist schools will decide which students to take.

The Minister retorted that McDonald's restaurants are all the same, whereas under new Labour all schools will be different. 'We celebrate diversity.'

Isn't excellence more important than diversity? Sir Patrick Cormack, Conservative MP for South Staffordshire, thinks it is. He asked what plans the Government has to encourage youngsters who seek a career in what he called 'the crafts'. The Minister said the Government desperately wants to give the crafts a higher status.

One hopes she does not include gimmickry among these favoured 'crafts'. That has far too high a status already. We later learnt that the way Mr Blair proposed to favour crafts was to treat them as equivalent to scholarship. In February 2002 Ms Morris announced a scheme to this end. I had the following letter in the *Sunday Times* –

Blair's Education Minister Estelle Morris says she thinks studying law is on the same level as studying plumbing or carpentry. Having been a lawyer for more than 50 years I can tell her that is false. Law brings in the whole philosophy of a nation. It engages our values, and plunges to the depths of our being. Law is the sharp end of morality; and our morality is what, at the deepest level, makes us tick. I do not disparage utilitarian plumbing or carpentry, which helps our comfort. Law on the other hand penetrates deep into our lives. It reflects our basic values, or should do. It deserves corresponding respect from educationists.

22

Red Ken and Hunting Pink

That noted Cockney MFH (Master of Fox Hounds) Mr Jorrocks had a high opinion of his vocation in the hunting field. 'Of all sitivations under the sun, none is more enviable or more 'onerable than that of a master of fox 'ounds' he is reported as saying in Robert Smith Surtees' classic novel *Handley Cross*. As I write in 2002, Mr Jorrocks' rural vocation is under severe threat from crass townees, backed up by a large number of urban and suburban Members of Parliament who can't see the point of hunting.

Mr Jorrocks did not think much of Members of Parliament. 'Talk of a MP! vot's an MP compared to an MFH?' To which one can only add vot indeed! Yet here these pampered creatures are, bunched up in the electrically warmed House of Commons, elected en masse with a democratic mandate and speaking out accordingly. Licensed to interfere, one might say. Even to interfere with things they know nothing about. That is democracy, worse luck.

Mr Jorrocks would have used fruity language about a Bill promoted in 2000 by the MP for Brent East and at that time candidate for London mayor Mr Ken Livingstone. Called the Wild Mammals (Hunting With Dogs) Bill, it had a second reading as a private Member's Bill on 7 April 2000. Suitably enough, there were high jinks in the Commons. They began with a procedural trick played by Mr Andrew Dismore (Labour) to get Livingstone's Bill on ahead of one higher in the order. When Mr. Iain Duncan Smith (Conservative) solemnly complained to the Speaker that this was a massive abuse of the process of the House she told him the trick was not new and supporters of his Bill should have made sure enough of them were present at the crucial time. Hansard then recorded –

Mr Ken Livingstone (Brent, East): I beg to move, That the Bill be now read a Second time.

May I make it clear that I had no idea. . . [*Laughter*]

Mr Livingstone went on to deny that his motive in putting forward this anti-hunting Bill was to gain publicity and win favour for his mayoral bid. I will, he said, always put animal welfare ahead of human pleasure. He continued (and many MPs were moved at this) -

> I believe that animals have the right not to be torn apart on a grand scale. . . 100,000 foxes, deer and hares are torn apart by dogs every year. That is totally unnecessary cruelty and suffering on a scale that is rejected by the vast majority of the British people. . . I am proud today to be able to build on the work of colleagues who introduced earlier Bills on the subject, and once again to give the vast majority of honourable Members the right to ban the unacceptable face of cruelty and to end the appalling abuse of our responsibility to protect the life that shares these islands with us. I have foxes in my garden, and it has been a source of amusement to the media that one of them bit off the head of one of my tortoises. I have no illusions about foxes: they are wild animals and they themselves hunt, but we are not wild animals and we can make a conscious choice about the degree of cruelty and pain that we impose on other human beings and on the wildlife in these islands. . . We have a duty to protect wild animals in exactly the same way that we protect our domestic pets.'

The Conservatives might have pointed out that it is the hounds, acting according to their feral nature, who actually tear foxes apart. Instead they continued to moan in a fourth-form way about the procedural trick that had been played on them. Then they groused that Mr Livingstone kept leaving the chamber and coming back, like a fox going in and out of cover. The Deputy Speaker upheld this complaint: 'It is the convention of the House that when one has made a speech to the House, one should stay and hear at least the response from the other side'. Where is he? demanded Mr Douglas Hogg, then answered his own question: 'Talking to the press no doubt'. At that point a mobile phone went off.

Mr Deputy Speaker: Order. Madam Speaker takes an extremely strong line on electronic devices that are not under honourable Members' control in the Chamber.

The Conservatives then started to filibuster. Mr Hogg, objecting that angling was also cruel, told an inordinately long story about how his wife's inefficiency with the rod had added to the sufferings of the fish. For the Liberal Democrats Mr Lembit Opik told an incredulous House that, after listening to the arguments favouring hunting, he had changed his mind on the issue. The idea that anyone should change their mind after listening to a House of Commons debate was beyond most MPs.

The Minister, Mr Mike O'Brien, said the Government thought the Bill should wait until an inquiry Mr Blair had launched under someone called Lord Burns had established the underlying facts. The former actress Glenda Jackson asked why, if hunting was so effective, were numerous foxes living and breeding in her Hampstead garden? There was no answer. Nobody had really said that hunting was all that effective. Its justification was that it had being going on since William the Conqueror and gave a lot of pleasure to a lot of people. The subtext was that people matter a great deal more than vermin. Not everyone agreed.

Finally the Bill was talked out when only 74 of its supporters (instead of the necessary 100) turned up to vote for the closure. Mr James Gray (Conservative) said that Labour MPs should remember that small number next time they tried to argue that their party is overwhelmingly opposed to fox hunting.

Mr Jorrocks would have rubbed his hands at that last crack.

Lord Burns duly reported that, after carefully weighing the evidence, he had come to the conclusion that on the whole there was a lot to be said for controlling foxes by hunting with hounds, provided certain simple safeguards were met. The Labour oiks, led by the vociferous Tony Banks MP, were unimpressed by this. Careful arguments, and the weighing of evidence on either side, were not what they had in mind. It was abolition, and nothing less, that they continued to demand.

23

The Human Rights Act

If anyone should happen to ask you what Thatcher and Blair have in common, tell them this. When the poll tax of dismal memory was imposed on a surprised citizenry by Margaret Thatcher, it was tried out first in Scotland. The very same thing happened when Tony Blair wanted to give his gratified subjects all the benefits of the Human Rights Act (HRA).

While it was provided that the HRA would not come into force generally until 2 October 2000, the Scotland Act 1998 s 29(2)(d) had already provided that legislation enacted by the new devolved Scottish Parliament would be ultra vires (beyond the powers and void) if incompatible with any of the Convention rights under the European Convention on Human Rights. Members of the Scottish executive had no power to issue subordinate legislation or do any other act if it would contravene the Convention.

One dramatic output of this shrewd Blairite move was the decree of the Scottish High Court of Justiciary in the *Starrs* case, based on article 6 of the Convention (right to a fair trial). That article says that in the determination of any criminal charge against him or her, a person is entitled to a fair and public hearing by an independent and impartial tribunal. In Starrs it was put to the High Court of Justiciary, and they perforce agreed, that a judge could scarcely be regarded as 'independent' if, having been appointed by the executive on a temporary basis, he was liable to be sacked next day by that same executive if his performance was not considered up to snuff.

In response, and well in advance of 2 October 2000, the Government announced that all this nonsense of temporary judges was to disappear pronto throughout the United Kingdom. On 12 April 2000, Jane Kennedy, Parliamentary Secretary in the Lord Chancellor's Department, was asked about this. I give her reply, as recorded by Hansard.

Jane Kennedy: The Lord Chief Justice of England and Wales, and the Lord Chief Justice of Northern Ireland and the Lord Chancellor have agreed new arrangements for part-time judicial appointments for which the Lord Chancellor is responsible. We accord the highest value to the maintenance of judicial independence for all judges, full-time and part-time, and the arrangements have been fashioned for that purpose.

The announced changes affected a variety of judicial officers including Recorders, Deputy District Judges, Acting Stipendiary Magistrates, Deputy Masters or Registrars of the Supreme Court, Deputy High Court Judges, and Deputy Circuit Judges, together with retired Lords of Appeal in Ordinary, Lords Justices and High Court Judges. Furthermore the Lord Chancellor decided that no useful purpose was served by retaining the separate offices of Assistant Recorder and Recorder. He said that he would, accordingly, be recommending to Her Majesty that all serving Assistant Recorders should be appointed Recorders. In future, appointments will be made direct to Recordership through an openly advertised selection procedure. Many other judicial posts are affected, but perhaps I have said enough to whet the appetite.

The next day (13 April 2000) it was the turn of the Solicitor General (Mr Ross Cranston) to face the music on preparations for the coming into force of the HRA. Mr Andrew Mackinlay (Labour) questioned him on the HRA s 19, which provides for a statement of compatibility from Ministers when introducing legislation into Parliament.

Mr Mackinlay: Is it not time that we revisited section 19? It is inadequate, and will lead to embarrassment for the United Kingdom and to work for the Law Officers, who will have to defend our statute book in the European Court and other courts. Did my honourable and learned Friend notice this week that my right honourable Friend the Deputy Prime Minister was unable to give a human rights compliance notice in relation to the Local Government Bill? On the advice of the Lord Chancellor, he is unable to explain why he is not able to give that notice. It is nonsense. Private Members' Bills and private Bills are passing through the House, and with them there is apparently no need for human rights compliance certification. Again, that is nonsense. When these measures reach the statute book, the Law Officers will sometimes have to defend the indefensible. We should recognise that we are being sloppy and that these issues should be taken up with expedition.

The Solicitor General acknowledged that Mr Mackinlay had a point. He said the matter was being considered. Perhaps all would be ready by 2 October 2000 (or perhaps not).

When the Conservatives tried to cash in, the Solicitor General was ready for them. He pointed out that under the changes noted above Edward Garnier QC, the shadow Attorney General, was in clover. He was no longer a mere Assistant Recorder. Overnight he had suddenly become a full-blown Recorder.

It was one way to keep the Opposition quiet.

24

Corporate Homicide

If in 2000 the Blairite MP Mr Andrew Dismore's 10-minute rule Bill had been enacted (which was always unlikely, and did not in fact happen), one result would have been a marked shortage in the future of those useful creatures company secretaries, as I shall show.

Dismore's proposed measure, entitled the Corporate Homicide Bill, was read a first time by the Commons on 18 April 2000. There was no debate on it – just a brief speech by the promoter, the said Mr Dismore. It is not I suppose his fault that the very name conveys a dismal message, coupled with the notion that there will be more dismality to come – I know that is not a word, so don't write in. Still Mr Dismore MP does live up to his name.

Before becoming a Member of Parliament this dismal Dismore, a Labour backbencher, practised as a personal injury lawyer. In doing so he represented many families who had been bereaved by accidents. His clients included people who had lost relatives in major incidents such as the Zeebrugge ferry disaster and the King's Cross fire. Of the latter he told the House of Commons: 'As I took statements from victims, distraught relatives, firefighters and tube staff, and as I sat through the public inquiry day after day hearing over and over again about the failures of the senior management of London Underground Ltd, it struck me as outrageous that neither the company nor any of its managers would face criminal proceedings over those 31 deaths'.

Mr. Justice Sheen said during his inquiry into the 192 deaths on the *Herald of Free Enterprise*, sunk at Zeebrugge in another unnecessary disaster –

All concerned in management, from the members of the board of directors down. . . are guilty of fault. From top to bottom the body corporate was infected with the disease of sloppiness. . . The failure on the part of. . .

management to give proper and clear directions was a contributory cause of the disaster.

However, Mr Dismore went on, the prosecution in the Zeebrugge case collapsed owing to those same inadequacies of the criminal law.

The Dismore Bill sought to enact changes first proposed by the Law Commission. In its report 'Legislating the Criminal Code: Involuntary Manslaughter', published in March 1996, the Law Commission recommended a new criminal offence of 'corporate killing'. Here the Commission for some peculiar reason (not explained) disdained two accurate words (the Old English/Norse 'manslaughter' and the Latin-inspired 'homicide') in favour of the wider term 'killing', which of course includes (though here that is not intended) such forcible deaths as foxhounds inflict on foxes (see chapter 22).

According to the Law Commission, there appear to have been only four prosecutions of a corporation for manslaughter in the history of English law. Only one of these resulted in a conviction. That was the Dorset canoeing case, where because the corporation in question was a one-man company the problem of identifying the necessary 'controlling mind' did not arise.

The Law Commission say the problem is that, under the present law, prosecutions for corporate manslaughter can be brought only where a corporation, *through the controlling mind of one of its agents*, does an act which fulfils the requirements of the crime of manslaughter. Usually the effective acts of carelessness are diffused through the company, and no one person can be pin- pointed for blame.

The Law Commission saw no reason why companies should continue to be effectively exempt from the law of manslaughter. It thought they should be liable to prosecution for a homicide offence if they caused death through conduct sufficiently blameworthy. The Commission therefore made the following recommendations –

(1) There should be a specific offence of 'corporate killing', broadly comparable to killing by gross carelessness on the part of an individual.

(2) A corporation should be liable to prosecution for corpo-

rate killing if (a) a management failure by the corporation resulted in a person's death, and (b) that failure constituted conduct falling far below what can reasonably be expected of the corporation in the circumstances.
(3) Companies charged with corporate killing should be tried only in the Crown Court.
(4) Where a company is convicted of corporate killing, the judge should have power (a) to fine it an unlimited sum; and (b) order it to remedy the cause of the death.

In its Fourth Report, published on 2 February 2000, the Select Committee on Environment, Transport and Regional Affairs endorsed this Law Commission proposal. They said that a departmental working group set up to consider the proposal had now submitted recommendations to Ministers, and that there may be a consultation exercise later. They added: 'We recommend that the Government brings forward legislation to introduce a crime of corporate killing as soon as possible.'

Mr Dismore's Bill would also have punished individuals. To show the pitfalls involved, I return to what I said at the beginning about those useful functionaries company secretaries. Under the Dismore Bill a company secretary (as well as the chairman, managing director and chief executive) would be guilty of corporate killing, and liable to a fine and/or imprisonment, if the way the company's operational activities were managed or organised fell far below the reasonable and resulted in death. Yet company secretaries are not normally concerned in the detail of operational matters. Nor for that matter are company chairmen and directors. So why should they be penalised? If the word got round that they were being so penalised, who would apply for their jobs? And then what would happen to the corporate structures upon which our economy depends? It seemed Mr Dismore had not thought of that.

If one who is near and dear to you perishes or is injured in some ghastly accident on corporate premises you naturally seek – what? Money, apologies, abased contrition, revenge, the public disgrace of the company? You might want all of these, but the question is what should you be entitled to seek and allowed to have? Often money might be the sole answer. It is carrying revenge too far to demand to strike at, and put in the dock, company employees who intended no harm and were merely trying to do their job. Even if they did their job badly, that is not unusual. It is not expected to land people behind bars. So I would say, come off it Mr Dismore.

That in fact was what Parliament in effect said. The Bill was lost, but there are plenty of people who would like to revive it.

25

The Sad Case of Mrs Loizidou

What has the Cyprus problem to do with that of Northern Ireland? Very little if anything, you might suppose. Yet there is a link, as I will show.

Mr Tom Cox, Labour MP for Tooting, chairs the Cyprus Commonwealth parliamentary group in the House of Commons. In the adjournment debate on 20 April 2000 (just before the Easter break), when backbenchers were free to raise any subject under the sun that took their fancy, Mr Cox chose to raise the case of Mrs Loizidou. She is a Greek Cypriot, who found herself on the wrong side of the Green Line when Turkey decided to take over Northern Cyprus in 1974. What was worse, her home and possessions in the northern town of Kyrenia were on the wrong side of that line too. The Turks forced her to leave everything behind and retreat to the southern side of the line. That Green Line has divided the island of Cyprus (through the middle of its capital Nicosia) since 1974, and did so to some extent even before that. From 1974 Mrs Loizidou has been refused access to the Turkish occupied area. The Turkish military authorities barred her way, and they are quite definite, even cruel, in imposing their will. Poor Mrs Loizidou.

Since that time, Mrs Loizidou has fought to regain her property. She went to the European Court of Human Rights at Strasbourg, citing article 1 of the First Protocol to the Convention. This states that no one shall be deprived of his possessions except in the public interest and subject to the conditions provided for by law (including international law). The case of *Loizidou v Turkey* went before the Court at Strasbourg in July 1998. The Governments of Turkey and Cyprus had every opportunity to present their views on the case, and they did so. The court found by 15 votes to two in favour of Mrs. Loizidou. That should have concluded the matter, since both Turkey and Cyprus are members of the Parliamentary Assembly of the Council of Europe. The United Kingdom is also a member of that Assembly, as well as being one of the guarantor powers for the original, entire Republic of Cyprus.

Unfortunately, as so often in these matters, *realpolitik* got in the way. Mr Cox told the House of Commons that following the Court decision there have been many attempts by the Council, by the Secretary General of the Council and by the Committee of Ministers (which represents the member states of the Council) to ensure Turkey's compliance with the judgment. Still Turkey refuses to recognise the Court's decision. Still Mrs Loizidou is debarred from her rights.

At a meeting of the Parliamentary Assembly of the Council of Europe in Strasbourg in January 2000, the Chairman-in-Office of the Committee of Ministers, the Irish Minister for Foreign Affairs, Mr. Brian Cowen, made a statement of regret that the Committee of Ministers had made no progress towards the execution of the judgment in the Loizidou case. He said that it was the unanimous view of the committee that the compulsory jurisdiction of the court is an obligation that is accepted by all contracting parties, which obviously includes Turkey. He added that he had sent a letter to the Turkish Foreign Minister Mr Cem, emphasising the Committee's concern at Turkey's continued failure to meet its obligations.

Recently, added Mr Cox, he approached the Secretary General of the Council of Europe on Turkey's attitude. 'He said clearly that he deeply regretted the lack of response and commitment, and that it cannot be allowed to continue indefinitely.' This was at a time when discussions were taking place about Turkey's possible future membership of the European Union. That is still in the balance.

It was also a time when the British people were bracing themselves for the coming into full effect of the Human Rights Act 1998, which explicitly incorporates the crucial article 1 of the First Protocol. Will that get Mrs Loizidou any nearer achieving her aim? That is most unlikely. The reason? Why *realpolitik* of course.

The Republic of Cyprus (what is left of it) is up against *realpolitik* in the same way as, over a much longer period, in fact since its creation, Northern Ireland has been. For a variety of reasons, it is very much to the substantial interest of the United Kingdom and other nations of the European Union that Turkey should be kept within the Western fold. Turkey is needed by the west as a bastion against the Islamic forces that lie to the east of her. It would be seen as a catastrophe if Turkey turned round and became instead the front line state of those eastern Muslim forces.

In a similar way, the United Kingdom sees itself as unable to afford to please the majority of the people of Northern Ireland at the political cost of displeasing not only the Republic of Ireland but the United States too.

Beneath such mighty forces of geopolitics, little people like Mrs Loizidou are apt to find themselves crushed. Mr Blair might have thought it right to come to her aid, since right is obviously on her side. The idealist Mr Blair might have felt ashamed at the craven part Britain has played, as the protecting power, in confronting the Turkish occupation of northern Cyprus. But Mr Blair had other things to worry about, such as retaining power in his own country and winning the next election.

26

A Professional Body for Teachers

In my book *Professional Ethics*, published in 1969, I said of school teaching in England that its lack of a representative body (apart from purely trade union aspects) prevented it from being a true profession. Even from the point of view of trade unionism it has lacked a single body to represent it. Division is weakness; and the teaching profession has suffered accordingly.

It is to the credit of Mr Blair's Government that that particular deficiency has at long last been remedied. Chapter I of Part I of the Teaching and Higher Education Act 1998 provides for the setting up of a General Teaching Council for England and another for Wales. Scotland has had one since 1966. In what follows 'the GTC' refers to the English council; arrangements for Wales will be similar.

The GTC became operational in September 2000. Elections were held for the 64 places on the Council, consisting of –

- 25 elected teachers;
- 9 teachers appointed by the main teaching unions;
- 17 appointments by various representative bodies, mostly from within the education system, and
- 13 Secretary of State appointees.

The elected teachers consist of 11 primary teachers, 11 secondary teachers, 1 primary headteacher, 1 secondary headteacher; and 1 special school teacher.

It is officially said that the GTC will be the independent professional body for all teachers, and will provide an authoritative voice for the profession. Its aims are to maintain and enhance the profession's standards; and to improve the public standing of teaching. It is claimed that the GTC will be a leading player in shaping the education service of the future, and will bring a fresh and authoritative perspective by drawing on the experience and knowledge of over 400,000 teachers. It will advise the Secretary of State and others on a wide range of issues, including:

- the recruitment and supply of new teachers;
- initial training and induction;
- ongoing professional development, and
- medical fitness and professional conduct.

A key role will be to advise on teacher training and professional development. The GTC will have a legal right to be consulted on any future change in the standards required for entry to teaching. It will keep a register of qualified teachers, and registration will be a requirement for practising as a teacher in a maintained school. Other fully qualified teachers will also be eligible to register. The GTC will draw up a Code of Professional Conduct and Practice. It will have powers to remove individual teachers from the register if it finds them guilty of serious professional misconduct or incompetence. Initial funding is by the Government, but after that financing of the GTC will be by an annual registration fee, ensuring independence from the government of the day. Teachers in Scotland currently pay £20 per year to the GTC for Scotland.

The Act enables the Secretary of State to require the GTC to give him such assistance as he may specify under the Education Reform Act 1988 s 218(2) to determine whether a person is a qualified teacher. He may require the GTC to maintain records relating to such categories of persons (including persons not eligible to be registered) as may be prescribed; and the records must contain prescribed information relating to those persons. The GTC must carry out such additional functions as the Secretary of State may direct, so his or her authority over them is considerable.

All this is laudable no doubt, but there is a question mark. School teachers in the state sector are required to register with the GTC; for those in the private sector registration is optional. Why should this be? Other professions do not observe this distinction. If the teaching profession is really intended to be independent of the Government should not registration with the profession's ruling body be compulsory for all members? This would require that all school teachers, and not just those in maintained schools, should be required to register. There is a long history of strife between the public and private sector in teaching, illustrated by the fact that, in the days of teacher probation (abolished by Kenneth Clarke, who characteristically declared it 'a complete Horlicks'), service in independent schools was not recognised for probation.

My anxiety over this is shared by John Sayer, whose book *Towards the General Teaching Council* (1989) was instrumental in furthering the GTC movement which led to the passing of the 1998 Act. In his 2000 book *The General Teaching Council* (Cassell) Sayer says that what the Act effects is not yet the GTC constituency which has been suggested by its proponents. He adds: 'The GTC is about the protection and trust of the public, about the quality of education and the skills and qualities and morale of teachers. How is the public protected until all teachers are required to be qualified and to register?'

This criticism is not intended to stand in the way of rejoicing that at long last school teachers have found themselves a comprehensive professional body. As the first national chairman of the Professional Association of Teachers I could say nothing else.

27

The House of Lords Inspects Itself

The scene was the House of Lords, in the Bishops' Bar (yes, there is such a place). The year was 1987. Maurice Peston, Professor of Economics at London University, had just been raised to the peerage and was fortifying himself before entering the chamber to speak. The ex-Prime Minister Lord Home of the Hirsel (Baillie Vass to *Private Eye*) sat down beside the nervous professor and made himself agreeable. 'What do you think of the House?' he asked in his marvellously mellifluous upper class voice. 'I love it', said Peston, 'the only thing that troubles me is the enormous length of the working day here'. The former 14th Earl of Home responded: 'Oh yes, dear boy, I fully understand that. It's a big change. When I first came here in 1951 we had difficulty keeping the business going till tea time'. (And then of course they went off for toasted scones.)

1951 was about the time when I too first became acquainted, as a novice parliamentary draftsman, with the workings of their Lordships' House. I can confirm that it was then indeed a place where business was slack. Lord Peston told the story retailed above on 10 May 2000, when he opened a debate on his motion to call attention to the case for a review of the workings of the House of Lords in the 21st century. The Leader of the House, Baroness Jay (who mysteriously held the office of Lord, rather than Lady, Privy Seal), thought they should sit in the mornings instead of the evenings so as to accommodate the family life of peers and peeresses. She met her match.

> **Lord Strathclyde:** I shall say one thing about 'family friendly'. I am the father of three small children. They are in bed in the evening and therefore I am free to do my work in this House. But my children revel in playing with me in the mornings.

This riposte by the spokesman for the Conservative Party summed the whole thing up really. What suits one person does not suit another, so you might as well leave things as they are. We should not, Lord Strathclyde told the House, make changes in our procedures for our own personal convenience – still less that of Ministers. Anyway, changes had recently been agreed by the House, such as (it says in Hansard) 'sparing the noble and learned Lord the Lord Chancellor from the necessity to wear breaches [sic] or to read out the Queen's Speech'. Lord Strathclyde disliked Lord Peston's motion because it implied that the workings of the House are somehow outdated and unfit for the 21st century 'and that they should therefore, in the cliché of Blairism, be "modernized" or changed to fit into what Baroness Jay calls "contemporary life"'. The gathered Lords shuddered. They cling to standards of the past.

That sturdy survivor of the Gang of Four, Lord Rodgers of Quarry Bank (now alas deceased), thought the recent ejection of most hereditary peers had led to the House becoming more confident, in a way that could not have been foreseen. He went on to say that all professional people, certainly in mid-career, have very demanding hours, adding –

> Those hours involve evenings away. I hope that we do not complain too much about the life that we lead. Most of us rather enjoy it. I say that both in relation to Members of this House and Members of another place as well. Let us not complain too much. It is a hard life for many men and women pursuing their careers, whatever those careers may be.

The Bishop of Durham praised the ethos of the House of Lords, which he said the Bishops very much appreciate. He said that it was not perhaps professional in the political terms of the House of Commons. 'That does not make the House less effective but it does make for a different approach to debate and decision-making. . . we should retain something of that distinctive ethos.' However he complained about the Bishops being compelled to wear 17th century dress. 'We are quite ready to continue with our dog-collars as a sign of the proper humility that would be expected of us, but robes simply make for billowing in the corridors and perspiration in the Chamber'.

It was left to the former Conservative Home Secretary and Governor of Bermuda Lord Waddington to sound a sour note. He said that improvements in facilities do not necessarily improve the working of a place any more than do changes in procedures. More office accommodation and more secretarial assistance had accelerated the decline in attendance in the Chamber of the House of Commons and, consequently, the importance and influence of debates there. He complained that Mr Blair had adopted a policy of bypassing Parliament whenever possible, 'which time and time again has attracted adverse comment from Madam Speaker'. The Government have sought, he continued, to take a very firm grip on the Parliamentary Labour Party, threatening with draconian penalties those who step out of line. 'When the House of Commons has been weakened', he concluded, 'let us for goodness' sake be jealous of our own procedures'.

28

Prohibiting Fur Farming

What are human beings? The traditional Judeo-Christian belief, expressed in Genesis 1.26, is that they are the lords of creation. That bit of the Holy Bible tells us God gave mankind dominion over the fish of the sea, and over the fowl of the air, and over the cattle, and over all the earth, and over every creeping thing that creepeth upon the earth. It's a nice idea, and was graciously accepted by mankind (which of course includes womankind) for over two thousand years, though it is not known whether the creeping things agreed.

Some in our generation, such as Mr Blair, think themselves wiser than Genesis 1.26. So, as already mentioned in chapter 6, our Prime Minister (otherwise a devout Bible-reading Christian) introduced into Parliament a penal measure contradicting it: the Fur Farming (Prohibition) Bill (now the law of the land). This Bill was opposed (surprise, surprise) by the British Fur Trade Association, the Fur Breeders Association of the United Kingdom, and the International Fur Traders Association. The Bill made it a criminal offence, punishable on summary conviction by a fine not exceeding £20,000, to keep animals solely or primarily for slaughter for the value of their fur or for breeding progeny for such slaughter.

The Bill was given a second reading in the Commons on 15 May 2000. As befits the level of the creeping things concerned, Mr Blair deputed the task of handling it to a lowly Parliamentary Secretary, Mr. Elliot Morley. The history of fur farming in the United Kingdom, earnestly maintained Mr Morley, has not been a happy one. It has been dogged (?) by escapes from fur farms resulting in large public sums being spent on eradication. The coypu eradication programme cost £4 million. Attempts to eradicate escaped mink cost £1 million. Mr Morley added that with the associated escapes (he meant associated with the escapes) have come damage to the environment, to indigenous wildlife, and to stock and feeding birds.

That is not all. Mr Morley went on to tell a breathless House that concern about how animals are reared and kept in fur farms had been expressed by the Government's very own advisory body, the Farm Animal Welfare Council. There are also, he added, complaints from people who live adjacent to fur farms about smells, nuisance and flies.

I once lived opposite a pig farm in Surrey. I could tell Mr Morley a great deal about the smells, nuisance and flies that issued from that. My family and I suffered agonies, and finally moved away, but it never crossed our minds to demand that pig farming be made a criminal offence in England.

Mr Morley then passed to the moral issue. Mr Blair and his colleagues, forgetting or contradicting Genesis 1.26, believe it is morally wrong to keep animals to slaughter for their fur. Animals should not be destroyed or bred for destruction without a sufficient justification of public benefit. Research shows that the majority of the British public (notoriously sent swooning by little furry animals) share that view.

I interpose to enquire whether Mr Morley has asked the Esquimaux, sorry Inuit, about this. But you don't need to travel to Alaska to know that people of all generations till ours have cheerfully worn animal fur for warmth. They thought it was the sensible thing to do. Out of a thousand examples I think of André Gide, travelling not so long ago in Switzerland, attired in what his recent biographer describes as 'his new winter wardrobe of fur-lined coat, waterproof boots lined with sheepskin, fur hat etc'.

However Mr Morley insisted that fur farming, being distinct from food production, is immoral. He said that if the primary purpose of keeping animals is the production of food, that provides a sufficient public benefit to justify breeding them for slaughter (ask any vegetarian or vegan whether they agree with that). He said nothing about shoe leather. Animals, he assured us, are live creatures. They should not be killed for the sake of it, or just for the business of stripping the skins off their backs – not in the 21st century (do animals check the calendar?). Then came a crushing intervention.

Mr James Gray (North Wiltshire): The Minister will be aware that because of the current state of the sheepmeat market some sheep are kept specifically for the purpose of producing sheepskin. Will that be banned?

Caught out, Mr Morley did his best for Mr Blair. He said sheep are skinned in the production of wool. Or their skins are a by-product of the slaughter industry. Sheep, he added defiantly, have no bearing on the Bill. What about bears?

Well there you are. Logic chopping was what it all came to in the end. But the result will be one more addition to the list of penal offences our new rulers impose on people hitherto thought to be blameless good citizens.

29

The Whitsun Adjournment - and Multiculturalism

If, as I do, you believe in the value of the House of Commons as the tribunal of the people you should pay some attention to its adjournment debates. This is difficult, because they are ignored by the media. However they show our elected representatives, who are then granted a little freedom, talking about what concerns them personally – regardless of what ministers and whips think. What concerns them personally is likely to be what, as transmitted to them in 'surgeries', personal letters, confrontations in the village pub and otherwise, concerns their individual constituents. In other words you and me. We are not told about adjournment debates because we are in the grip of a 'media' who earn their money (and money is mostly what counts) by stirring up trouble on a national scale. What does not stir that up does not interest them much, so adjournment debates are beneath their notice. They are not beneath mine, so let me give you a brief account of the Whitsun adjournment debate held on 25 May 2000.

Mr Gareth Thomas, backbench MP for Harrow West, kicked off. He raised what he admitted to be three entirely different subjects: alcohol misuse, the siting of mobile phone masts and the social responsibility of corporations. That scattering of shot is what tends to happen in adjournment debates, when ministers and whips are absent and backbenchers are freed to let off steam and talk to themselves.

On alcohol abuse Mr Thomas gave us some worrying statistics. One in six people who attend accident and emergency units do so as a result of alcohol-related incidents or problems. 31,300 hospital admissions are due to alcohol dependence syndrome. 70 per cent. of men convicted for assault on their partner committed the assault while under the influence of alcohol. Heavy drinking by parents is a factor in 50 per cent. of child protection cases. 65 per cent. of suicide attempts are linked to excessive drinking. One in five men and one in six women admit to having unsafe sex after drinking too much. Alcohol consumption by 11 to 15-year-olds rose from 5.3 units in 1990 to 9.9 units in 1998. 20 per cent. of excluded pupils were suspended for drinking at school. Between 20 and 30 per cent. of all accidents are alcohol related. 15 per cent. of drownings and 39 per cent. of deaths from fire are linked to alcohol. Half the rough sleepers are alcohol dependent. And so on.

Depressing indeed, but there was no countervailing mention of the magnificent job alcohol does in oiling the wheels of social interplay and inspiring writers to release their fruitful thoughts. The same thing happens with sex, when those who rule us get talking about it. The downside is all they think of, except of course in private.

Mr Stephen Day MP (Cheadle) also had three disparate topics to address. Mrs Ann Cryer MP (Keighley), who followed him, made a valiant attempt to provide continuity where none existed by beginning: 'It is appropriate that Mr Day should have spoken about a long, dark tunnel because I want to talk about our railway heritage'. In support of the Keighley and Worth Valley Railway, of which she is a shareholder, she went on-

> I want to say a few words in praise of railway preservers or preservationists. . . They are not, as they are sometimes described in the media, railway buffs, anoraks, amateurs or people playing at trains. . . They simply want the pleasure of preserving the nation's industrial, transport and, often, architectural heritage, so that we and future generations can understand and appreciate what went before.

Next came the obstreperous Mark Oaten MP (Winchester), who first entered Parliament as recently as 1997. He showed none of the natural diffidence of the new boy. On the contrary, he was highly dissatisfied with the way he found the House of Commons functioning. It should, he said sternly, adopt a fixed working week with fixed hours, preferably finishing at 7 p.m. Instead of trooping through the division lobbies (where he had failed to observe that much essential socialising is done), MPs should, he said, engage in instantaneous electronic voting. There should be no bobbing up and down to catch the Speaker's eye, but MPs should be allotted a timed slot. Instead of having to refer to 'the Honourable Member for Winchester' one should be able to talk about 'Mr Oaten'. And so on. Altogether a crass exhibition of the failure of a new boy to grasp the essential workings of an ancient assembly he has been fortunate to be elected to.

Dr. Ashok Kumar (Middlesbrough, South and Cleveland, East) raised the case of Mr. Whittaker, a now elderly gentleman who served this country in uniform in a largely forgotten episode. Dr Kumar said that unbelievably, though Mr. Whittaker and his colleagues were conscripts in what was essentially a war zone, they have never received official acknowledgement of their service and bravery by the award of the General Service Medal. That Dr Kumar should take up his precious slot in the adjournment debate by raising that particular matter is a striking example of the benign face of multiculturalism (it has other faces).

Mr Blair is very fond of multiculturalism, so let us finish this chapter by examining it. It can be defined as the belief that a human society is best with numerous cultures, which give it richness and variety. In particular it stresses that a society should accord equal prominence and respect to the culture of every person living within it. By a social transformation, England is said by the Blairites to have converted itself into a multiculture. Mysteriously, the same is not said of Scotland, Wales or Northern Ireland. These are agreed to remain monocultures, out of respect for their ancient ways and a perception that these should be preserved. Similar agreement prevails regarding the Irish Republic. Don't ask me what the logic of all that is.

The essence of a multiculture is that within the one locality two or more distinct cultures seek to flourish alongside each other, while each remains more or less separate. It is not a case of the original exclusive culture assimilating the incoming cultures. That is a familiar phenomenon, not conflicting with the idea of a monoculture. Multiculture is rather the idea that the incoming cultures will jostle for possession with the host culture while insisting on retaining their own distinctive features. At the same time separatism is eschewed.

Why do people seek to reverse the trend of human history and set up a multiculture? First we must ask why people of one culture seek to move in on those of another. They become immigrants within the local territory of the host culture, but what makes them do this? The answer is simple. They think they will be better off living in the new territory. They will escape oppression, or improve their standard of life, or acquire some new freedom. Perhaps it is all three. Why, having shifted their lives from the old territory to the new, do these immigrants not respect their new host culture and try to fit in with it? In the past most have done this, following the advice of Saint Ambrose –

Si fueris Romae, Romano vivito more
Si fueris alibi, vivito sicut ibi.

This may be translated as: if you live in Rome, live according to the Roman culture; if you live anywhere else, live as they do in that place. Popularly shortened to 'when in Rome do as Rome does', it is the recipe whereby the host culture gradually absorbs the alien, rejecting what does not fit in but welcoming new enriching features. One name for it is assimilation or the melting pot, but nowadays it is often pejoratively called cultural imperialism. The United States of America is the classic example.

Under Blair's preferred multiculturism written or visual output, such as examples given in educational materials, ought not to belittle any of the local cultures by omitting or underplaying it. A London education authority circular said –

Sometimes writers and illustrators try to make mathematics materials friendly and appealing by dressing them up with illustrations of soldiers in busbies, steam-trains, teddy-bears, candlesticks, elves on toadstools. . . While some of these are things that children may be familiar with, many are in fact more significant to the nostalgic adult than to children today. These images mostly stem from the nurseries of the nineteenth or early twentieth centuries. But whatever their history, their flavour is definitely European and, on the whole, middle class. Children who have not been brought up to know about these myths will view them as alien, and the images as strange, and so they will not serve their purpose of making the mathematics friendly.'

Does multiculturalism apply in favour of whites? On the whole no. Many Africans refuse to accept that it applies at all to whites living in Africa. The Zimbabwe government under Mugabe has stripped many thousands of third and fourth generation white citizens of their Zimbabwean nationality On secondment to Ghana from Whitehall, I drafted a new citizenship law that was duly enacted. During this time my wife gave birth to a daughter in Accra. Having drafted the new law, I knew my baby was a Ghanaian citizen by birth. When I went to the appropriate government office in Accra to register her as such, this was refused. I explained the new law, and said I had drafted it. Still my application was refused. The incredulous black official said: 'You are English; your wife is English: your daughter cannot be Ghanaian'. End of story.

This leads to the topic of discrimination.

Once discrimination was considered the mark of a gentleman. One was discriminating in one's tastes, being able to distinguish a good vintage from a bad or a high quality cigar from a cheroot. Now 'gentleman' is problematic and 'discriminate' has moved on. Under Blairism it has OED meaning 3b: to discriminate against: to make an adverse distinction with regard to: to distinguish unfavourably from others. It is in this sense that the BBC said that their aim was to 'eradicate discrimination and to find ways of dealing with it whenever it arises'. It is not concerned with discrimination against an individual on grounds peculiar to that individual, for example that he or she is known from past actions to be devious or heartless, or by reason of poor hygiene smells unpleasant. The subject is *generalized* discrimination against certain categories of persons on grounds related to perceived characteristics of that category when compared to another

category or categories. The usage also extends to discrimination against animals on the ground of their
perceived inferiority to humans.

British laws against sex and race discrimination define it
by saying that a person discriminates against another
person if he treats them 'less favourably' on the ground of
sex or on racial grounds than he would treat other persons.
This may be taken as a general definition of the acts that
constitute discrimination under Blair. The harm inflicted
may be economic, as in the case of those Bostonians who,
when advertising a job vacancy, used to add 'No Irish need
apply'. Or it may be a deprivation of services or facilities,
as with the theatre or cinema whose entrance steps do not
allow the passage of a wheelchair. In extreme cases there
may be danger to life, as happened with segregated
hospitals in South Africa or the US South whose doors
were closed to black sufferers even when *in extremis*.
However the type of act we are mainly concerned with here
consists in a particular use of language, as by labelling a
person with learning difficulties 'backward', or calling a
black a nigger or an ephebe a pansy, or using pronouns that
assume the entire population to be masculine when half of
it is feminine.

The interest in use of discriminatory language is that it
may be hurtful. A prime impetus of the political correctness movement was the perceived need to avoid offending
people, or hurting their feelings, by inappropriate words or
actions. Michael Day, when Chairman of the Commission
for Racial Equality, called for 'remedies appropriate to the
hurt caused by racial discrimination'. On the other hand it
has been said that 'if you move around for ever with the
expectation of being discriminated against, the chances
are you won't ever be disappointed'. When Dean Peter
Steiner of Michigan University was asked for a new
initiative aimed at increasing the number of blacks
employed as university teachers he not unreasonably
pointed out that this would require a revolution in blacks'
attitudes towards higher education comparable to that
which had recently occurred among white women. For this
the United Coalition Against Racism branded him a racist.

The grounds for discrimination are multifarious. In late

nineteenth century England the Socialists complained that police discriminated against them 'on account of their opinions'. This indicates that it may be relevant who is doing the discriminating. We feel that the police, as paid public servants, ought not to be discriminating against anyone on account of their opinions, at least where these do not comprise advocacy of illegal acts. To private individuals we may be inclined to grant this freedom. However in relation to certain grounds, which differ with time and place, society is less willing to yield dispensations. At the present time western society is strongly, though not universally, opposed to the following types of discrimination.

By whites against non-whites (racism).
By males against females (sexism).

A substantial body of opinion is also opposed to the following types of discrimination by society generally.

Against persons with physical or mental disability (ablebodiedism).
Against the old (ageism).
Against the overweight (weightism, stoutism or fattism).
Against the ugly (lookism).
Against the educationally disadvantaged (élitism).

Minorities in our society are opposed to yet further types of discrimination.

By heterosexuals against homosexuals (homophobia).
By heterosexuals and homosexuals against bisexuals (biphobia).
By humans against animals (speciesism).

There also needs to be mentioned a type of discrimination currently in issue which may be called cultural discrimination, for example by the English against other cultures (Anglocentrism) or by Europeans against Third World cultures (Eurocentrism).

Freedom from discrimination is sometimes numbered among human rights. In fact it is usually more realistically a claim than a right. Nor is it always very clear what kind of claim (or right) it is. There are at least three possibilities.

A moral claim (or right).
A legal claim (or right).
A social claim (or right).

None of these can exist in a vacuum. To appraise the first we need to know of which system of morality it is a part. Some are asserted by adherents to be universally valid, as with Christianity or Islam. Others, such as Judaism or modern-day humanism, are seen as partial or optional, in which case the claim (or right) not to be discriminated against has the same quality.

There is little meaning to a legal claim (or right) unless we know by which system of law it is said to be conferred. Of a social claim we need to know which is the society in which it is said to be recognised. There is a reference above to 'western' society. This provides some degree of context, but it is a vague one. In the west there are many different societies, each with its own package of values. Moreover within a given society there are many layers of conformity. What a man or woman professes in public they may deny among friends. What they profess among friends they may deny in the family living room. What they profess in the living room they may deny in the bedroom. Even what they profess in the bedroom they may deny in their secret heart.

So we see that when faced with a given claim, for example not to be subjected to ablebodiedism or homophobia, we may need to look at it in several ways. Under what systems of morality is the claim valid? Does one of these apply in this case? Is there a law binding on us by which the claim can be enforced? Does our own society recognise the claim? Is that recognition universal or partial? In many societies there is deep dispute about some alleged 'human rights', for example a woman's right to choose abortion (as opposed to the right to life of her foetus) or everyone's right to free speech (as opposed to the black's right not to be racially insulted). There is further conflict when rights protected by law, such as the right to hunt foxes or experiment on animals, are said to conflict with supposed animal rights.

We need to remember all this when we encounter the person, so common nowadays, who confidently asserts that so and so 'has a right' to something or other. We need to ask 'what kind of right is that?' We need to check on its validity, or otherwise. A right is only unquestionably valid if it is conferred by some system of law, and even then it binds only those whom that system binds. Some people consider themselves morally entitled to break the law. Some laws, for example those of Nazi Germany or Stalinist Russia, any of us would feel entitled, if not bound, to break. If the claim (or right) is said to be against society, or some segment of society, we would all want to have our say about whether society really should recognise it, or should do so without exception – and if so what the exceptions are.

30

Inspecting the Crown Prosecution Service

There is a growing Blairite itch to set up, for each aspect of public activity, a separate Inspectorate. Each one of these is yet another taxpayer-financed Quango, staffed by self-important people out to make their mark. This development is worrying. Such over-the-shoulder inspecting enfeebles the individual worker's self respect and pride in the job. Until recently it was indeed a matter of self-respect to do one's job properly without snooping supervision. Now we think no one can be trusted to do this, so we set up Inspectorates to check on them. Snoopers squinting over a worker's shoulder undermine confidence and get in the way of the work. Latest to suffer are the staff of the Crown Prosecution Service (CPS). There is a special reason for regretting this.

I will explain why we should be particularly worried about this development. Our prosecution system deploys what may be called the prosecutive power of the state, or ability to put persons on trial. This sensitive and important power is *sui generis* – for justified reasons historically separate from all other powers of the state. For centuries it has lodged with the Attorney General, who on his own initiative has always been able to start or end a prosecution.

In this aspect of his functions the Attorney is supposed to be independent both of the executive and the judiciary, though that constitutional principle is untaught, little known and often flouted. Overweening Governments have increasingly encroached on it, for example by starving the CPS of the funds and staff it needs and promoting legislation to constrict its activities. Another undermining factor is the expansive self-given powers of the courts, most recently manifested in the decision of the Lord Chief Justice that in certain cases the CPS must give reasons for a decision not to prosecute. Thus the judiciary unjustifiably encroach on the distinct prosecutive power of the state – but who notices that, or cares?

The latest intrusion is the Crown Prosecution Service Inspectorate Bill which, having been passed by the Lords, was given a second reading in the Commons on 23 May 2000 and duly passed into law. It turns out, as I shall shortly show, that another (perhaps unwitting) such legislative encroachment was the Race Relations Act 1976, which set up the Commission for Racial Equality (CRE).

In the Commons on 25 May 2000 the Solicitor General, Mr Ross Cranston MP, announced that Sylvia Denman (another sort of Inspector, and a black woman) had presented her interim report on race discrimination in the CPS on 10 May 2000. The report (he said) recognised that some of the most glaring deficiencies in race equality in the CPS had been remedied recently, but concluded (surprise, surprise!) that race discrimination and institutional racism had nevertheless operated to the disadvantage of black and Asian CPS staff. The Denman report, he said, recommended various areas for future work, which would now be addressed by the CPS in consultation with Ms Denman and the CRE. At this point the Liberal Democrat spokesman on legal affairs, Mr John Burnett MP, thought fit to interject a comment on the 'collapsing morale' of the CPS. One was not surprised to hear of this.

The Crown Prosecution Service Inspectorate Bill provided for the appointment of an official to be called by the grandiose title of Her Majesty's Chief Inspector of the Crown Prosecution Service. No further details about the functions of his new department were set out in the Bill, but in the second reading debate on 23 May 2000 the Solicitor General gave us some. His remarks, echoed by the Conservative spokesman Mr Edward Garnier QC, betrayed the usual incomprehension of the importance, or even existence, of the Attorney General as the totally independent holder of the prosecutive power of the state.

Interference by the Government in CPS functions was celebrated throughout the Commons speeches. Interference by the courts was again shown by the fact that the very idea of the Bill originated with the 1998 report of a committee headed by a retired Lord Justice of

Appeal, Sir Iain Glidewell. The new Quango itself was proudly set up in open competition with the CPS. It would, insisted Mr Cranston, be separated from the CPS. It would be financed separately and located in a separate building. As respect the wielders of the prosecutive power, it will thus be a rival, criticising, interfering, force. Its staff members will have a background and experience quite distinct from those of the CPS staff – or so said that very Solicitor General who by statute shares in deploying the independent prosecutive power supposedly wielded by his senior colleague the Attorney General.

Far from jumping in to safeguard our constitutional liberties under this ill-informed attack, the Conservative Party even claimed credit for a lamentable Bill. When Sir Nicholas Lyell was Attorney General, boasted Mr Garnier, the Conservative Government decided that an inspectorate of the CPS was needed. It was indeed set up informally by that Government. Once the Bill was enacted, enthused the foolish Mr Garnier, 'the inspectorate will have a status equal to the other statutory inspectorates with which we are already familiar – such as those for prisons, the probation service, magistrates courts and the constabulary'.

What then will be left of the independent prosecutive power of the state, with its built-in protection for the citizen? No one could say, because evidently no one participating in the debate had the least idea about all that. Ignorance prevailed in this culture where history is almost entirely neglected. Yet those who ignore mistakes committed in the past are compelled to repeat them.

On 21 December 2000, last sitting day before the Christmas break, the Solicitor General, Mr Ross Cranston MP, was questioned (again) about low morale in the Crown Prosecution Service. I discussed above this strange 'low morale' syndrome (what is the civil service coming to?) in connection with the Bill to set up a CPS inspectorate. I noted that the Liberal Democrat spokesman on legal affairs, Mr John Burnett MP, had perceived 'collapsing morale' in the CPS. Has this strange infection got any better? Or has it even got worse?

Before answering I should note that the Bill received

royal assent on 20 July 2000 as the Crown Prosecution Service Inspectorate Act 2000, and was brought into force on 1 October 2000. As we now definitely know the key wording I can tell you that section 2, the only substantive provision, orders the new statutory Chief Inspector of the CPS to investigate 'the operation' of the service and submit an annual report to the Attorney General on his findings. This must be laid before Parliament.

Concerning that vexed question of morale, on 21 December 2000 the following interchange took place –

Mr John Burnett (Torridge and West Devon): Earlier this year, a survey on the Crown Prosecution Service was published. It disclosed that morale was at rock bottom. Since then, additional funding has been made available to the CPS. Will the Solicitor General conduct, or cause to be conducted, another independent survey into the CPS? If he does so, when will the results be published?

The Solicitor General: As I have confessed to the House previously, the survey showed that there was a problem of morale. I have also explained that, historically, the CPS was underfunded by the previous [Conservative] Government. The honourable Gentleman acknowledged that we are investing much more money in the CPS. This year, we are investing another £15.8 million and there will be an 8 per cent. real-terms increase over the next three years – I emphasise that that is a real-terms increase and will not occur merely in money terms. In addition, a pot of money containing more than £500 million is available to the various criminal justice agencies. My right honourable Friend the Home Secretary and the Lord Chancellor have said that the CPS claim on that pot of money is a priority. Decisions will soon be made about the matter. Inasmuch as money and resources are the problem, we are remedying the situation that we inherited from the previous Government.

Less interest than might have been expected was taken in that intriguing 'pot of money' (in fact none at all). Instead the House turned to how the criminal justice system was coping with the demands of the Human Rights Act 1998. It was coping very well, insisted Mr Cranston. For the Conservatives Mr Edward Garnier QC tried to fight back by suggesting that the greatest present attack on human rights was the Government's proposal to introduce, for the third time, a discredited measure to restrict the right to jury trial (see chapter 9). Wearily the Solicitor-General responded that they had been around that particular track a number of times.

Mr. Jim Fitzpatrick (Poplar and Canning Town) brought the House back to the question of CPS morale. The Solicitor General replied that on his frequent visits to CPS offices up and down the country he had been impressed by the commitment and professionalism of the workers (well he would say that, wouldn't he?). The CPS board had agreed to a number of measures to improve morale – for example, enhancing the support systems for keeping staff better informed of changes. Long-term planning had also been addressed through the 'staff attitude survey' and the 'stress audit steering group'. (Now we see what the civil service is coming to.)

A Conservative, Mr. John Bercow, thought morale in the CPS would rise if staff felt they were delivering an improved service to the public. Mr Cranston told him new targets had been set, and were constantly monitored by the CPS inspectorate. As a result of being put on a statutory basis, he added, the inspectorate is better resourced, does much more work and constantly reports on the operation of areas. Would all that really raise CPS morale – or send it into steep decline? What does a professional body like that need with 'targets' monitored from outside? This is Blairism at its worst.

A parting shot was fired by our old friend the Beast of Bolsover.

Mr Dennis Skinner: Does the Solicitor General think that CPS morale would be improved or otherwise if it were to deal with the cases of about eight members of the Equitable Life board who have scuttled away like rats leaving a sinking ship?

The Solicitor General: If it were a responsibility of anyone under my aegis, it would be the Serious Fraud Office, but I am not saying that it has gone that far.

As a trusting Equitable Life investor I appreciated that crack by the dearly loved Bolsover beast. Not that it will do us gullible investors any good.

To end this chapter, I return to my starting theme of castigating Blairite inspectors. The 2002 BBC Reith lecturer, Lady O'Neill, principal of Newnham College Cambridge, is quoted by the Times (6 April 2002) as saying that our new culture of accountability is taking us in the wrong direction. 'We are requiring those in the public sector and the professions to account in excessive and sometimes irrelevant detail to regulators and inspectors.' Lady O'Neill adds that we must give up childish fantasies that we can have total guarantees of others' performance. We need, she warns, to free professionals and the public service to serve the public. So I am not the only one saying this. Mr Blair, please listen.

31

Laura Spence and the Hallowed Halls of Academe

The House of Lords debated higher education on 14 June 2000. They considered what to do about Government Ministers who play around in this area for crude political reasons, and came up with an answer. I will give that answer later.

The problem was perceived to centre on Gordon Brown's prevarications concerning the comprehensive school pupil Laura Spence, coupled with Baroness Jay's prevarications on what she alleged to be her 'ordinary' grammar school education (in fact she went to a fee-paying Girls' Public Day School Trust school just like Croydon High School, the one my own three daughters attended). In the debate Lord Skidelsky referred to the Chancellor's 'recent clumsy attempt to make a class-war issue of the Oxford selection system'.

Ken Baker, former Conservative education secretary, spoke of Gordon Brown's 'infamous' attack on Baker's old Oxford college, adding as respects the President of Magdalen's wining and dining of this man to explain to him what Oxford is doing to widen participation in its courses: 'if you invite the Chancellor to dinner, remember that he bites the hand that feeds!' Lord Baker went on: 'He got his facts hopelessly mangled. Of the five students accepted at Magdalen, two came from state schools and three from ethnic minorities.' Which of these worthies of our time does Brown suggest should have been discarded in favour of Miss Spence, who had not even taken her A-levels? Answer not known.

The Chancellor of Oxford University, Lord Jenkins, then weighed in concerning what he called Chancellor Brown's 'little blitzkreig on Oxford'. He identified the historical event which Brown's attack most closely resembled as Chairman Mao's cultural revolution in China. This, said the other Chancellor, was designed to achieve not any practical result but just to stir things up for political purposes, to spread unease and to create damage – which took a lot of repairing. Lord Jenkins added: 'Mr Brown's diatribe was born of prejudice out of ignorance. Nearly every fact he adduced was false. I only hope he is better briefed when dealing with Treasury matters'.

The Liberal Democrat leader in the Lords said there must be no question of governments, or agents of government, deciding which individuals should or should not be admitted to particular universities. Baroness Young said Gordon Brown's attack was 'extraordinary and intemperate'. It was 'utterly disgraceful' to use a young girl in this way. Oxford, said she, will not lower its standards, and should not be ashamed to be élite. 'We surely do not want third-rate institutions of any kind.'

Baroness James of Holland Park (the novelist P D James) agreed that the Laura Spence affair was a scandal, though not in the sense Mr Brown intended. She added –

> We have to assume that rational men intend the natural results of their actions. This means that the Chancellor, to propitiate those members of his party who require regular skirmishes of the class war to satisfy their passion for social indignation, and perhaps to pursue some private ambition, deliberately insulted one of the world's greatest universities, slandered a distinguished academic, and, perhaps most serious of all, put back, perhaps for years, the patient work of Oxford in persuading young people from the state system that Oxford welcomes them and that they can be happy there.

Winding up for the Conservatives, Baroness Blatch said that Baroness (Tessa) Blackstone, who was later to wind up for the Government, must say precisely why Mr Brown described what happened at Magdalen College as a scandal. She went on to give details showing why it was in no way a scandal, ending: 'Finally, does the Minister believe that Magdalen College did discriminate unfairly against Laura Spence? If not, the college should receive an apology. Does the noble Baroness think that they will receive one?' In fact the ignoble Baroness failed even to mention the Laura Spence affair or Magdalen College in her rambling and waffling winding up speech. Such is the way of seasoned politicians.

Before coming to the solution proposed I will mention one other relevant matter. Government control over university funding brings insufferable bureaucracy involving innumerable quangos. Moreover the quangos get less and less efficient. Lord Morris pointed out that the old University Grants Committee was made up of experts who did not need to be taught what questions to ask because they already knew most of the answers. Their replacement, the English Funding Council, is far less knowledgeable.

The solution proposed was the obvious one: get Government out of higher education. Lord Skidelsky said that universities must wean themselves of their present dependence on the state. Lord Baker said they started as private institutions (this is doubtful), and should become private institutions once again. He added: 'They should become independent, free-standing bodies, totally in charge of their own affairs.' Baroness Young agreed. Lord Desai said that particular option had great attraction.

Perhaps the days of clumsy politicos like Gordon Brown are numbered in the hallowed halls of academe. One would like to think so, but one has one's doubts.

32

More Feet on the Beat in London?

Capital cities attract capital crime. Gangs from around the planet congregate on London, whether Yardie crooks from Jamaica, Triad creeps from China, Mafiosi majors from Sicily, or Columbian cartel kings – and many more besides. But still, as has always been so, the main crooks infesting what William Cobbett called the Great Wen are Londoners born and bred. The answer to the social problems this causes is policing.

The annual House of Commons debate on London's policing took place on 23 June 2000. The Home Secretary, Mr Jack Straw, told the House that the Met, as it is now popularly known (at the expense of its authority and dignity, but who cares about that?) was established by the Metropolitan Police Act 1829 as the nation's first police force. The 1829 Act's progenitor, and Straw's distinguished predecessor as Home Secretary, was Sir Robert Peel He showed a sort of genius in setting up the Metropolitan police force (now feebly renamed a 'service'), but that was not immediately appreciated at the time. The so-called Peelers were also known because of the colour of their uniforms as 'raw lobsters' or 'blue devils', and public hostility to them was immediate and universal. Nonetheless by the end of the 1850s they had gained the public's approval (Mr Straw dubiously said 'affection') and, by the latter half of the 19th century, their activities had led to a steady fall in the capital's crime rates.

Not everything went smoothly with the new police force. In 1872, 180 officers mutinied over pay. Pay and appalling living quarters were major causes of the 1918 and 1919 police strikes, in which more than 1,000 officers were dismissed. The collapse of the 1919 strike led to the outlawing of industrial action by the police and the formation of the Police Federation. This was designed to represent police officers while withholding the strike weapon from them. It proved a success, and flourishes to this day.

Throughout its history until now, the Met has been the responsibility of the Home Secretary, who has acted as its police authority. The ever-modernising Mr Blair has put a stop to that useful piece of history, as to so many others. Mr Straw dishonestly said it was an impertinence for one man to seek to represent London on policing matters. The truth is of course that the 'one man', the Home Secretary, has had all the resources of the Home Office behind him. This long-standing and successful arrangement ended on 2 July 2000, when the newly constituted Metropolitan Police Authority or MPA (yet another Quango) took over.

Sir Robert Peel showed foresight by establishing geographical boundaries for the Met that were far wider than those of the then City of London. They still encompassed three times the area administered by the London County Council on its establishment in 1888, and even extended well beyond the boundaries of the Greater London Council in 1964. Blair's Government took the opportunity of the creation of the new MPA to realign the Met's boundaries to make them correspond to those of the new Greater London Authority. That will ensure that there can be borough policing in each of the 32 London boroughs, which, in turn, means a reduction in the number of local operational command units from 60 to 32.

Despite all this restructuring the key question for the public remains one of bobbies on the beat. For the Opposition, Mr Oliver Heald MP, quoting the new Metropolitan Police Commissioner Sir John Stevens, said that the numerical strength of the Met – the number of officers available, rather than the budgetary strength – had taken a battering recently. When Blair's Government came to power in 1997, the strength was 27,166. Now the figure was 25,480, a drop of nearly 1,700 in just over three years. That is just the figure for the Metropolitan police; the City of London police have lost more than 100 officers in the same period. The thin blue line, mourned Mr Heald, is becoming even thinner.

Sir John Stevens said he needed to maintain at least 25,600 officers if he was to police London properly. He insisted we had reached a point where he was going to have to say that he didn't have enough officers to do that job of proper policing of London. The chairman of the Police Federation, Glen Smyth, put the matter in a different way. Referring to the old quip about having one's collar felt by the filth, he was reported by Mr Heald as saying that you've got to have feet on the beat to put hands on collars.

Mr Straw undertook to do his best to put more feet on the beat, but one felt his heart was not in it. The police culture of today is for filling in forms and sitting in cars, not pounding pavements in all weathers. Not that I would blame the police for that. It is the politicians I would blame.

33

The Right to Roam

Blair's Countryside and Rights of Way Bill, which had passed the Commons, was given a second reading by the House of Lords on 26 June 2000. As Baroness Byford remarked, it was really three Bills in one. The first part conferred the controversial right to roam. The second part tidied up the general law concerning rights of way. The third part gave greater protection to wildlife. I shall concentrate on the first part.

For the Government, Lord Whitty opened the debate. He said the access provisions did not, as some opponents have said, confer an unfettered right to roam. They are restricted to mountain, moor, heath and down, as well as existing common land. They apply only to persons on foot. A landowner will remain entirely free to farm, fence, improve or develop his land and will be under no obligation to facilitate or improve public access. Moreover he can exclude the public for up to 28 days a year, and more if the countryside bosses let him. So what were the landowners complaining about?

Baroness Byford was the first to tell him. For a start, said she, this part of the Bill shows the Government do not understand the country. In 1999 18,000 farmers gave up in despair, and many more are hanging on by their finger-nails. The Bill not only further reduced their already dwindling incomes, but also demanded more of their time. It was, she said, overburdensome, heavy-handed, regulatory and impracticable. It made insufficient allowance for land management techniques, especially management of heather moorland where grouse are bred. The Bill's 28 days of peace and quiet was wholly inadequate to accommodate birds' need for solitude during courtship, nesting and fledging.

Lord Brittan (formerly Sir Leon) criticised the fact that the right to roam was to be exercisable at night, as well as in the daytime. Given the rising level of rural crime and the number of isolated farmhouses, the fears expressed about night-time access are, said he, neither unreasonable nor excessive. It is one thing to be allowed to walk at night on a known footpath; it is a completely different matter to be allowed to roam everywhere. The legitimate dawn bird-watcher can be catered for by the proposal that access should be permitted for one hour before sunrise and one hour after sunset. 'As regards the people who are alleged to gain special pleasure from contemplating an unimpeded night sky, is it too much to ask them to do so from a footpath?'

Lord Moran reminisced –

At home in Wales, ramblers left the gates open on our small farm. Our cows got out and into a rocky river, where one of them damaged her leg. It took us seven hours to get them out of the river and back where they belonged. That evening I was not particularly enthu-siastic about the right to roam. Nor was I a couple of weeks ago, when I came across a youth trying to cut down a small tree in our woods. He seemed quite unaware that there was anything wrong about that.

Ramblers, added Lord Moran, do not put anything into the countryside, unlike farmers or the young volunteers who help the Royal Society for the Protection of Birds, the wildlife trusts and those in the British Trust for Conservation Volunteers. 'When, during lambing, a farm-er and his wife have to set their alarm clock to go off every two hours or need to sit up half the night to tend a sick cow, the ramblers are not there.' No, they are tucked up in their beds, fast asleep. Unlike the poor farmers, the ramblers' enjoyment of the countryside does not take place in unsocial hours. They go there when it suits them.

Then came Lord Denham on dogs. 'Dogs are like children, in that we all know that everybody else's are disobedient and totally unreliable, whereas our own are perfect'. More trouble between land managers and visitors arises from dogs than over anything else. But this Bill allows access to owners with dogs without leads at certain times of the year. 'Surely a complete ban is necessary; otherwise, people who innocently think they are obeying the rules may make a genuine mistake about the date. For the sake of avoiding acrimony, dogs on leads at all times is a small price to pay.'

Lord Denham had another worry. Landowners and farmers may find themselves victims of an ever-increasingly litigious society. 'Putting one's foot in a rabbit hole and breaking a leg may be covered, but slipping off a bridge over a stream, falling off a rotten fence or slipping on damp concrete – all these being man-made – may not be. The Peak Park agreements and by-laws rightly ensure that the people who enjoy access do so totally at their own risk.'

There will no right to compensation for this curtailment of landowners' property rights. Blair's ministers were deaf to argument. The Bill was passed into law as the Countryside and Rights of Way Act 2000. Lawyers for the landowners are already leafing through the Human Rights Act.

34

Pub Names: True Courage and Good Manners

Like sex, ale showed up as an early need of man. Ale's providers displayed an early trait of man: to cheat one's fellows. Hence the Assize of Ale at the medieval University of Oxford. For the benefit of students, medieval dons joined townsfolk in seeking to suppress this infamous cheating. Early legislation backed them. A 1502 enactment required that 'euery barell, kilderkyn and firken of ale and bere kepe ther full mesur'. The full measure of a firkin of ale was eight gallons. And it was meant not to be watered.

Some shallow minds of today see a risible connection between the ancient word for a small barrel, namely 'firkin', and an activity related to that other early human need I mentioned, namely sex. Unhappily, some who nowadays own pub chains employ people with such shallow minds to be their marketing agents. Hence a rash of juvenile name changes. The *Red Lion* of old becomes the *Firkin and Fuggle*, or suchlike. Does this matter?

Some people think it does matter, and this forms a nice illustration of the perennial question how far law should intrude on everyday life. It came before the House of Commons on 10 July 2000, when Mr Ben Chapman MP (Wirral, South) asked Blair's then Secretary of State for Culture, Media and Sport (Mr Chris Smith MP) what steps he was taking to support local heritage initiatives.

Mr Smith: We welcome the heritage lottery fund's decision to make local heritage one of its four main priorities. It has committed £8 million to its local heritage initiative, which is designed to help local communities to investigate, explain and care for their landscape, landmarks, traditions and culture.

Mr Chapman: I thank and congratulate my right

honourable Friend. What role does he envisage for the local pub in any local heritage initiative?

Mr Smith: My honourable Friend is right to draw attention to the role of the British pub as an integral part of the local heritage in many parts of the country. Not only buildings but the names of pubs often reflect local history or events. Many pubs have changed their names for various reasons over the years, but there appears to be a growing fashion of rebranding pubs with names such as 'The Dog and Doughnut' or 'The Goose and Granite' – names which appear to have little relevance to the history of any area. We are surely in danger of losing an important part of local history and folk memory. It is up to the owners of a business to choose its name, but I hope that breweries will bear in mind the unique historic role that many of our public houses have and think twice before destroying that link with the past.

This was the signal for a free for all.

Mr Geoffrey Clifton-Brown (Cotswold): I am pleased to hear that the Secretary of State is so keen on pub names. Will he undertake some research and tell us how many pubs are called 'The Spinner', as that might be of some benefit to the Labour party?

Mr. Smith: I suspect that the number is similar to that of pubs named 'The Silly Question'.

Robin Young in the Times of 11 July 2000 filled in the background. In the past five years 700 pubs in Greater London had had their names changed. In 1999 Ann Winterton MP (Congleton) put forward a Bill that would have made it illegal to change the name of a pub without first consulting local opinion and obtaining planning permission. It failed. The Campaign for Real Ale (CAMRA) coined the phrase 'firkinisation' to describe the process whereby brewery chiefs impose identikit formats on old pubs.

The craze for change affects not only *old* pubs. After the last war a new pub in London WC1 was named *The Escape* to commemorate the feats of prisoners of war. The pub was opened by two distinguished escapees, Oliver Philpot, who escaped from Stalag-Luft III by using the famous wooden horse copied from Troy, and Air Vice Marshal Burton, who was the first to reach England after escaping from a German camp. For no particular reason, this pub was later renamed Mabel's, thereby tossing out history, albeit recent history.

All right, maybe we could do without some common pub names like *The Red Lion* or *The Fox* or *The Marquess of Granby*. But in doing so we might lose an interesting slice of our history. The eighteenth century John Manners, Marquess of Granby and heir to the Duke of Rutland, is commemorated by many pub names. This is because, having been Commander in Chief of the Army, this particular noble Marquess charitably and at great personal expense set up retired former troopers as tavern keepers. The following lines written on his death celebrate this interesting man.

> What conquest now will Britain boast
> Or where display her banners?
> Alas in Granby she has lost
> True courage and good Manners.

35

Madam Speaker and the Sultan of Spin

A flower of British civility recently abandoned us. On 12 July 2000 Madam Speaker, Mrs Betty Boothoyd MP, erstwhile Tiller girl, told the House of Commons of her intention to resign. Hansard records that she added:

> I believe there is clear advantage in a new Speaker being elected during the course of a Parliament. In particular, it ensures that all Members are familiar with the qualities of potential successors. My decision will give my successor a run-in before the general election. My statement today also gives notice to my constituents in West Bromwich, West that, at the same time as relinquishing the office of Speaker, it is my intention to retire as their Member of Parliament. [Honourable Members: 'Oh.'] Be happy for me.

Those poignant final words strike an uneasy chord. We remember what made Madam Speaker *unhappy* in her final years. It was the tendency of Mr Blair to downgrade Parliament. Under him, Government announcements are first made anywhere but in the Commons. Ms Boothroyd's protests about that are said to have angered the Prime Minister. Did she freely go or was she pushed?

Three days later the true Blairite agenda was uncovered by the BBC 2 TV programme *News from Number Ten*. Here one saw handsome, youthful, charming, capable Tony Blair being continuously processed for presentation to the media (and through them to the public) by his equally handsome, youthful, charming and capable press secretary Alastair Campbell, who modestly described himself as His Master's Voice and was elsewhere in the programme called the Sultan Of Spin. The Commons itself, though past its best, still would not stand for such slick processing. Does that explain the phenomenon of Mr Campbell, and the sad disgruntlement of Ms Boothroyd?

News from Number Ten said that the lunchtime news bulletins all reflected what Mr Campbell had said to the

Lobby that morning in his dungeon beneath Number 10. Someone remarked that Herr Geobbels, the news manipulator of Nazi Germany, would have rejoiced at achieving so much. One struggles to remember the essential democratic principle that every citizen must have equal access to all statements made on behalf of Government.

In *News from Number Ten* Mr Campbell explained that a new special unit in the Cabinet Office, the Media Monitoring Unit, scrutinised output on behalf of Mr Blair. It was assisted by the equally novel Strategic Communications Unit, which responded to that output in suitable terms. It was later announced that the Prime Minister had stood down the eager Mr Campbell from this duty of daily briefings, so that he could concentrate on policy matters. A deputy then took over, and so the position remained substantially the same: disgraceful.

Why do I say the Campbell role is disgraceful? Because it was until recently a principle of public life that the news media received little special consideration from Government. Sir Trevor Lloyd-Hughes (press secretary to Harold Wilson 1964-1969) said in the *Daily Telegraph* of 19 July 2000 that in his day he just gave the plain facts and avoided party-political varnishing like the plague. Campbell, paid by the taxpayer, openly encroached on the party political sphere. In *News from Number Ten* he said (and later repeated) that Mr Blair would never allow the Labour Party to play the race card over immigration and asylum seekers. As a supposedly impartial civil servant, paid by the taxpayer, he should have nothing whatever to do with what the Labour Party might or might not do.

In *News from Number Ten* Mr Campbell complained, as is indeed the case, that today a news story is often not presented to the public directly but dressed up in the slants and glosses imparted by privily-briefed reporters, being now a form of comment. Yet he is a prime cause of this abuse. The skeleton of that old editor of the *Manchester Guardian* C P Scott, who told his reporters that while comment is free facts are sacred, must be revolving once again in some sooty Mancunian cemetery. Or perhaps I should have said 'spinning'.

In the programme a journalist indeed said that Campbell's job was spinning. On the other hand 'ours', he said 'is decoding'. To which Mr Blair replied: 'it is important to get on top of the news'. Any democrat would find it intolerable that the news should be officially stage-managed in this way. Democracy requires a level playing field. Constant behind-the-scenes briefing from on high is a grave threat to it.

The new mayor of London, Mr Ken Livingstone, said Parliament has been reduced to a holding pen for eager young hopeful ministers in waiting. Yet Parliament is supposed to be the place where elected representatives of the people are not confined in a holding pen, but hold their rulers to account. If it is not that, what that is of any use is it?

Mr Campbell is one of the new breed of civil servants known as special advisers (or political advisers). In chapter 67 we shall meet another of that breed: Jo Moore.

36

Rising for the Summer Recess

I return to the interesting topic of adjournment debates, which I mentioned in chapter 29. Parliament rose for the Summer Recess on 28 July 2000, and the adjournment debate in the Commons took the usual form. Twenty-two backbenchers had their say on a variety of issues, and one humble parliamentary secretary strove to answer all their points on behalf of Mr Blair's Government. Of course he strove in vain, but that was expected.

There was the usual petty sniping. Mr. Martin Salter (Reading West, Labour) criticised Sir Richard Body (Boston and Skegness, Conservative) for making 'offensive' comments, adding 'he did not even have the courtesy to be here at the start of the debate; I caught the 7.40 train'. Sir Richard had boosted his own area, a harmless fault surely. Skegness, in my constituency, he carolled, is a marvellous place for a holiday. 'Come to Skeggy. I shall be there with my grandchildren, though not with my bucket and spade.' Why not?

Some people choose Cyprus, rather than Skeggy, for their summer holiday. The Cyprus problem, which I mentioned in chapter 25, was again taken up by Tom Cox (Tooting, Labour) and Dr Rudi Vis (Finchley and Golders Green, Labour), supported by Andrew Love (Edmonton, Labour). Mr Cox, who chairs the Commonwealth Parliamentary Association Cyprus group, once more complained that Turkey, having occupied Northern Cyprus since 1974, showed no sign of giving it up. Yet another round of talks had begun, but the doughty Turk Mr Denktash would not budge. Denktash was undeterred by the fact that Turkey is the only country in the world to have recognised his Independent Republic of Northern Cyprus. The United Nations and the Council of Europe also refuse recognition. The eastern seaport Famagusta, once one of the most beautiful resorts in Cyprus, remains a ghost town. Its return to life was promised by Mr. Denktash. He reneged on his promise, Mr Cox complained, so great opportunities for Greek and Turkish Cypriots to live and work together were sadly lost. Mr Cox urged the British Government to act.

Dr Rudi Vis backed Mr Cox. He pointed out that there are more than 1,600 missing people in northern Cyprus. Others live in enclaves, surrounded by occupied territories. The new Anatolian settlers from Turkey are not at all the same culturally as the old Turkish Cypriots. Blair's vaunted multiculturism, which I discussed in chapter 29, does not seem to work there. There are tens of thousands of Turkish troops on the island, and all Christian churches in the occupied territories have been destroyed. It was enough surely to make a British Government representative sit up. However the reply on behalf of Blair's Government by the Parliamentary Secretary, Privy Council Office (Mr Paddy Tipping) was anodyne to the point of rudeness. I give his statement in its entirety –

> We do need to make progress. The Government are committed, as guarantor, to a settlement in Cyprus. We fully back the efforts of the United Nations. We take every opportunity to press human rights issues with the Turkish Government.

Feeble or what? The point was not pursued in this rag-tag debate at the end of term, before the boys and girls ran out to play for the summer.

Mr Andrew Rowe (Faversham and Mid-Kent, Conservative) disarmingly complained, in relation to teaching in schools, that 'the Government, building on the bad example set by us, have so increased the bumf and the controls that professional staff prefer to walk away from the stress'. Perhaps even more important was his point that the new forms of electronic communication mean that the age of representative democracy is drawing to a close. Governments can quickly discover the (uninformed) opinions of the populace on any topic, and then fashion policies accordingly. They no longer need an input from the constituency MP, who is thus rendered redundant.

Mr David Amess (Southend West, Conservative) announced that the Kennel Club had advised him that the

German Government are attempting to pass legislation to ban the breeding and import of bull breeds, including the Staffordshire bull terrier. This he said is causing great distress to dog owners in Britain. No one seemed to mind about that.

Mr Paul Tyler (North Cornwall, Liberal Democrat) said that air passengers are far more likely to suffer serious ill health – even death – from the conditions in the aircraft cabin than they are to be victims of an air crash. Partly this arises because organophosphates are used as lubricants in aircraft engines, and dangerous vapours from these can leak into the cabin. There were one or two shrugs, but otherwise no reaction. MPs were thinking about seaside shores and bathing. They longed to get off.

Mr Dominic Grieve (Beaconsfield, Conservative) wound up this messy debate for the Opposition. He said the key points MPs make in Adjournment debates would have more impact if they were to be met by written replies from the various Departments. He ended with a crack at Mr Blair who, he said, suffers from the Tinkerbell factor –

> When the light starts to go out, or something goes wrong, he needs reassurance so that the light can shine again. As he is not receiving that reassurance at present, I think he needs a long holiday. I am happy to wish him a good holiday. Indeed, I wish every Member of the House a good holiday.

There was no graceful response from Mr Blair. This was simply because he and his family were already on their way to the borrowed holiday home in Tuscany – that blissful territory John Mortimer (recently knighted at Blair's behest) calls Chiantishire.

37

The Religion
(Relief from Trivialisation) Bill

A Protestant has the right to work as a maths teacher in a Muslim school. A Roman Catholic has the right to teach geography in a Jewish school. An atheist linguist is entitled to a job grinding French into Greek Orthodox pupils. So claimed the opposing Dr Evan Harris, LibDem MP for Oxford West and Abingdon, when on 24 October 2000 the House of Commons considered a 10-minute rule Bill introduced by Mr Edward Leigh (Conservative). These were not Dr Harris's own ideas. They are, he assured the House, enshrined in the latest European Union employment directive. All Dr Harris himself contributes is a warm embrace for modish concepts.

The European directive is not course saying that any and every Protestant has the right to teach maths in a Muslim school, and so forth. That would be absurd. What it is saying amounts to this. Suppose two candidates are shortlisted for a post teaching French in a Muslim school. Let them be Jane Smith (a Protestant convert to Islam) and Mohammed Jones (a Welsh Muslim suddenly persuaded of the validity of Anglican orders). Suppose each is a competent French teacher, but Mohammed is just a smidgeon better than Jane. The selection panel think this slight superiority unimportant. Their school is committed to Islam, and they would prefer a current follower of the Prophet.

The directive (supported by Dr Harris) tells them they must not give way to this natural preference. What they must do is appoint the Muslim apostate Mohammed Jones. Mr Leigh feels it is not right to coerce Muslims and others in this way, and that is what motivated him in introducing his Bill. It did not in fact have the short title I have given it at the head of this chapter. It was truly called the Employment (Religious Beliefs) Bill. But my title fits better, as I shall show.

Mr Leigh began by saying that we British have a very fine tradition of tolerance in our society. Long before the

American melting pot was consolidated or even dreamed of, we were creating our own melting pot among the English, the Scots and the Welsh. (Sadly, he added, our record with the Irish was not so successful.) So we came to the conclusion that we had to be tolerant towards all religious organisations, though there are limits. 'Some westerners', said Mr Leigh, 'may have difficulties with the Hindu caste system or with Muslim dietary laws.' Even the opposing Dr Harris admitted there are limits. 'We do not', he said, 'allow the religious freedom to carry out *fatwas* against inhabitants of this country because, to put it mildly, that would damage the rights and interests of other people'.

This points to a basic flaw in the concept of outlawing religious discrimination. It is generally, if not universally, admitted that the dogmas of a religion may include items that are unacceptable in our society, so one is forced to pick and choose. Religious discrimination must be allowed, not outlawed, wherever unacceptable dogmas are in issue. But there is inevitably hot dispute over what is and is not acceptable, so the concept is unworkable and has no place in our legal system.

Another flaw was spelt out by Mr Leigh. Surely we have the sense, he said, to accept that other religions should run their religious schools, organisations and bodies in the way they want. No one doubts that Jewish organisations should be able to insist that people cannot be appointed rabbis unless they are Jewish. 'But what about teachers who do not teach religious studies? What about people employed in Church social organisations? Surely, the raison d'être of many religious organisations, what drives them and gives them impetus, is the fact that they are believers.'

Following, Dr Harris disclosed his real worry. 'There is concern that too wide an exemption for religious bodies to discriminate on the basis of religious ethos or views would mean that anyone employed, regardless of his or her role, by a private religious organisation or a public organisation with a religious input is likely to be discriminated against – not employed or sacked – because of private *sexual* behaviour. . .' Once again, sex had reared its ugly head.

To respect a religious belief is to respect the sincerity of those who hold it. If a religious employer thinks it important that all members of her or his staff should be practising members of the religion, what right has any outsider to interfere with this? If, as is to be expected, the religion in question holds strong views about morality, including of course sexual morality, then its adherents would naturally be expected to conform to them. Liberty too demands this right of free employment. It is surprising that it is not accepted as one of those precious human rights we hear so much about nowadays.

Worse was to follow on this front, in fact the converse. It is shown in a letter of mine the Times published on 19 November 2001 –

> The Blair Government's Anti-Terrorism, Crime and Security Bill, introduced on 12 November 2001, punishes religious hatred. This it describes as hatred against a group of persons 'defined by reference to religious belief or lack of religious belief'. The Bill does not define 'hatred' or 'religious belief', which are both notoriously inexact. It will be punishable 'religious hatred' to criticise a bunch of atheists. Is this really what we want our laws to do?
>
> The penalty for this newly-invented thought crime will be imprisonment for up to seven years. That might be inflicted on a comic who jeers at so-called religions that chop off a thief's hand or stone to death a woman caught in adultery. Is this really what we want?
>
> Or an earnest do-gooder might be imprisoned for criticising so-called religions that prevent a desperately ill child being given a blood transfusion. Again, is that what we want?
>
> I myself am an agnostic, with no desire to defend atheists who presume to have greater knowledge of the Universe than is given to mankind. I claim the right to criticise them. Do I really deserve to be locked up?
>
> The same goes for the multitude of people who endlessly debate faith, and argue for ever about our place in the cosmos. It is what humans have done from time immemorial, so far without challenge.
>
> Will Mr Blair kindly get off our backs?

This letter, with similar objections, appeared to do the trick. Blair was frightened, and dropped his iniquitous proposal from the Bill. But that is not quite the end of the story. Somehow there was left behind, and crept on to our statute book, a provision, in what became Blair's Anti-terrorism, Crime and Security Act 2001, which adds greater penalties to various offences, such as assaults and criminal damage, which are what it calls 'religiously aggravated'. This is defined as prejudicial to a group of persons defined by reference to religious belief or lack of religious belief. So we are almost back where we started.

It is iniquitous that a society which has for long advocated freedom of speech should have religious shackles placed upon it by Mr Blair. Religions have caused more cruelty in the world than anything else – except possibly jealousy and greed. We should not be prevented from attacking a religious creed that we believe is harmful to human welfare – as many undoubtedly are.

I end with the transcript of a television interview I gave about Salman Rushdie on 10 January 1991.

Q. You say that Mr Rushdie is not worth defending. Why?

A. Because he has let the side down.

Q. What 'side' do you mean?

A. The side that is engaged in the battle for free speech. The battle is against religious persecution – an old enemy of libertarians. Most religious creeds prohibit freedom of speech. They know they are right, and no argument is tolerated. It might undermine the faith, or insult the deity. Besides, it's disrespectful to the controlling priests or mullahs – or whatever else they call themselves.

Q. Mr Rushdie says it's no one's business but his own if he converts to Islam.

A. Why did he make a public announcement about it then? That's nonsense. Mr Rushdie's conversion strengthens the Islamic religion in Britain. This is of concern to all of us.

Q. But if you believe in religious freedom. . .

A. I support religious freedom, but like all freedoms it has limits. If any religious dogma or practice harms society it is our right and duty to oppose it by law, and in every lawful way. That is why British law forbids the Hindu caste system, under which large numbers of people are treated as untouchables.

Q. Are you saying that Islam threatens our society?

A. I am not free to answer that.

Q. What do you mean?

A. When last week I said Islam was a bigoted creed because it sentenced a novelist to death for what he wrote in a novel I received death threats. A letter was published in a national newspaper saying I must not be allowed to get away with it...

Q. Are you going to allow yourself to be silenced by such threats?

A. Not completely. But I have to recognise that the danger is there. Already our freedom of speech has been damaged by Muslim fundamentalism.

Q. Why then do you not stay on the Rushdie Defence Committee?

A. Because the Committee is ineffective, except as a source of comfort and moral support for Mr Rushdie personally. It is paralysed by fear – fear that whatever it does will make matters worse, fear of the wrath of Islam.

Q. How then can we defend free speech?

A. Free speech is only part of the issue. We have to stand on the principle that the British state, which is all of us, will not tolerate any religious practice which damages society. The state has both a moral right and a moral duty to ensure that the tenets and actions of any religious system operating within it do not adversely affect the social wellbeing of any citizen, whether a believer or not. Our forbears did not struggle for many centuries to establish a civilised society in order to have its values undermined now. Those values are important.

Q. The Muslims attack western values.

A. Yes. They attack our values, but we are not permitted to attack theirs. They label America as the Great Satan, and dismiss our secular values as worthless. They are not worthless. I am proud of them, and mean to defend them.

Q. I believe you have a book on secular ethics coming out soon. Was that why you wrote it?

A. Yes. The book is about *sexual* ethics only. It is called *The Sex Code*, and will be published by Weidenfeld & Nicolson in the Spring of 1992. In it I am trying to show how most people behave morally in their sexual actions even though they reject religious teaching on sex. There is such a thing as secular, or non-religious, morality. We need to proclaim it.

Q. How can we do that?

A. The main way is through education. Young people, all people, need to learn the history of how our secular values were won. Let me give just one example from history. In 1222 a provincial council or synod of the Christian church met at Osney Abbey, near Oxford. It tried a young Christian man for apostasy, which is what Salman Rushdie was convicted of over *The Satanic Verses*. The young man had fallen in love with a Jewess, who would not return his love unless he became a Jew himself. The Church council found him guilty and delivered him up to the civil power for punishment. He was burnt alive in the grounds of Osney Abbey.

Q. What is the present relevance of that story?

A. Through the struggles of Lollardism and the Reformation, the British people have persuaded the Christian Church not to act in that cruel way. If the Church tried to act in that way again today it would not be allowed to. It has to be the same with the Moslems.

Q. What of the hurt feelings of the Moslems over *The Satanic Verses?*

A. Hurt feelings are more tolerable than murder. It is vitally necessary that those who consider that any religious creed is harmful to society should be free to challenge it with all weapons available. These include the weapons of satire and ridicule used by Rushdie.

38

Open Letter to an Asian Would-be MP

Dear Mohammed Khamisa,

Your article in the *Sunday Times* of 9 April 2000 complained that, no matter how often you apply for selection as a Conservative parliamentary candidate, you are ignored by the constituency parties. You tell us you are an Asian Muslim. In 1972 you were ejected from Kenya, with the rest of your family, by Idi Amin. England took you in. Around that time I founded a housing charity, the World of Property Housing Trust. (It was later amalgamated to form the present Sanctuary Housing Association.) I mention it because we campaigned to allow British passport holders like you to be admitted to Britain. I remember devising the advertising slogan, which we used for fund-raising, 'Honour this passport!'. So I am very well disposed towards you.

You made good in England, and now you want to be elected as one of our Members of Parliament. That, as you must know, is a great privilege. Our English Parliament has a long history. With no false modesty you say your record is impeccable, and you are 'perfect' Conservative candidate material. Called to the Bar in 1985, you now work on criminal cases. You allege that we British are one nation, a family made up of different races, cultures and faiths, and that when it comes to parliamentary selection neither colour, culture nor faith should enter the equation. I wonder about that. I agree about colour. On culture and faith I have my doubts, and this is why.

I am a white English man, whose forbears have lived for centuries in England and have for long embraced the Christian religion that marks this country. Once, like you, I was a would-be barrister MP (Conservative), also unsuccessful in being selected by any Conservative constituency party. At around the time you were allowed to enter Britain from Kenya I, like you at a later time, persuaded Central Office to put me on the list of approved

Conservative candidates. I got very close to being selected, even being the runner-up in such safe Conservative seats as Knutsford, Stretford, Macclesfield and Twickenham. But it was not to be. At the last resort the selection committees did not like the cut of my jib. Even though my ancestry was white English for endless generations, even though I had fought as a volunteer RAF pilot for five years in the Second World War, even though I was an Oxford University graduate and former don, they still preferred somebody else. That was their right.

I hated it, but bit the bullet and accepted their decision (what else could I do?). I felt that perhaps I was not after all really suited to being an MP. I could not blame for non-selection my colour, culture or faith since my family have been white Anglo-Saxon Protestant (known as WASP) for many generations. I realised that there may be lots of reasons why a Conservative selection committee decides that one's face does not fit. One just has to accept it: stiff upper lip and all that. After all, the essential nature of an MP is to be a *representative* of the constituents.

To my regret, my own MP at the present time is Dr Evan Harris (Liberal Democrat). He is not what I personally want, but a majority round here in Oxford West and Abingdon have decided otherwise. Harris sits in the House of Commons to reflect my views, along with those of 60,000 other constituents of all parties. He is not a delegate, and in the last resort exercises his own judgement on issues of the day. But of course he does pay attention to his constituents' opinions. He plays the game, and I have to accept it.

Now if you asked me as an elector what sort of person I would like as my representative I would have to answer: someone as like me as possible. No doubt the other electors in my constituency would say the same. It is the normal human response. You can apply it to any sphere of life. If I were unable to attend a planned meeting with you, and had to send a representative, I would want that person to be someone who thinks the way I do, and is as much like me as possible. It stands to reason. Anyone would think the same.

It stands even more to reason when the representative is supposed to defend my vital interests in the place where all important matters of government are decided, the House of Commons. So I suspect that most Christian people round England who are looking for a new MP to represent them might not feel entirely happy when they see that the applicant is a Muslim. England is still basically a Christian country. Christians and Muslims have been at each other's throats ever since the foundation of the Islamic religion in the seventh century. In many places, they still are.

Consider, just as one example, what is currently going on in Nazareth, the birthplace of Christianity. Local Muslims have been given state permission to erect a mosque on land adjoining the Basilica of the Annunciation, where the Virgin Mary learned of her Immaculate Conception. That is indeed a holy place for Christians. Their local church leaders think the siting of this mosque is insulting to Christianity. Those sincerely holding this view include the Latin, Greek Orthodox and Armenian Patriarchs in the Holy Land and the Franciscan Custos. So strongly do they object to this projected mosque that they temporarily closed all Israeli Christian churches in protest. The Times of 5 November 1999 called this 'a national strike by Christ's servants'. It is a serious matter.

Islamic terrorist leaders like Osama Bin Laden actively recruit British Muslims (Times, 14 April 2000). Many Islamic countries forbid worship by Christians of the Christian God, and indeed persecute them if they attempt this. English people with a Christian background feel deeply unhappy about all that. So we English might not think a Muslim was really the sort of person we wanted to represent us in Parliament. There are plenty of alternative candidates offering themselves. Many might strike us as more appropriate. What is wrong with that? Nothing that I can see.

I do not know if all this explains your own problem of non-selection, or whether there are other reasons. If it does, it raises obvious difficulties. Who is to represent the British Muslims in the British Parliament? Are they to have their own MPs? That does not seem desirable. Yet obviously they should be represented. You see that I do not have a solution. However I do suggest that your grievance is perhaps not as straightforward as you seem to think. The trouble with the current entanglement with so-called racism is that it overlooks the fact that there are a great many reasons why people might reject one person in favour of another. The anti-racist philosophy, worthy though it may be, must never forget the fact that there are a thousand reasons, in addition to race, why a person might dislike someone. Being selected as a representative is a complex matter. I think you should be a little bit more circumspect – and modest.

Yours sincerely,

Francis Bennion
15 April 2000.

Afterword

The above was not published in my weekly political series because the Editor objected. What he said was -

I am extremely worried that you would be accused either of conscious or unconscious racism and we along with you. I do not think you can say in today's multicultural society that a predominantly white community would be justified in being unhappy about having a Muslim representative. Strictly speaking I accept that the thrust of your argument is on religion and not race but I do not think that is how readers will read it. Rather than asking you to cut and amend I think the best thing will be to pay you your usual fee in lieu of publication.

I declined my usual fee for this abortive effort, and sent in something else more acceptable to the modern world of political correctness. However that was not the end of the matter. I later wrote the following about the subject of the above effusion, Mohammed Khamisa.

Andrew Bowman, prominent Uxbridge Tory, would like a quiet word with Mohammed Khamisa. Mohammed had a go at the Conservative Party in the Times of 3 April 2000, under the provocative heading 'Is race the reason?' He said that, having applied to be a Conservative candidate for 13 seats, he had never even been offered an interview by any of the local Tory associations. That assertion is what

Andrew would like a word about.

Andrew Bowman says to Mohammed Khamisa that when he met you he was very impressed by you as a person. However he thinks there are enough barristers in the House of Commons. His view was influential, because at the time in question he was Chairman of the Uxbridge Conservative Association and you had applied for the vacancy there caused by the death of Sir Michael Shersby MP. Andrew says you were interviewed by Uxbridge at two successive stages, and made the shortlist of 12. That's what he wants to have a word with you about. Why did you tell a lie and say you had never even been offered an interview by any of the local Tory associations?

39

Word Hijacking – Discrimination Again

A worldwide cultural battle is going on, and language is a powerful part of it. The opulently rich English language, well on its way to becoming the dominant world tonguespeak, is at the centre of this contest. I now choose, as an example of the current planetary language war conducted in English, the word 'discriminate' and its variants. This adds to I wrote about it in chapter 29. The topic bears elaboration.

In his *History of England* Macaulay wrote of some hero that 'No man observed the varieties of character with a more discriminating eye'. In a recent parliamentary answer Tony Blair said his government 'has always stood firmly against discrimination in all its forms'. Macaulay thought discrimination a good thing; Blair thinks it a bad thing. That shows how our language has degenerated. Why has this happened? One answer is this. The word 'discrimination', like so many others in recent times, has been *hijacked*. Its original meaning has been overturned to suit the aims of persons who care little if anything for the true meaning of words in our splendid English language. Heedlessly, they suborn our tongue to suit their own narrow psycho-political ends.

As a gormless youth many years ago I was taught that to be discriminating was an excellent thing. A discriminating palate knew bad wine from good. A discriminating mind could tell false arguments from true. A discriminating judge could distinguish the liar from a decent honest citizen. In the old days to possess the ability to discriminate was to be able to *distinguish*. It showed one had nous enough to tell the sheep from the goats. There was nothing new in that. As long ago as 1687 George Barrow wrote 'We take upon us to discriminate the goats from the sheep'. The Blairite world holds goats and sheep to be indistinguishable, and equally worthy of respect. In that falsity lies the trouble and the threat.

On the meaning of 'hijacking' the Oxford English

Dictionary gives this example: 'When a virus enters a cell it hijacks it, and makes it do what it wants'. That justly describes the activities of Mr Blair and his politically correct cohorts. Unscrupulously they seek to hijack the English language, and make it do what they want. In that they delude themselves, for the English language is more robust than they, and does not knuckle under so easily. People will not let it.

I hope and believe that there are still enough intelligent people in command to see through this Blairite miasma and ensure that we dismiss the absurd notion that all peoples, all faiths, and all cultures are equally worthy of respect and emulation. To believe in such dull undiscriminating equality overturns the laborious work of human history in its striving towards civilised standards. Tennyson said: 'We needs must love the highest when we see it'. It follows that we must do the opposite when we see the lowest. That is what civilisation is all about. It requires discrimination (in the old true sense).

When Tony Blair said his government 'has always stood firmly against discrimination in all its forms' he had particularly in mind discrimination against Roman Catholics. People who know no English history often cavil at the fact that Prince Charles would forfeit the throne if he were to marry a Roman Catholic, though not if he were to marry a Christadelphian, a Rastafarian or even a Seventh Day Adventist. To those ignorant of history that seems absurd, but we are not all so ignorant. Some of us know just why that constitutional restriction is in place. In the middle ages there was a conflict between the idea that England was a small corner of Christendom (that vast European tract regarded as an ecclesiastical unity ruled by the Pope) and the idea that England as a distinct political entity was entitled to govern itself without Papal interference.

The current British engagement with the European Union reminds some of us that this ancient dichotomy is not defunct, but still very much alive. Today the European Union aims to wipe out England, and reduce it to little provinces on a population level with Scotland or Wales. It would make more sense to remember the Anglo-Saxon heptarchy. That term derived from Greek words meaning *seven rule*, and designated the period of English history between the arrival of the Anglo-Saxons in 449 and the union of the English kingships under Egbert in 828. The term was first used in the sixteenth century, being adopted because of the belief of Camden and other historians that during this period there were seven identifiable kingdoms, namely Mercia, Wessex, Northumbria, East Anglia, Kent, Essex and Sussex. The European Union, in its desire to obliterate the great name of England, might, if it had any historical sense, revive these ancient kingdoms for its regional titles. But what would mighty England say to that?

All that does not mean I necessarily support the continuation of this constitutional rule directed against Roman Catholics. Historically justified rules become spent when history departs, and one must recognise this. Perhaps the time has indeed come to jettison the Act of Settlement. I would have more respect for Mr Blair if he openly accepted the need to examine in depth this ancient piece of history. Instead, seeing trouble ahead, he dips his head in and wishes all such problems away. He fears they might interfere with his urgent longing, born of vanity, for more new Labour terms of office with himself at the head.

I end this piece on words and their political meaning with a salutary story. In Washington DC David Howard, a local government officer, lost his job for using the word 'niggardly'. This word has no relation whatsoever to 'nigger', but was nevertheless absurdly deemed by his colleagues to be offensive in that sense. Howard, who is white, used the word to explain at a meeting that he was going to have to be miserly with a government fund. 'I will have to be niggardly with this fund because the project is going to cost a lot of money' he said. Two black aides looked stunned, and one stormed out. Mr Howard tried to apologise but to no avail. No one would listen to him. Ignorance was in the ascendant, as nowadays it so often is.

So 'niggardly', a bleak Anglo-Saxon word meaning sparing or mean, is hijacked by race relations cranks and politically correct idiots to give it a derogatory meaning for blacks. It derives from *niggard*. In the year 1374 the

English poet Chaucer wrote: 'So parfite joye may no negarde have'. One is reminded of the illiterate English fools who in the year 2000 thought a pædiatrician was some sort of pædophile, and wrought their revenge on a learned doctor accordingly.

Words are powerful. All of us users of words need to respect this power, and never ever subvert their true meaning – not even in the august cause of race relations and political correctness.

Afterword

Again the above was not published in my weekly political series because the Editor objected. What was said was only that the Editor had decided it was unsuitable for publication. Nothing more was uttered (cringing is a symptom). Obviously the ground was again political correctness.

If these craven editorial creatures had their way the funeral message for the magnificent English language would be R.I.P. (rest in peace). Fortunately they will not have their way, I sincerely hope. Wake up England!

40

Jimmy Hood and the Fuel Crisis

This is about the debate on 24 October 2000 when the House of Commons considered the fuel protests of the previous month, which began at Stanlow refinery in Cheshire. The debate was held on an Opposition Day, so the Conservatives selected the topic. In search of nuggets of truth, I have to pick among innumerable party-political points scored or missed in the usual House of Commons way. Several such nuggets were offered by Mr Jimmy Hood, Labour MP for Clydesdale since 1987. He includes in *Who's Who* the information that he was 'Leader, Nottingham striking miners, 1984-1985', so when it comes to direct action and its effect on democracy Jimmy knows what he is talking about. Jimmy said –

> I do not accept that a cut in the fuel tax levy would automatically reduce the price of fuel. What would there be to stop the oil companies making more profit?. . . Many small road haulage businesses in my constituency are in trouble, usually as a result of the cut-throat approach of a lot of the big road hauliers who run the industry through the Road Haulage Association [which] was faxing, e-mailing and telephoning its members in my constituency days before the protests. It sent people to the demonstrations and protests. To say that the event was spontaneous is just a bit rich, and I do not accept it. . . On the Wednesday of that week, the Prime Minister had another meeting with the oil companies and the police. Within hours of that meeting, the protest was being called off. It is in that context that I raise my point about the defence of democracy, and the need to ask how we, as a Parliament, can defend it. If what happened was a spontaneous act – a popular uprising which happened just like that, and was called off just like that, as it was – questions must be asked. What led to its being called off?. . . A Member of Parliament, the late Norman Buchan, told me when I arrived as a new

Member, 'Jimmy, always suspect a conspiracy until proven different'.

What the ex-miner Jimmy Hood failed to mention, and we cannot blame him for that, was that the law which provides for the prevention and punishment of such criminal conspiracies is for some unexplained reason not being used by the prosecuting authorities, a point I shall return to. Jimmy Hood was shortly followed by the Labour MP for Ellesmere Port and Neston, Andrew Miller –

> I want to explain to the House what happened on the night of 7 September 2000 at Stanlow refinery in my constituency. . . Stanlow is a major hazard site to which unimpeded access for emergency vehicles 24 hours a day is vital. . . A few minutes after 10 o'clock on 7 September the refinery was blockaded, and the main oil terminal entrances were physically blocked. That is intolerable as it puts my constituents at physical risk. . . the shadow transport spokesman had prior notice of the incidents that were to take place in my constituency and put my constituents at risk. When reading the report of my speech, I hope that he will consider that next time he might have the good grace to tell me, so that I can inform the police and the relevant authorities because of the major safety issues involved. Intimidation has been mentioned, and there was intimidation. A total of 185 incidents have been collated across the country. . . In one incident a driver was boxed in with a white van at either end of his vehicle, and was prevented from proceeding. Is [Mr David Maclean MP] saying that that is not intimidation? Is he saying that the leader of the protest, whom I met at about 3 o'clock in the morning on 8 September, was not being intimidating?. . . The leader of the protest said 'Our only objective is to stop all fuel getting out of the plant. . . If the riot police move on us tonight, what happened in France will seem like a picnic. I do not care if Stanlow blows up.

I could have mentioned many party points made in the debate by the political leaders, such as the fact that it was the Tories who introduced the fuel escalator by which taxes have been increased by much more than the rise due to inflation. However I thought it best to concentrate on the above extracts. They reinforce the complaint I have frequently made about the failure of the authorities in such cases to prosecute for criminal conspiracy. This is the most potent weapon in the police and Criminal Prosecution Service armoury, which is to proceed against the organisers of disruption for the indictable offence of criminal conspiracy. For some undisclosed reason this weapon is not nowadays used.

I have been fighting for its use for the past thirty years or more. My battle began when in 1970 I set up Freedom Under Law, an organization opposed to unlawful direct action by protesters. It had a go at several targets, including the Hunt Saboteurs, but its chief claim to fame was the successful prosecution of Peter Hain, now a Labour Government Minister, for disruption of sporting fixtures in the UK involving South Africans. The offence of which Hain was convicted at the Old Bailey in 1972 was criminal conspiracy. The jury convicted, despite a remarkably sympathetic summing-up by Judge Gillis (featured by criminals in the cells by the graffito 'Gillis is good for you'). When he appealed against the conviction three judges of the Court of Appeal dismissed his appeal with costs. As reported in *The Daily Telegraph* of October 23 1973, the court said his conviction was 'fully justified'. Lord Justice Roskill said Hain had not elected to give evidence, adding 'He gave no explanation of his part over the incidents with which he was charged'. Now Blair thinks this man is fit to be his Minister for Europe.

The principle governing the prosecution of criminal conspiracy was laid down by the Court of Appeal in the case of the so-called Shrewsbury Six, *R v Jones* (59 Cr. App. R. (1974) 120). Lord Justice James said-

'The question whether a conspiracy charge is properly included in an indictment cannot be answered by the application of any rigid rules. Each case must be considered on its own facts. There are, however, certain guiding principles. The offences charged on the indictment should not only be supported by the evidence on the deposition or witness statements, but they should represent the criminality disclosed by that evidence. It is not desirable to include a charge of conspiracy which adds nothing to an effective charge of a substantive offence. But where charges of substantive offences do not adequately represent the overall criminality, it may be appropriate and right to include a charge of conspiracy.'

Support for conspiracy charges was expressed to the Law Commission by the Society of Public Teachers of Law in the statement that they can be used 'to charge in one count a number of persons who had taken part in various ways in the commission of a crime, or series of crimes, and the gravity of whose acts could only be judged in the light of the whole criminal enterprise, particularly where the exact extent of individual participation was not clear' (cited The Law Commission: Report on Conspiracy and Criminal Law Reform (1976) LAW COM. No. 76, para. 1.68).

The Law Commission held that the only justification for indicting as conspiracy an agreement to commit summary offences is 'the social danger involved in the deliberate planning of offences on a widespread scale'. An advantage of conspiracy charges was pointed out by the Law Commission as follows –

> Another reason adduced for the retention of conspiracy as a crime is that it provides a useful means whereby persons who plan or organise crimes but take no active part in them can more easily be brought to justice. It is, of course, true that, strictly, proof that someone has planned or organised crime is all that is needed to make him guilty of the offence itself if it is committed, but it is said to be easier to explain to a jury the simple requirement of proof of an agreement than to make it clear that someone who has not actually "one"anything can be guilty, by reason of complicity, of the substantive crime. We accept that there is some merit in this argument.

It seems that the police and CPS have adopted a deliberate policy of not prosecuting offences of criminal conspiracy, even though the adoption of such a policy by them is unlawful. There are many examples of this neglect. I single out a few.

In 1998 the port of Shoreham in Sussex was overwhelmed by animal rights protesters objecting to shipments of live animals. In *R v Chief Constable of Sussex, ex p International Trader's Ferry Ltd* Lord Nolan said: 'The result may be seen as the acceptance by the courts of a victory for the violent elements in the crowds at Shoreham over the forces of law. I would describe it myself as an acceptance of the plain fact that there are limits to the extent to which the police can control unlawful violence in any given situation. If these limits are felt to be too narrow, the remedy lies in increasing the resources of the police'. Lord Nolan inexcusably failed to mention that an answer may be found in reducing the violence by *prosecuting the main organisers for criminal conspiracy.*

In 1999 there occurred the biggest triumph of lawlessness in recent Oxfordshire history, the forcible closure of the cat-breeding Hillgrove Farm by animal rights demonstrators. These highly organised protesters broke the law incessantly over several years, and by brute force compelled Chris Brown, the law-abiding owner of the farm, to close down. Mr Brown is reported as saying that this was a loss to medical research, upon which we all depend. The organizers of these mobs should have been prosecuted, but Thames Valley Police ignored this important aspect of the criminal law. Did the Home Office criticise them for this neglect? Not so far as the public aware.

A final example is the scheme of digging up the turf of Parliament Square by 'guerrilla gardening'. It was plotted in advance on the internet and widely known. The organisers of this criminal conspiracy should have been apprehended well before May Day 2000, when the acts of vandalism were committed, but this did not happen. We, as a democracy under the rule of law, have surrendered. We are giving up.

In a democracy (if we had remembered), a minority is not entitled to use illegal force where no force is used against it. To use such force in the promotion of a private opinion is tyrannous. As José Marti said, the dagger plunged in the name of Freedom is truly plunged into the breast of Freedom. What do we care now for democratic freedom? Lying down on our backs, pressing the remote control to change the channel, we gaze stupidly at the electronic screen. We no longer know what people like José Marti are talking about.

I return to this theme in chapter 49.

41

Misgivings on the
International Criminal Court

Another self-inflicted wound by Blair. On 7 November 2000 his Minister of State in the Foreign and Commonwealth Office (Peter Hain MP) made a statement concerning the establishment of an international court to try war criminals and others who gravely transgress canons of civilised behaviour. He told the House of Commons that twenty-two countries have ratified the Rome treaty, out of the sixty needed for establishing this court. Naturally those ratifying did not include any states, like Libya, Yugoslavia, Iraq, Syria, Iran, Rwanda, Zimbabwe, North Korea or Burma, from which the vilest such criminals emanate. Nor did they include the country with by far the largest of the world's populations, China. Nor, very significantly, did they include the most powerful country in the world, the United States. President Clinton was too wily a political animal to entangle his country in such a nightmare scenario. His successor Mr Bush, though perhaps not quite so wily as Clinton himself, is likely to be of the same mind. Mr Hain banged away at his Blairite drum –

> We encourage all countries, including Libya and China, to sign up to the international criminal court. In our bilateral diplomacy with all countries in the world, we consistently pressure them to do so. We are committed to the court. It is a way of catching war criminals and ending the situation whereby the Pol Pots, Pinochets and all the dictators of the world continue to act with impunity. It is part of our agenda for human rights, of which we are proud.

Others in the House of Commons rose to contribute their ideas.

Dr Julian Lewis (New Forest, East): When the war crimes tribunals sit, there should be retribution for the past and a deterrent to obscene atrocity in future. I express some concern that it is taking as long as it is for Britain to ratify the process and to get it under way.

Mr Hain: We are committed to achieve ratification as quickly as possible. I am delighted that we shall have the honourable Gentleman's support. It is a unique experience for me, but I am delighted to agree with virtually everything that he said.

Every MP who spoke in the debate expressed support for the Bill which Mr Hain indicated would soon be introduced into Parliament to enable us to ratify the Rome treaty (it was indeed included in the Queen's Speech). Mr Huw Edwards (Labour) was sure this Bill would have cross-party support, and incredibly it seems he is right. He urged the United States to 'take a greater role and ensure that those who commit crimes against humanity are brought to justice'. To this there was not a note of dissent in the whole brief debate. One longed for the good old days of University seats (Oxford and Cambridge only), and the salty common sense that an A P Herbert would have injected.

What common sense do I mean? How dare I impugn this obviously worthy project? It may seem worthy to the likes of Peter Hain, but there are other viewpoints on our planet. What we in the west think of as canons of civilised behaviour are not shared elsewhere. What we regard as obvious cruelty others dismiss as commonplace, unworthy of mention. We in Britain, led by the immigrant from South Africa Peter Hain, seek to impose as a universal standard a code many others reject. In the planetary context, our endeavour is flawed.

An international criminal court should not be set up before an established and agreed international criminal code is in place. The function of a court is to administer law. If there is no law, there should be no court (unless we want the court to invent the law). Mr Hain's enterprise, backed by Amnesty International, puts the cart before the horse by seeking to establish a court before establishing an agreed system of law for that court to apply. But then Mr

Hain's personal history shows he has little regard for the law.

As stated above, Dr Julian Lewis (Conservative) said in the debate that when the war crimes tribunals sit there should be retribution for the past and a deterrent to obscene atrocity in the future. The trouble with this is that one person's justified action is another's obscene atrocity. Gerry Adams and Martin McGuinness would say that many routine British military operations in Northern Ireland constituted 'obscene atrocities'. If they insisted on taking this claim to the International Criminal Court they could not be stopped, and then where would our brave soldiers be? Where would their leaders be? Where even might our Prime Minister Mr Blair himself be? Are we happy at that thought?

I close with an even more potent question. We have recently seen Tony Blair and others apologising on behalf of the nation for so-called crimes and misdemeanours committed long before they were born. When Hain's new regime comes into effect shall we see Her Majesty the Queen as head as state indicted on some foreign state visit for alleged atrocities committed on past occasions in India, Cyprus, or anywhere else in the territories of the dead, lamented ? No one can guarantee that we shall not.

42

In Honour of Mrs Dunwoody

I am neutral when it comes to party politics, standing fair and square behind each and every backbencher as democracy requires. Mrs Gwyneth Dunwoody, who first entered the House of Commons in 1966 as the Member for Exeter, is a backbencher who is one of the champions of backbenchers. Her high ability and character are what would be expected from the daughter of the late Morgan Phillips, ablest of post-war Labour Party secretaries.

I have two reasons for celebrating Mrs Dunwoody. One is that on 23 October 2000 she bravely stood for Speaker. The other is that on 7 November 2000 she held out against her own party in the worst piece of buffoonish Blairite chicanery to have been inflicted on the House of Commons in recent times.

Mr David Davis MP, a former Conservative whip, now Chairman of the party, proposed Mrs Dunwoody for the office of Speaker. He said he wanted a Speaker of strength, independence, integrity, passionate commitment to the Commons in its role of scrutinising Government and holding them to account and, within that, a relentless devotion to the rights of backbenchers. The Speaker must be not just independent of the Government of any persuasion, but determined that that Government will subject themselves to the democratic will of the House of Commons – upon whose support they are constitutionally based. Mr Davis said –

> The honourable Lady has the experience: she has served the House for a total of 30 years; 26 of them continuously. She has served in government; she therefore understands only too well the pressures and imperatives of office. However, it was long enough ago for her not to be biased by it today.

Mo Mowlam, Minister for the Cabinet Office, seconded this motion, saying –

With a strong Executive, it is crucial to have an independent, gutsy, hard-hitting Speaker to stand up for the House, its Members and the people whom it represents. . . Honourable Members should be in no doubt about how hard my honourable Friend will work on their behalf, irrespective of their attitudes, beliefs or individuality. In the thirteen years that I have spent in the House, I have come to respect her many qualities and singular character. She has been thoughtful and attentive to me and other honourable Members across the political spectrum and to the many staff who work here. She does not do that in public. When the going got tough in Northern Ireland, she would call, not necessarily to agree with what I was doing, but always to offer solidarity and support from one Member to another. I also like her direct, honest and straightforward approach to life in the House. She is a hard-working Member who does the business. She stays late for division after division. She is never seen slipping out; she is always seen standing in the taxi queue after voting and doing her duty to the House.

Mrs Dunwoody herself told the House she was disturbed by the gradual erosion, under many names, of the rights of backbenchers. Sadly the House rejected her by 341 votes to 170. So passed a great opportunity. Instead we got Gorbals Mick, of whom more later.

It was because she believes it right to 'stay late for division after division' that on 7 November 2000 Mrs Dunwoody voted against her own party on the nonsensical proposal to defer divisions to a later date if they fell after 10 o'clock at night. This notion, which was coupled with another to facilitate guillotining of debates on Bills, originated with Mr Blair's select committee on so-called modernisation. On the guillotining proposal, Mrs Dunwoody objected that the ability of backbenchers to speak for their constituents would be reduced to a series of administrative decisions. 'Although many people may deeply disapprove of honourable Members expressing views that are not regurgitated from their Front Bench, that is fundamentally what Parliament is about'.

Mrs Dunwoody also objected to the fact that under the proposal the views of the official Opposition would be taken into account in drawing up a timetable, but not those of backbenchers of any party (including the Government's). To her everlasting credit, Mrs Dunwoody voted against her own Blairite Government in all three divisions on the iniquitous modernisation proposals.

To underline my impartiality I end with Mr Dominic Grieve MP (Conservative). In the modernisation debate he echoed other Conservatives in saying that separating the process of debating from the voting process, especially for short debates, would degrade the House of Commons. It would, he said, remove the chance that one's vote could be influenced when matters are fresh in one's mind, and it would prevent the Chamber from being a focus for any informed or sensible debate in which people could be influenced by what was said. 'One thing that I have learned since I came to the House is that if one bothers to spend six hours listening to a debate, one learns an enormous amount, usually from one's opponents'.

This late deployment of reason proved useless; and the voting steamroller trundled out. New Labour finally put paid to the House of Commons as an honest and reflective debating chamber. Such is the mark of our times, well past the best in terms of true democracy. The people read about this in their newspapers, but turned the page. More boring nonsense from Parliament.

43

Lord Donaldson of Lymington and the Parliament Acts

Lord Donaldson of Lymington, former Master of the Rolls, had a bee buzzing in his recently ennobled but still essentially plebeian bonnet. The discomfort that brings can afflict any elderly gentleman (Lord Donaldson was eighty). We do not know whether this particular baronial buzzer was a homophobic bee or a constitutional bee, but it does seem to have been one or the other (possibly both). Out of its hive came Lord Donaldson's Parliament Acts (Amendment) Bill, introduced by him into the House of Lords on 8 November 2000.

What woke up the Donaldson bee from its dozy slumbers and started it buzzing was the Blair Government's threat to use the Parliament Acts to force into law, against the desires of the majority of His Lordship's noble House, a measure that would if passed become the Sexual Offences (Amendment) Act. It was based on Blair's notion that. . . and here I must pause.

This Blair notion can be expressed in various ways. One is that youths of sixteen and seventeen must have the same legal right to engage in sexual commerce with willing males as they have to engage in sexual commerce with willing females, which puts it as an equality issue.

Another way to describe it is that Blair aches to give disgusting perverts the legal right morally to debauch, and physically to injure, inexperienced boys by thrusting sodomitically into their chaste semi-childish bodies.

Which of these descriptions commends itself to Lord Donaldson of Lymington I have no means of knowing, and do not presume to guess. Professedly, the Donaldson worry was that if the Government did use the Parliament Acts to force through this Bill they might come unstuck. His Lordship professedly wished to save Blair from this dismal fate by removing what he fancied was a doubt about the constitutional validity of such a procedure. Here I must get down to technicalities. The Parliament Acts consist of the original Act of 1911 and the amending Act of 1949. The former said that, in relation to a Bill introduced into the Commons, that House would prevail against Lords disagreement, and the Bill would become law, if it were passed *three times* by the Commons. The 1949 Act substituted two times (or twice, as we used to say). At the time the Lords disagreed with this change, so the 1911 Act in its unamended form was used to effect it.

In explanatory notes to his Bill Lord Donaldson says doubts have been raised by, amongst others, the constitutional lawyers Sir William Wade, Professor Zellick and Professor Hood Phillips. He ought to have added the references to the relevant writings of these gentlemen, so that those interested could have inspected for themselves the arguments deployed. I will not attempt to guess what they were.

Lord Donaldson explained what he was up to in an article published in the *Daily Telegraph* on 14 November 2000. Here he showed how chummy he intended to be by signing it with the plebeian name 'John Donaldson'. It was chummily headed (with scant justification) 'The muddle and fuddle of the Parliament Acts'. Donaldson accepted that on a literal construction the 1911 Act permitted the 1949 amendment, but insisted that in constitutional law 'a literal construction of a statute may well be rejected if to accept it would conflict with the statute's purpose'. This is very dodgy territory, for who can be sure when the purpose requires the literal meaning to be rejected? What court would engineer such a crass conflict with the Government and Parliament?

My 1000-page textbook *Statutory Interpretation* was originally published in 1984 and has gone through three editions and half a dozen supplements. It deals exhaustively with the Parliament Acts but does not mention these supposed doubts. The various editions have been reviewed worldwide, but no reviewer has mentioned them either. That suggests that Donaldson's doubts were misconceived, as I believe is the case.

The Donaldson Bill sought to validate certain Acts that had previously been passed under the 1949 Parliament Act procedure, namely the War Crimes Act 1991 and the

European Parliamentary Elections Act 1999. It asked the House of Lords to signify agreement to these measures, which it had rejected at the time. Why would the House do that? It was one more attempt to rewrite history. This Blairite tendency is evidently catching.

The House of Lords Information Office told me that no date had been set for the second reading of this Bill. With the end of the Session near, it would proceed no further – as everyone concerned well knew. So why did Lord Donaldson bother? And anyway Blair's Act for the buggery of innocent boys passed into law anyway. It now sits on our statute book as the Sexual Offences (Amendment) Act 2000. An innocent enough title, you might think, for what some consider a debauched measure.

44

Rooted in Dishonour?

The very first day I walked into the Parliamentary Counsel Office (PCO) in Whitehall as a tyro legislative draftsman (the year was 1953) the venerable Chief Clerk Frank Heritage, seated almost in rags on his high stool, took pen (as one said in those days) and scribbled a calculation. He then showed me what he had written and said: 'that's the date when, if you keep your nose clean, you will get your KCB'. Those initials stood, and still stand, for the Whitehall big chief award of Knight Commander of the Most Honourable Order of the Bath. Heads of the PCO then, as now, stood automatically to be awarded this prestigious honour, after which they could posture for ever as cardboard Knights of the Realm (horses and swords optional). In retirement, old ladies loved them for it – and constantly asked them to tea and whist.

I felt uneasy at this dizzying prospect, since it occurred to me that it was a rather too obvious way of trapping clever folk into a job that should have paid far more than they were actually getting. It was not at all why I had responded to an invitation to take up this career. I had the much more egotistical aim of *making the laws*. So at once I saw through this clumsy ploy. It was, I felt, calculated to trap only the second class. And so, in my subsequent experience, it has proved. I gladly escaped from the PCO before any such drab Whitehall honours were routinely conferred on me. And ever since I have of course been envious of those who wore them.

A few years after joining the PCO I was seconded to help Kwame Nkrumah produce Ghana's first republican constitution. As a reward for my labours for a full two years in what used to be called the White Man's Graveyard, the local Attorney General Geoffrey Bing QC (formerly a Labour MP at Westminster) kindly recommended to Her Majesty's Government that they award me an OBE (Officer of the most Excellent Order of the British Empire). For some reason never vouchsafed, that recommendation was ignored by the powers that be in Downing Street and Whitehall. To this day my loyal bosom remains chastely undecorated in any way. I make no complaint whatever about that: it is how I prefer to be. I do not lust for cups of tea or hands of whist from the old ladies. It shows however the hit-and-miss chances and hazards of our ridiculous pasteboard honours system.

Should this system exist at all? Harbouring grave doubts, Mr Fraser Kemp MP (Houghton and Washington, East) moved in the House of Commons on 22 November 2000 a 10-minute rule Bill. It would he said replace the arcane panoply of honours currently available, from knighthoods to baronetcies, from the Order of St. Patrick to the Order of the Thistle, including the Star of India, the Order of the Indian Empire, and the Furred Diadem of the Persian Cat (Second Class).

Replace them with what, you may ask. If they are that bad should they not be swept away altogether? Well not quite, Mr Fraser Kemp thought. In *Who's Who* he gives his recreations as the cinema and reading, so he is a man of culture. If he has read his Tennyson he might think some current honours recipients reminiscent of Lancelot –

His honour rooted in dishonour stood,
And faith unfaithful kept him falsely true.

Such an outdated arrangement as we now have, said Mr Kemp, does no credit to a nation that has just entered a new millennium. We should strive to break down social divisions, not reinforce them by clinging to an honours system based on an empire which has ceased to be. I sympathised with that, though I have never understood what is supposedly wrong with social divisions, which have been found to exist in every human society so far recorded. I am and always have been a fervent supporter of the great British Empire, except in its propensity to rely on pasteboard honours – otherwise known as Maundy Gregory gimcracks. Yes that word is a noun, defined by the Oxford English Dictionary as 'a showy, unsubstantial thing; especially a useless ornament, a trumpery article, a knick-knack. Knick-knack paddy whack one might say – until remembering the IRA. Do they award honours – as well as gun salutes at funerals of their grisly tribe?

Next we were given Mr Kemp's most powerful penseé.

How are we to quantify public service, or judge one person's contribution to society as more important than that of someone else? Why should we honour a first-rate diplomat and ambassador about whom many of us have not heard, rather than an exceptional nurse who has looked after people throughout a professional career? Why should one grade of honour be awarded rather than another? How can we make a judgment about television presenters or celebrities, and whether they should receive an honour of one grade rather than another? The same applies to authors – ultimately a literary judgment would have to be made, which I am not sure the honours unit, the Prime Minister or anyone else, is qualified to make.

Mr Kemp believed they do things better down under. He told the House that Australia had replaced the old British-based honours system with one simple Order of Australia. 'Whether someone worked in the outback as a postman for 40 years or was Prime Minister, he is proud to receive the Order of Australia.'

This is a worse nonsense even than what went before. A nation that really thinks working as a postman is equivalent in the nation's annals to serving as Prime Minister can only be called myopic – if not worse. I would say very much worse.

But Mr Kemp did sincerely want us to follow Australia-

'We should replace the present panoply of honours with an Order of the United Kingdom. That should be the way in which this country honours its worthiest members. I think that recipients would be proud to receive the honour. It would be awarded on the basis of what someone has done to make society a better place, irrespective of where he stands in the pecking order.'

How absurd to ignore the pecking order, and pretend that everyone is as useful to society as everyone else is. Every human community ever known has had its pecking order. Why should we British, under the saintly leadership of Blair, be so arrogant as to think we can rise above that and dispense with it? It is obvious rubbish, born of the silly idea that all people are created equal. Obviously, that is very far from being the case. On the contrary, communities need, for their own good, to value as is fitting their cleverest members. To do so will serve them best. They need clever people to survive. Always have done.

Mr Kemp's Bill was opposed by Mr Eric Forth MP, whose social club is the Bromley Conservative. His chief argument was what I can only describe as goo on stilts-

'Surely, the acid test of whether the current honours system is appropriate is the pleasure with which people accept honours. It is all very well for the honourable Gentleman to patronise people who happily accept various honours, but he does not seem to have given any thought to those recipients who, when they accept, are honoured – and say so – and make no secret of the fact that they are delighted. They reveal the great pleasure that they take in being recognised in many different ways.'

Ah well! Such is the dismal quality of the modern generation of MPs of all parties. I really do not know what to make of the fact that Mr Kemp's Bill was approved by 153 votes to 58. It went no further of course. It will never be law. Thankfully, our system does in the end filter out that sort of tripe.

45

Jokes and the Queen's Speech

Those who know it know that the House of Commons is a rare and precious flower of our country. It is to be cherished. That is why I ransack Hansard to show you some of its many felicities, ignored usually by what used to be called Fleet Street and is now known as the media. One felicity is the joke.

Jokes are important in the House of Commons, feeding as they do the camaraderie that is a feature of the place. It used to be exclusively male camaraderie, and that lingers. Women are not much good at camaraderie. Few of them even know what the word means, and that especially goes for the incoming ladies disdainfully known as Blair babes.

On 6 December 2000 we had the debate on the Queen's Speech, which thankfully featured many jokes. As usual on such occasions the two front benches (largely composed of men) faced each other cheerfully, mouthing good-humoured putdowns with appropriate gestures. I will give you some of the jokes delivered first by the Leader of the Opposition and then the Prime Minister.

William Hague started – this is another tradition – by remembering MPs who had recently died. The late Sir Michael Colvin, he recalled, had many interests. He was even a pub landlord – a qualification much praised in the modern Conservative Party (first joke). The also late Donald Dewar, Mr Hague recalled, was only happy when he was thoroughly depressed (second joke).

Mr Hague then congratulated Sir John Morris on his speech opening the debate. Although an MP for a continuous 41 years, Sir John has said he does not regard himself as a professional politician. This, said Mr Hague, is quite a statement for someone who has spent 33 years on the Front Bench as Minister of Defence, Secretary of State for Wales, Attorney General, etc. With that record, said Mr Hague, he would have to be a professional politician to claim that he was not one (third joke).

Mr Hague then got down to business. The Gracious Speech was so skimpy, he said, that obviously a May election must be in the offing (it was). It was very good of Her Majesty to come down to deliver it at all (fourth joke). He quoted at the Prime Minister Paddy Ashdown's autobiography, page 276, adding 'not many people have reached page 276' (fifth joke).

Mr Hague ploughed relentlessly on. Mr Prescott said about the recent European summit 'I had not been home for three weekends, so I admit. . . wanting to go home that night'. A human touch? Mr Hague was merciless. Why are the Government bothering to recruit the star of 'One Foot in the Grave' when they already have the star of one foot in the mouth? (sixth joke). Very clever ambitious youngsters are chained to dripping stone walls in the Central Office dungeon while they work out these jokes for their Leader. And still they pile mountains on top of Mr Hague's political grave, clearly visible in the very near future. In politics, those elevated too soon to have acquired the necessary savvy (short for savoir faire) inevitably die early. So it was to prove with the cheerful and likeable William Hague.

The Prime Minister, Mr Blair, rose to reply. He said the first half of Mr Hague's speech, in which he made his jokes, was excellent. The rest was not so good. Then Mr Blair, following custom, paid tribute to the Member for Aberdeen South, Anne Begg, who had seconded the Loyal Address. 'She was a teacher and used to say that, having taught 15 to 16-year-olds, being in the House of Commons was no problem for her'.

At this point the new Speaker from Glasgow (later to be known as Gorbals Mick) found it necessary to intervene. What he said was not meant as a joke, though some found it faintly risible.

Mr Speaker: Order. Private conversations are going on in the Chamber. [*Interruption.*] Order. If honourable Members find the debate boring, they know what they can do – they can leave. They will not be missed. If honourable Members wish to become involved in private conversations, it is only courteous for them to leave the Chamber. That is the case no matter which honourable Member is addressing the House.

The Prime Minister resumed. He was still on about Mr Hague's jokes. 'As I have said, the jokes were good – they are always good. Probably there is a little debate in his office: 'Do we go for jokes or for policy?' Let me congratulate him on at least one sound judgment. Frankly, I think it is better to stick with the jokes. I think he has taken the right tactical decision in that respect.'

Then Mr Blair sprang a joke of his own. It arose from the tiresome idea that parties can win elections by promising to lop items of government expenditure, when everyone knows this is like the poisonous Upas Tree – lop one branch and a dozen will spring up in its place. 'The right honourable Gentleman says – this is my favourite one – that he will save £205 million from not creating regional assemblies, but there is no £205 million budgeted for regional assemblies, so where does he get it from?'

A good question, to which no answer was given. Mr Blair rammed home his advantage. 'If the Conservatives want to save £1 billion on fraud, they can start with their own programme.'

We may leave them there, battling it out.

46

Finding Britain's Place in an Enlarged Europe

Not surprisingly, France since the end of World War II has been determined to hold its neighbour Germany in check. Having been overrun three times in seventy years might be expected to arouse that response in a spirited people. Seeking allies to this end, the French conjured up the image of a Europe united, perhaps a federal Europe – even a European unitary state. Some nearby nations, also sickened by the waste caused by two grotesque internecine struggles within a mere thirty years in the first half of the twentieth century, were inclined to support the French in this and did so. The shamefaced apologetic Germans fell in, which presented we forthright British with a problem that has straddled our domestic politics for two generations.

The British genius is to be independent, to go our own way. Foreigners may learn from us, but we have little to learn from them. It is we who are the destined world leaders, as testified by our magnificent unwitting creation of an Empire on which the sun never set. Remember that that included the United States of America, which was once a vital component of the burgeoning British Empire and then decided to leave. Now the USA is accepted as the World's policeman, and many are grateful for it. We British can claim some credit for that, not that it is ever accorded.

That is all very well you may say, but there is another side. We British cannot deny belonging to Europe. For two thousand years or more, our populations migrated to Britain from the continent and beyond. Our culture owes much to Europe, and to that further extended Europe which was instituted when in the 17th century the Pilgrim Fathers set sail from Plymouth to the west. Let no one doubt that the United States, indeed the entire American continent, is culturally a European enclave. It began that way, and still is that way – even though we may find it difficult to keep this progeny in check.

In that European bind, what were we British to do? As always, some genius sprang to the rescue. The name of that genius I do not know, but he or she is deserving of our praise. The answer was TO ENLARGE! The European Union of a few nations was too small to shrug off the monolithic power of Germany, confined only by feeble Gallic constraints. So let us bring in tough eastern nations such as Poland, Hungary, the Czechs and the Slovaks. Are they not European? Of course they are, who can gainsay it? This unknown genius in the British cause perceived that there is safety in numbers.

That brings me to the present day and the Nice summit, where once again a hapless British Prime Minister was required to square the circle. Mr Blair delivered his report to the House of Commons on 11 December 2000. He said that the summit was the culmination of a year-long conference called to deal with issues on which agreement could not be reached at Amsterdam three and a half years before. Agreement was essential to open the door to the enlargement of the European Union, the goal of successive British Governments. Enlargement will mean that the EU will ultimately comprise 27 nations, 'embracing all the countries of Europe – east and west – in a way that would have been unimaginable throughout most of the troubled history of our continent'.

The Leader of the Opposition, William Hague, had little useful to say in reply. On a key issue for lawyers, the Charter of Fundamental Rights, he feebly cited the Commission's website, which says that the Charter's causing a large rise in the number of lawsuits cannot be excluded. The Charter means, says the website, that the European Union has entered a new, more resolutely political stage of integration. It boasts that the Charter will be a very important milestone on the road towards this political Europe.

Hague made nothing of this, whereas he should have stressed its utmost importance. We have just gone through a lengthy, detailed process to get the Human Rights Act 1998 on to our statute book. This sets out articles of the European Convention on Human Rights. Our courts, acting in the shadow of the Human Rights Court at

Strasbourg, have to set these articles beside our ordinary Acts of Parliament and other laws to check whether the latter measure up. It is a shameful equation, but still we have accepted it.

Also to impose in addition a somewhat different, partially overlapping, set of rules laid down in the EU Charter of Rights must cause additional confusion and conflict in our legal system, as well as giving the Luxembourg Court unwarranted additional power. It was already very difficult for the British citizen and his or her advisers to find out just what the law provided on any matter. The Human Rights Act 1998 makes these problems of legal uncertainty far worse. The Nice proposal to pile on yet another tier in the shape of the Charter of Rights must inevitably lead to unspeakable confusion. The entire concept of law as an instrument for the just government of society is being overturned. People need to know what the law says about their case. That is what law, as a social tool, is all about. We need certainty in our law, or we are lost. Thanks to European influences, certainty in our law is for ever receding in this age that prides itself on being enlightened.

But what did poor little William Hague know of the rule of law, its value to society, and what was needed to preserve it? The short answer is nothing. Which all goes to show that if you try to place raw youths in positions of high authority you will inevitably come unstuck. Nice chap, but it was not enough. It is never enough just to be nice, when you have been inserted into a position of high authority.

47

Gazumping, Gazundering, Daisy Chains etc.

English law, as we all well know (or should do), has the fine principle of domestic sanctuary, summed up in the ancient maxim that every man's house is his castle. However we have regrettably not gone nearly so far in protecting the householder as our former colony New Zealand, where in 1999 there was created a special criminal offence, with increased penalties, called *Home Invasion*. Mr Blair please copy.

The best our Mr Blair has so far done for the house-holder, and it is not very much, is to produce the Homes Bill. This was given a second reading in the House of Commons on 8 January 2001, the Conservative Party forbearing to divide against it (in other words sitting on the fence as usual).

Part I of the Bill dealt with house sales; Part II with homelessness. As I had been trying unsuccessfully to sell my Oxford house since June 2000, I thought I would concentrate on Part I. As it happened it was Part II that was passed into law by itself, as the Homelessness Act 2002. Part I thankfully remains in limbo.

In England there are very many problems involved with house sales (Scotland is said to do better). I am no stranger to what in the second reading debate was referred to as the daisy chain, though this casts an unjustified aspersion on a loved and innocent wild flower. I prefer simply to call those grim, yet too easily broken, house-dealing shackles *the chain*. (My long-suffering wife, when I talked this over with her, said she would very much like to *pull the chain*.) The chain arises because very often each person who wants to buy a house also has one to sell. Usually he or she also has a mortgage on that house, and needs another mortgage to finance the purchase of its replacement. The same applies to the person to whom he or she aims to sell the house, and so on *ad infinitum*. It only needs one link in the chain to snap and every shackled person suffers.

Another problem is gazumping. If the market is rising, and the above rigmarole continues for too long, the owner who has informally agreed to sell to Mrs X for £Y finds that from someone else he could get £Y + Z, and yields to temptation. Where on the contrary the market is falling Mrs X may find she can get the same sort of house elsewhere for £Y-Z, and so commits the act known as gazundering. Either of these natural human activities causes grief, so well-meaning souls want them stopped. That includes the Conservative Party, here as so often false to its free enterprise philosophy.

The second reading of the Homes Bill was moved by the Minister for Housing and Planning, Mr. Nick Raynsford. He said –

> The Bill was published on 13 December 2000 alongside our policy statement 'Quality and Choice: A decent home for all – The way forward for housing'. That statement sets out our strategy for ensuring that everyone has the opportunity of a decent home. It followed our housing Green Paper. . . and our spending review announcement in July 2000, which confirmed our commitment to more than double the capital investment in housing that we inherited in 1997, improving the quality, affordability and supply of housing and the choices available to all.

The Minister went on to say that every MP would have had direct experience of the failings of the current house buying and selling system and know someone who had suffered frustration, heartache and, often, financial loss. The delays and uncertainties in the current system, he added, put home buyers and sellers under enormous pressure: 'Planning with confidence is impossible, and too often the end is dejection as the deal fails'.

What is the solution? Mr Raynsford gave his answer. 'The Bill requires sellers to arrange for the key information about their homes, including searches and a mid-level survey, to be prepared up front, in the form of a seller's pack, before marketing starts. The pack will enable sellers and their agents to have the information that they need to set a realistic price, and buyers will be able to make a well-informed offer safe in the knowledge that they are unlikely later to encounter any nasty surprises'.

If only it were true! We would all rejoice. One after another, experts in the shape of chartered surveyors, solicitors, conveyancers *et al.* stood up to demonstrate to the House that it is not true. The Conservative MP for Eastbourne, Nigel Waterson, even moved an amendment to that effect (heavily defeated on a division). He added –

I am tempted to say that this measure is a large sledgehammer to crack a small nut, except that the nut is signally absent. The Bill does not. . . tackle gazumping [or] its uglier sister, gazundering. . . the Bill has not a friend in the world apart from the Minister.

So far house sellers and buyers have not actually been troubled by this silly proposal of a seller's pack. It may be described as dead in the water.

48

Improving our Tax Law: a Brave Try

Do we want our laws simplified, or do we not? My own experience of more than fifty years in law making is that many law users bitterly complain of obscurity, yet find the topic supremely boring when it comes to doing anything about it. Yet something is at last being done.

On 15 January 2001 the House of Commons gave a second reading to the Capital Allowances Bill, the first in a series designed to simplify our tax laws. As a former Finance Bill draftsman and long term would-be reformer I welcome this aspirational Bill.

As respects statute law, the reform story began in 1968 when I founded the Statute Law Society. Its main object was (and I believe still is) to procure technical improvements in the form and manner in which legislation is expressed and published so as to make it more intelligible. The Society's first report, drawn up by a committee chaired by the late Sir Desmond Heap and published in 1970, said the primary rule should be that the procedures must be *governed by the needs of the user*. This was endorsed in 1975 by the Renton Committee, set up by the Government to deal with the Society's criticisms.

Dissatisfaction continued. In the debate on 15 January 2000 Mr David Ruffley MP mentioned vitriolic comment from accountants and solicitors in 1986 about the complexity of provisions of the Finance Act of that year relating to capital allowances, the subject of the present Bill. In 1994 the Institute of Fiscal Studies set up a tax law review committee which concluded that the tax system is too complicated and not working as intended. An Inland Revenue report published in 1996 admitted that the language of the existing law could be simplified. The rewrite project was born.

Introducing the project, the then Chancellor of the Exchequer, Mr Ken Clarke MP (Conservative), had said it was as ambitious as translating *War and Peace* into lucid Swahili. 'In fact', he added, 'it is more ambitious. . . *War and Peace* is only 1,500 pages long, while Inland Revenue tax law is 6,000 pages long and was not written by a Tolstoy'. He might have added that neither is *War and Peace* a palimpsest of a thousand disconnected fragments from many different legislative years.

Moving the second reading the Paymaster General, Dawn Primarolo MP, said the Capital Allowances Bill was produced by an Inland Revenue project team. (In fact of course it was largely produced by the labouring drafters known as parliamentary counsel, to whom Mr Michael Jack MP, a former Financial Secretary to the Treasury, paid warm tribute.) The project team was supervised by a high-level steering committee chaired by the former Chancellor of the Exchequer Lord Howe of Aberavon, well known in committee circles for his almost inaudible utterance. An attack by him was famously likened by Dennis Healey to being savaged by a dead sheep. From my own experience I can confirm that impression, though (I write in 2002) Lord Howe does seem still to be breathing, if only faintly.

There was also a consultative committee drawn from professional users of tax legislation. The consultation process involved four separate exposure drafts, published at relatively early stages between October 1998 and February 2000. A final round of consultation on a draft Bill was published in August 2000. The procedure cannot be faulted for thoroughness.

Ms Primarolo quoted, without naming, 'a leading figure in the tax world' who had told her that the Bill represented a revolution in accessibility. He added: 'It has a logical structure and for the first time in my experience it has actually been designed to help the user'. She said that other features of the rewrite include shorter sentences, modern language, clearer signposts, more effective definitions, and greater use of reader aids. There were however some critical voices.

Mr John Burnett MP, a LibDem solicitor, raised a key point when he asked for an assurance that future Finance Acts would tailor changes to fit the format of the new Capital Allowances Act. He added: 'We do not want to go back to the position of taxpayers and practitioners having to hunt around numerous Finance Acts to get to the law on capital allowances'. He did not receive that assurance, but his question was crucial. During the consultation process I raised it myself, also without result.

Mr John Redwood MP asked whether Ken Clarke would have been pleased had he known that '903 pages of legislation, annexes and explanatory notes would result, just for the purpose of capital allowances'? Mr Jack said some people would say of the Bill 'It doesn't look any less complex to me; but now I can understand the complexity better'. Mr Peter Lilley MP, also a former Financial Secretary to the Treasury, retorted that the complexity was largely due not to perverseness or incompetence but to policy decisions to discriminate between different classes of assets. It is policy that produces complexity.

More such measures are to come: also on 15 January 2001 the House of Commons voted to set up a select committee to join with one from the Lords as the Joint Committee on Tax Simplification Bills. We shall see what that produces. I am not hopeful. It is not a subject that promises simplicity, even though simplicity is highly desirable.

49

Why this Conspiracy of Silence?

18 January 2001 was an Opposition day in the House of Commons. The Conservatives had elected to debate police numbers (for the umpteenth time). Usual accusations were bandied about concerning whose fault it is that there are too few bobbies on the beat in our cherished towns and villages.

The shadow Home Secretary, Miss Anne Widdecombe MP, entertained the House with a lively story of the Pontefract pensioner who is daily beset in his own house by gangs of rowdy youths. They wouldn't know a bobby on the beat if they saw one (which of course they never do). The besieged pensioner thus finds it necessary to ring his local police station for help almost every day. So, said Miss Widdecombe, he has cleverly added the police telephone number to his British Telecom facility called *Friends and Family*.

When the Home Secretary, Mr Jack Straw MP, rose to answer the case put by the redoubtable Tory lady rudely known as Doris Karloff he was interrupted at the start.

Mrs Anne Campbell (Cambridge): On the subject of investment in the police force, may I thank my right honourable Friend for the £1 million that he announced yesterday as extra funding for the Cambridgeshire police force? Will he commend that force for achieving a 2.9 per cent. reduction in recorded crime since the election, despite its considerable difficulties in policing the protests against Huntingdon Life Sciences (HLS)?

We know Mrs Campbell shouldn't have talked about the police *force*. For years its correct name has been the police service, just to show how servile and non-forceful it is nowadays. But I rather warm to Mrs Campbell for not having caught up with this. It is not, after all, what one would expect – unless one had suddenly become aware of the new and dreadful trends in the policing of our beloved country. Her intervention referred to the fact that a group of illegal agitators had impudently announced its determination to 'close down' HLS, so the police were being given an extra £1m to combat this. As I explained in chapter 40 a similar unlawful group recently closed down Hillgrove Farm in Oxfordshire. Chris Brown, the law-abiding owner of this cat farm, meekly said its closure was a loss to medical research, then quietly departed. Thames Valley Police refused to prosecute the organisers for the offence they had undoubtedly committed, namely criminal conspiracy.

> **Mr Straw:** I greatly regret that it has been necessary to allocate £1 million to that force to deal with the outrageous intimidatory and, in some cases, violent attacks that have been made by so-called animal rights protesters against the perfectly lawful and important activities of Huntingdon Life Sciences.

Here a backbench Tory, successor to Julian Critchley as MP for Aldershot, intervened.

> **Mr Gerald Howarth:** Can he say why he and the authorities do not use the conspiracy laws to tackle the people who plan such attacks?

This was the key question raised in the debate. I will tell you in a moment how Mr Straw answered it, but first I will fill in some more of the background.

The 2000 scheme of digging up the turf of Parliament Square by 'guerrilla gardening' was plotted in advance on the internet and widely known. The organisers of this criminal conspiracy should have been apprehended and prosecuted well before it happened, but they were not. Why?

In the 2000 petrol crisis the Chancellor of the Exchequer, Mr Gordon Brown MP, stated that it was 'absolutely wrong for demonstrators to have decided who got fuel'. Yet the police and prosecutors omitted to use the law of criminal conspiracy. Why?

The port of Shoreham in the peaceful county of Sussex was overwhelmed by animal rights protesters objecting to shipments of live animals. Giving judgment in an unsuccessful prosecution (not for conspiracy), the Law Lord Lord Nolan said: 'The result may be seen as the acceptance by the courts of a victory for the violent elements. . . I would describe it myself as an acceptance of the plain fact that there are limits to the extent to which the police can control unlawful violence in any given situation.' As I said in chapter 40, Lord Nolan inexcusably failed to mention that an answer could have been found by prosecuting the main organisers of this illegal protest for criminal conspiracy, and so nipping their nefarious activities in the bud. Such a prosecution, if launched sufficiently early, does nip the plot in the bud. That means that numerous constables do not need to be deployed against the protesters, and so are freed to be, as we would wish, 'bobbies on the beat'.

The Home Secretary feebly attempted an answer to Mr Gerald Howarth MP.

> **Mr. Straw:** The police and the Crown Prosecution Service are determined to use all the powers and charges that are available to ensure that such outrageous activities are deterred and effectively addressed. If there is evidence that would add up to a conspiracy charge, such a charge would be laid.

That was a lie, and Mr Straw knew (or ought to have known) it was a lie. A sinister, behind the scenes, policy has decreed that conspiracy charges will not be brought in such cases as this – and they are not brought.

Did any MP rise to support Mr Howarth? The answer is no. Nothing else was said in the entire debate about the failure of the authorities to gather evidence and prosecute for criminal conspiracy. I ask again, why?

Democrats are always intrigued by Government malpractice, especially when the Government in question (like Mr Blair's) purports to be wholesomely democratic. As I said above, why are our well-established laws against criminal conspiracy not being used by the authorities to curb the criminals who organise unlawful animal rights protests?

The House of Commons returned to the topic on 12 March 2001. The hare was started (if I may so put it) by Dr Ian Gibson, Labour MP for Norwich North. He is an interesting man, this Dr Gibson. A trained biologist, he is a doctor of philosophy who once worked at Indiana University. That is where the late great Alfred Kinsey so strenuously studied the sexual habits of the human male (and the human female too, but he was rather more interested in the male).

Dr Gibson asked the Home Secretary about his discussions with trade unions representing workers engaged in animal experimentation about their intimidation by animal rights fanatics. Mr Straw said he had recently had a meeting with the Manufacturing, Science and Finance union (MSF), which represents employees in the biotechnology, pharmaceutical and medical research industries. Officials were also in contact with the MSF when preparing measures to combat animal rights extremists that have been included in the Criminal Justice and Police Bill.

Mr Straw: My honourable Friend is right to say that unfortunately many of those involved in extremist animal rights movements are. . .

Mr John Bercow (Buckingham): Poisonous.

Mr Straw: Poisonous and worse – and willing to go in for any kind of totally unacceptable tactics against people who are simply carrying out lawful and important duties. I have been very anxious, at an institutional level but above all at a personal level, to offer the support of the Government – and, I believe, that of the whole House – for the work that those people are undertaking. As I have said before, without that work many important scientific and medical advances would never have been made, and many people would have died prematurely or not been able to maintain the quality of their lives.

Fiona Mactaggart (Slough): Is the Home Secretary aware that it is not merely scientists who have been the targets of these vandals? The Horlicks factory in my constituency, for example, has been invaded by animal rights extremists. Will the Home Secretary congratulate Thames Valley police on their vigorous action against those responsible for the attack?

Mr Straw: I have no idea quite how targeting a Horlicks factory can help to propagate their aims; none the less, it was dangerous. I am very pleased, however, that Thames Valley police responded as they did.

Mr Ian Taylor (Esher and Walton): The Home Secretary might like to know that only last week there was another incident in my constituency, directed against individuals working in the pharmaceutical industry. This is intimidation verging on terrorism.

Mr Tam Dalyell (Linlithgow): When the chief executive of Huntingdon Life Sciences came to an all-party group, some of us were dismayed to learn the extent to which the cars of even relatively junior staff members had been vandalised. What can be done to protect junior members of staff? May I also ask, in the light of the Home Secretary's last answer, whether the Government are happy about the lack of backing from some who might be expected to show more courage in this matter, such as the Royal Bank of Scotland?

Mr Straw: To deal with the last point first, I am certainly not happy about the response of some of the United Kingdom's financial institutions, which I believe were pusillanimous in the extreme. If financial institutions give in to that type of intimidation, it will wholly undermine those who are on the front line of that very important scientific research.

I return to my opening question. Why are our well-established laws against criminal conspiracy not being used by the authorities to curb the organisers of unlawful animal rights protests?

An answer of a kind was delivered by the Home Office Minister Charles Clarke MP on 14 March 2001 when he said (erroneously) that the present law only covers the people who actually carry out the harassment, not those who plan it. On that day the Government put down a new clause to the Criminal Justice and Police Bill with the sidenote 'Collective harassment'. It proposes to amend the Protection from Harassment Act 1997 to cover aiding, abetting, counselling and procuring. This is a step in the right direction, but leaves my opening question still unanswered.

50

On the Morning after the Night Before

Another Sex Hater's Ball took place in the House of Lords on 29 January 2001. As usual, the dancing was led by Baroness Young on behalf of the Conservative Party. She moved that an humble Address be presented to Her Majesty praying that the Prescription Only Medicines (Human Use) Amendment (No. 3) Order 2000 be annulled. This order changes the law by allowing hormonal emergency contraception (the morning-after pill, known as Levonelle) to be sold by pharmacists to persons over 16 without a doctor's prescription. Much hot rage has been generated by that, fuelled by the Chief Stoker Baroness Young.

For the Government, Lord Hunt explained that the background to the order was an application made by Medimpex UK to the Medicines Control Agency. First, the Agency assessed the safety of the medicine in the light of the legal criteria for prescription-only status. Then the application was referred to the Committee on the Safety of Medicines, which initially reported favourably. The matter was then put out to public and professional consultation. Virtually all the main medical and pharmaceutical bodies which responded were in favour, and did not raise any concerns about the safety of supply in a pharmacy setting. Both the Committee on the Safety of Medicines and the Medicines Commission carefully considered all the evidence submitted. Finally they advised that Levonelle can be supplied safely under the supervision of a pharmacist.

In 1999 800,000 women were prescribed emergency contraception. To be effective Levonelle has to be taken very soon after sexual intercourse, and Lord Hunt said the order would assist this by ending the need next day to approach a general practitioner for a prescription. The Government had also made the order so as to reduce the level of abortions.

None of this satisfied the noble Lady.

Baroness Young: I have often been accused in the past of being concerned only about boys. That has never been true, but today I am concerned about girls. My concern, as always, is the protection of young people, and 16 year-olds are children in law. I have also said on more than one occasion that all law sends a signal. So what signal does this order send? First, it says that unprotected sex is all right. This is exactly the opposite of what the whole sex education industry has been saying for at least 20 years. It is of course a very dangerous signal because it will increase the incidence of sexually transmitted diseases. . . Secondly, promiscuity will be encouraged. Everyone, including GPs, health authorities and now chemists. . . nurses and youth workers, will be making the morning-after pill available to young girls. One can picture the scene. The boy will say to the girl, 'why not? you can take the morning-after pill' The girl will think: 'Why not? I could take the morning-after pill and be all right.'

Lady Young sought to strengthen this argument by citing the Government's Teenage Pregnancy White Paper, which quoted a boy as saying: 'I have used a condom, but I don't like it. It puts you off. What's the use of having sex if you don't enjoy it?'

Many will think the lad had a point, and echoing would ask What indeed is the use? Not the senescent Lord Longford (now alas deceased). He said it had been put to him that the morning-after pill reduced the number of teenage pregnancies. He accepted that such pregnancies were 'evil', but considered fornication a greater evil still. So he would vote against. What did this miserable old sinner know of fornication?

The Bishop of St Albans perpetrated the familiar solecism of equating a foetus with a child, falsely complaining that abortion wipes out 'villages filled with children week in and week out'. The Bishop of Southwark piously said, wringing his hands in their lawn sleeves, that sex outside marriage is morally wrong: '[w]e may preach against it, and we do; we may teach against it, and we do; but it goes on happening'. Surprise, surprise!

These holy bishops seem unaware that unmarried persons also need sexual fulfilment. That's the way they are made: it is not their fault. Their bodies demand it. They are equipped with various organs that are designed for this purpose, and insist on being respected. They include the many for whom, for one reason or another, marriage is simply not available. They also include pubescent youngsters made by nature hot with lust, and surely deserving of happiness.

In support of the proposed order, Lord Young introduced a shameful aspect. '. . .not all parents manage to talk to their children. Indeed, one study showed that one third of girls had not been told about periods before they started.' A peeress had the answer to this sort of prudish betrayal.

Baroness Walmsley: We could stop talking about sex as if it were some terrible immoral activity that causes untold harm to society and start accepting it as normal human behaviour. We should learn to discuss it with our children openly, frankly and without embarrassment. . . What we should be doing today is saying to the Government, 'Well done, keep going, extend the arrangements that make the product free to those for whom cost might be a barrier to getting help.'

To their credit, their Lordships were persuaded along those lines. Baroness Young's cruel and heartless motion was defeated by 177 votes to 95. The morning after pill went on sale. Even Tesco sells it, which for some reason adds to the fury of the Baroness Youngs.

51

When Religion Mattered

In the days when religion mattered in England it was thought that a priest should not also be an MP, or if you prefer, that an MP should not also be a priest. Each of these high vocations must, it was felt, be all-consuming of the energies and spirits of one human life. It was felt that the same man (it was always of course a man) could not conscientiously do both jobs, since each on its own required every ounce of his efforts. Hence the passing of the House of Commons (Clergy Disqualification) Act 1801, brought into law because a remarkable Church of England priest, Horne Tooke, won a parliamentary election for the unreformed rotten borough of Old Sarum.

Times have changed, and on 6 February 2001 the House of Commons gave an unopposed second reading to a Bill to repeal this archaism (as it is now described). In the debate MPs pontificated, one way or another, and some doubtful historical scholarship was on display. It reminded me of that time when the Bill to disestablish the Welsh Church was introduced and the barrister F E Smith, later Lord Chancellor Birkenhead (Conservative), publicly wrung his hands at the spiritual loss the passing of this unravelling Bill would entail. It was, he said, a Bill 'which has shocked the conscience of every Christian community in Europe'. The Roman Catholic poet G K Chesterton famously riposted -

> It would greatly, I must own, soothe me, Smith!
> If you left this theme alone, holy Smith!
> For your legal cause or civil you fight well and get your fee:
> For your God or dream or devil you will answer, not to me.
> Talk about the pews and steeples, and the cash that goes
>   therewith!
> But the souls of Christian peoples – chuck it, Smith!

What would the sublime Chesterton have made of the fact that the present Bill was brought forward to suit the convenience of just one man? This man was Mr David

Cairns, a former Roman Catholic priest who wished to stand as the Labour candidate for Greenock and Inverclyde at the forthcoming general election of 2001 (and at that election was in fact voted an MP).

The Government spokesman moving the second reading of the Bill, the Parliamentary Under-Secretary of State for the Home Department Mr. Mike O'Brien, confessed the truth, saying '[t]he case of David Cairns is clearly the reason for the Bill'. In other words it was an *ad hominem* Bill, and should therefore, under parliamentary rules, have been presented as a private Bill. In fact, on the orders of Mr Blair, it was presented as a public Bill and was therefore guaranteed the approval of Blair's huge parliamentary majority. What cares Blair for parliamentary rules when they get in the way of his majority? It shows what you can get away with when, like Blair, you have an overwhelming majority and no conscience – remember that Blair is a practising member of the Church of England who is married to a practising Roman Catholic. All very fishy.

Mr Eric Forth (Conservative) said the Bill was 'completely and grotesquely unfair'. Another Conservative, Mr Robert Key, slyly observed that the last MP on whose behalf a change in the law was specially engineered was the Conservative Neil Hamilton, who then promptly lost his Tatton seat. A third Conservative, Mr Gerald Howarth, pointed out that the Government spokesman had failed to disclose that Mr Cairns was employed by the House of Commons itself, and was moreover the paid researcher of a Labour MP. The Government spokesman found no difficulty is shrugging all that off. In the present Blairite climate, that is very easy to do.

Miss Anne Widdecombe MP presented the Conservative position. She had been a Roman Catholic convert for all of seven years, and still spoke with the enthusiasm of an *arriviste*. Yet she spoke wisely.

> I do not believe that being a Member of Parliament is compatible with the priestly vocation. Like the priesthood, it involves a huge commitment, both in this Chamber and outside. I do not believe that a Member of Parliament could represent constituents adequately

while continuing to serve as a full-time priest, or that a priest could administer to his flock adequately while undertaking duties as a full-time Member of Parliament'.

Then Miss Widdicombe touched on an interesting aspect. As a Roman Catholic she suggested that in an earlier intervention Mr Eric Forth (Conservative) had hinted 'that people of my persuasion are somehow dominated by some interesting European power, rather than by the monarch and Parliament'. This was a reference to His Holiness the Pope, who has for many centuries bedevilled religious affairs in England, having earlier claimed to rule our country from a secular as well as a religious viewpoint.

Mr David Winnick (Labour) here enquired whether Mr Forth was suggesting that Roman Catholics are not loyal to the United Kingdom or have a wider loyalty to an outside force? Mr Forth said that was a matter for Roman Catholics. Mr Winnick retorted that Mr Forth's questioning of Roman Catholic loyalty to this country 'was surely unacceptable and, indeed, downright disgraceful'. I wonder about that.

In docilely agreeing with Mr Winnick on this the Government spokesman overlooked one significant fact, which is this. Any religious devotee who rightly or wrongly believes that his or her faith possesses supreme truth in the higher realms of the universe must necessarily put all that above merely earthy secular values, such as loyalty to a Monarch. It stands to reason. What is more, it stands to faith.

The next speaker was a prominent Conservative Privy Councillor.

Mr John Redwood (Wokingham): Although the Minister has not been prepared to tell the House the date by which he wants the legislation to pass, we have now discovered that it is a rush job and that the Government failed to think about the matter in good time. Now they suddenly have a problem and they are trying to rush the Bill through before the general election.

In fact the Bill passed into law as the House of Commons (Removal of Clergy Disqualification) Act 2001, having received Royal Assent on 11 May 2001. In view of its importance, I end with some excerpts from the official memorandum on this interesting Act (in what follows I have corrected some errors in the official text).

OFFICIAL MEMORANDUM

The Act removes any disqualification from membership of the House of Commons that arises by reason of a person having been ordained in, or being a Minister of, a religious denomination, but continues the disqualification of Lords Spiritual from such membership. Prior to the Act, certain clergy were disqualified by statute from becoming members of the House of Commons. The statutory provisions were set out in the House of Commons (Clergy Disqualification) Act 1801 and section 9 of the Roman Catholic Relief Act 1829. The clergy specifically referred to in these two enactments were 'person[s] having been ordained to the office of priest or deacon, or being a minister of the Church of Scotland', and 'person[s] in holy orders in the Church of Rome'.

In 1951 (in *Re MacManaway*) the Privy Council decided that the 1801 Act not only disqualified persons ordained in the Church of England, but also all persons ordained by a bishop in accordance either with the order of the Church of England or other forms of Episcopal ordination. In the particular case of the Reverend James G MacManaway, this included ordination according to the use of the Church of Ireland. Thus, in broad terms, those clergy who were ordained by a bishop were subject to the disqualification whereas clergy and ministers of religion who were not ordained by a bishop were not subject to the disqualification.

The Clergy Disqualification Act 1870, however, provided a procedure which enabled Church of England clergy to relinquish their clerical positions and, after a period of six months, be freed from the parliamentary disqualification. There is no equivalent statutory procedure for clergy of other churches.

The Home Affairs Committee Report on Electoral Law and Administration (House of Commons Session 1997-1998) recommended reform -

> We therefore recommend that, with one exception, all restrictions on ministers of religion standing for, and serving as, Members of Parliament be removed; the exception would be in respect of all serving bishops in the Church of England who, for so long as places are reserved for their senior bishops in the House of Lords, should remain ineligible to serve as Members of the Commons.

The position of Lords Spiritual differs from others who sit in the House of Lords. Section 5 of the Bishoprics Act 1878, whilst not itself conferring the right of bishops to sit in the House of Lords, provides that the number of bishops who may sit is not to be further increased. The number is limited to 26. The Archbishops of Canterbury and York and the Bishops of London, Durham and Winchester are always summoned to sit in the House of Lords; the other 21 seats are filled by diocesan bishops summoned on the basis of seniority of date of becoming a diocesan bishop in the Church of England (other than the bishoprics of Sodor and Man and of Gibraltar in Europe). The House of Lords Standing Order No. 6 states that bishops to whom a writ of summons has been issued are not Peers but are Lords of Parliament. When sitting in the House of Lords, such bishops are 'Lords Spiritual'.

Siobhain McDonagh MP introduced a Private Member's Bill to rectify the position under the Ten Minute Rule Procedure on 16 June 1999. It had cross party support, but failed at 2nd Reading. The Government stated that it was sympathetic, but wanted to consult the churches before changing the law. The Church of England, Church of Scotland and Church of Ireland and the Roman Catholic Church in England and Wales and in Scotland and Ireland were subsequently consulted and were content for the statutory disqualifications to be removed.

52

When Shall We Join The Euro?

In his prime (the 1920s), my deceased father Thomas Roscoe Bennion was a strait-laced sombre auditor deployed at a humble desk in the august Whitehall office of His Majesty's Exchequer and Audit Department (as it was then known). Dad had a bothersome thing about freemasons. This obsession interfered with his work, supposed to be neutrally carried out in defence of all our interests. Freemasons troubled Dad more than somewhat (as, inspired by Damon Runyon, we used to say in those far-off days). What right had they to interfere in government? But it seems they do, and Dad could never accept this.

Dad once told me that a trick question Freemasons ask, when in doubt about the acceptability of some would-be joiner, is 'Do you know the meaning of words?' The correct answer, Dad said he had gleaned, is 'I've been taught to be cautious'. Not ever having been (or desired to be) a freemason, I do not know whether this ancient family tale is true or not. However I do know that my poor father really did have a pathological objection to the tribe of behind-the-scene conspirators known as Freemasons. Dad was under the rooted impression that because he had over many years steadfastly refused to seek admittance to their ranks his career in the Exchequer and Audit Department had wilted on the vine.

I was reminded of all that when I read Lord Rees-Mogg's column in *The Times* of 12 February 2001. His Lordship, a former editor of that newspaper, was holding forth about an exchange over the euro at Prime Minister's questions on 7 February. Rees-Mogg set out a passage which he portentously said 'needs to be quoted again and again until we all get it by heart'. He added: 'I take it from Hansard. It could decide the future history of Britain'. Well of course that made me sit up and take notice. I looked at *Hansard* on the internet and found that Rees-Mogg had got the crucial passage slightly wrong. Here is the correct version.

Mr William Hague (Richmond, Yorks): The Foreign Secretary repeated this week that the Government, if re-elected, would make an assessment on joining the euro early in the next Parliament. Does 'early' mean in the first two years of that Parliament?

The Prime Minister: 'Early in the next Parliament' means exactly what it says. It would of course be within two years.

This does not seem anything to make a fuss about, though Rees-Mogg said it was one of the most important announcements of government policy in that Parliament, since it disclosed 'the timing of the decision to hold a referendum'. Here we get back to that notion of the meaning of words, for obviously the Prime Minister's statement did not mean what Rees-Mogg said it meant. It referred to the making of an 'assessment'. As background Mr Blair said 'we favour Britain joining a successful single currency; in practice, the economic tests must be met'. So the assessment referred to was one which will determine whether at the relevant time the economic tests are met. If they are met, a referendum on joining the euro will be held. If they are not met, the matter will be deferred to a later date, when a further economic assessment will be held, and so on. In time the economic tests may ultimately be met, and then the referendum will at last be called. But it may take years. It may not happen at all.

Rees-Mogg suggested that in making his announcement on 7 February 2001 the Prime Minister outmanoeuvred the Chancellor of the Exchequer by without prior notice to him disclosing *when the referendum will take place*. Rees-Mogg said Labour policy had previously been to refuse to put any time on the referendum process 'because Gordon Brown thought the euro to be a damaging issue in election terms'. Now the cat was out of the bag (said Rees-Mogg).

All that was very great nonsense by the absurd Rees-Mogg. In fact Mr Blair did not disclose on 7 February 2001 when the euro referendum will take place. On the contrary he kept all his cats well within their bags. He accepted that 'early within the next Parliament' means within two years after the next election date, since it could not mean anything else. But he did not say that the referendum will be announced within those two years. It will be announced only if the economic tests are met then. If they are met then it will be sensible to hold the referendum. If not, not. That should be obvious, even to a silly Rees-Mogg.

I have to say that this new Labour policy on the euro, based on economic criteria, makes more sense than the Conservative policy, based on jingoism. Mr Blair had the last word in the debate, at the expense of the Leader of the Opposition.

> **The Prime Minister:** These stirring speeches in favour of the pound would be much more convincing if the right honourable Gentleman said that he was not ruling it out for just five years. That is an absurd position to be in . . . The truth is that our policy – to judge, according to the economic tests, what is good for British jobs, British business and industry – is the right one. The final decision will be for people to make in a referendum. The real reason that the right honourable Gentleman rules it out, in principle, as a matter of politics, is that he knows . . . that a large part of his party want out of Europe altogether.

The last word I would have is that all this is not, as the Prime Minister implied, just about economics. At some point in the future joining the euro may appear to suit Britain economically. But what about the political and constitutional consequences, which a statesman would think far more important? If a nation surrenders its right to rule its currency, it surrenders its right to rule. How about that, Mr Blair?

53

What shall we do about Derry?

What on earth is to be done about Wallpaper Derry? Shall we sweetly sing this Scottish interloper the London-Derry air, or smite him smartly on his London derrière? I speak thus disrespectfully of Mr Blair's Lord Chancellor because mockery is the only weapon left when puffed-up grandees show themselves deaf to reason. We long for almost any of Derry's predecessors. One cannot imagine Clement Attlee allowing William Jowitt to cavort in this gormless way. Not that Jowitt would have wished to do so; it would never have entered his decent, learned, level head.

Derry, otherwise Lord Irvine of Lairg, worships the one who appointed him (I do not refer to H M the Queen, who in fact appointed him, but to his old Bar pupil the said Mr Blair). Derry reminds me of the typical chuprassie in the far-off days of British India (and here I quote from an old source). 'The chuprassie paints his master in colours drawn from his own black heart. Every insinuation he throws out, every demand he makes, is endorsed with his master's name'.

It seems to me that Wallpaper Derry has tin ears. Inaudible to that humming, scheming brain of his are the subtle signals that his betters would detect, absorb and act on. These quiet signals tell the recipient what the people want, and also what they will not stand for. One remembers such humdrum political operators of yesteryear as Lord Hailsham of St Marylebone and Lord Mackay of Clashfern, who neither ever put a foot wrong. They were political, as a Lord Chancellor must be, but unlike Wallpaper Derry they instinctively knew where to draw the line.

One Sunday (18 February 2001), just after reading the newspaper report of Derry's Labour Party fund-raising letter, when he attempted to blackmail the Bar into contributing to Labour's coffers, I wrote to this man. I said, as one who was called to the Bar over fifty years ago, that for a currently serving Lord Chancellor to solicit from those subject to his powers of patronage contributions to the coffers of his own political party was disgraceful. It conveyed an obvious message: the bigger the contribution you make to Labour funds, the better your chance of receiving Derry's favours. And that was wrong. I said that as a barrister I felt sullied. I reminded this upstart Derry from Scotland of an English Lord Chief Justice's apophthegm. Lord Hewart famously said 'it is not merely of some importance but is of fundamental importance that justice should not only be done, but should manifestly and undoubtedly be seen to be done'. I received no answer from Derry, which is contrary to the etiquette hitherto prevailing in our ancient legal profession (always there to serve the public).

My old friend David (Lord Renton), who succeeded me as chairman of the Statute Law Society and served it valiantly for many years, joined in condemning Wallpaper Derry. He told the House of Lords on 20 February 2001 that as the second most senior Queen's Counsel in England he had a memory of these matters going back 70 years. With characteristic understatement he added: 'May I say that during that time there has never arisen such an occasion as this'.

With characteristic overstatement *Private Eye* joined in the general condemnation of Wallpaper Derry. A spoof item in the St Albion Parish News of 23 February 2001 (where 'the Vicar' is identified as the Rev A R P Blair MA (Oxon)) said that a Mr Lairg cordially invited all lawyers to a special 'Support the Vicar' cheese and wine party to be held in his office on Cash Wednesday. It added: 'the Vicar always remembers his friends'. How rotten of the stinking Derry to lay our learned and upright profession open to such mockery.

I believe his misconduct renders Derry liable to impeachment by the House of Commons, if only its members would do what is right and not blindly follow the party whip. The parliamentary bible *Erskine May* notes that impeachment of magnates has fallen into disuse, yet adds that it has never been formally abolished. A recent report by the Joint Committee on Parliamentary Privilege stated that the circumstances in which impeachment has taken place are now so remote from the present that the procedure may be considered obsolete.

And yet, and yet . . . The same used to be said of the High Court of Chivalry, which had not sat for centuries. Yet in 1955 the city of Manchester successfully applied to that court to protect its monopoly right to use the city's coat of arms. A constitutional procedure is not obsolete until it has been formally abolished. The wise and canny British are very slow to abolish institutions that might yet be found to have useful life. The remedy of impeachment has not been formally abolished. It should perhaps be revived for the iniquitous Wallpaper Derry.

After much pressure, Derry condescended to answer his critics on 21 February 2001. He said he had done nothing wrong. He added that he would do it again. I leave the last word to a master parliamentarian.

Lord Howe of Aberavon: Instinctively and intuitively, former Lord Chancellors recognised the conflict between the process of fundraising and the process of political campaigning.

Derry's instincts are as far astray as his intuition. Yet he continues to flourish, rank as a green bay tree. In 2002 he was reported as affronting a social gathering at Chequers, the Prime Minister's country estate, by demanding that 'the boy Blair' bring him whisky. Not once, but several times, did he call this out until at last Blair sprang to do his bidding. Lord Jenkins of Hillhead, who himself narrowly missed being a Labour Prime Minister, was said to be particularly incensed at Derry's impudence.

54

Opening the Doors of Libraries

The House of Commons briefly debated public libraries on 26 February 2001. Mr Blair's then Secretary of State for Culture, Media and Sport (Mr Chris Smith), since summarily removed, reminded the House that their provision is a statutory service under the Public Libraries and Museums Act 1964 (of which as it happens I was the draftsman). As always, Mr Smith appeared very pleased with himself. Smug might be the word. He paid for it in the end.

My own experience of Mr Smith in this connection suggests he should not have been so smug. Perhaps it was pride of authorship that led me to make a formal complaint to him under my 1964 Act concerning the poor library service in my then county of residence, Oxfordshire.

Mr Smith said on 26 February 2001 that he was prepared to intervene under the 1964 Act where unwarranted cuts are threatened in library services, and had done so on several occasions. Yet in the Oxfordshire case he declined to use his statutory powers. I will briefly describe these.

Section 7(1) of the Act states that it is the duty of the library authority (that is the local council) to provide a comprehensive and efficient library service, but that this does not extend to persons other than those whose residence or place of work is in its area or who are undergoing full-time education within the area. So this Conservative Act altered the previous law under which the provision of a library service by local authorities was a mere power, not a duty. It was entirely within their discretion whether they provided one or not.

Section 1(1) states that it is the duty of the Secretary of State (here Mr Smith) to superintend, and promote the improvement of, the public library service and secure the proper discharge by local authorities of their functions under the Act.

Section 10(1) states that if a complaint is made to the Secretary of State that any library authority has failed to carry out its duties under the Act he may, after holding a local inquiry, make an order declaring it to be in default. This may direct the authority to carry out such of its duties, in such manner and within such time, as may be specified in the order.

My complaint to Mr Smith relied mainly on a consultation document issued by the Oxfordshire County Council. This stated that to meet government spending targets the council intended further to reduce its spending. Figures given showed that at £9.90 per head of population per year its average expenditure was already considerably below the national average of £12.20. The document then said that in the previous seven years the authority had cut its library budget by a quarter. It went on –

> Opening hours have been reduced, mobile library services have been cut and many staff posts have been made redundant. Most newspapers and magazines have been cut in all libraries. We have not bought over 100,000 books which we would have done this year had the budget not been cut. This year we have to make [further] cuts of £620,000 in the library budget. Next year the library budget could be cut by another £280,000. . .

The document continued by detailing how the cuts would be effected. One of the proposed economy measures was the closing of up to 30 libraries in Oxfordshire, including the one in the Doomsday village of Kennington, where I then lived.

The reason given by the council for failing in its statutory duty was lack of funds. I pointed out to Mr Smith that this is not in law a sufficient excuse. As Lord Browne-Wilkinson said in a 1998 case, *R v East Sussex County Council, ex p Tandy*, the local authority 'can, if it wishes, divert money from other educational, or other, applications which are merely discretionary so as to apply such diverted moneys to discharge the statutory duty'. His Lordship added that to permit a local authority to avoid performing a statutory duty on the ground that it preferred to spend its money in other ways would be to downgrade a duty to a mere power. That, contrary to Parliament's intention, would return the public library service to the pre-1964 Act position.

Mr Smith remained unmoved, so I cited the Hansard report of the second reading debate on the Bill for the 1964 Act. The Labour spokesman quoted the definition by André Maurois of education as but a key to open the doors of libraries. The then Conservative Minister of Education stressed that one of the most valuable functions a library can perform is to cater for a large number of minority tastes. 'One must recognise that it is the books and other materials required by minority tastes which are often the most expensive'.

Mr Smith still remained unmoved, though my formal complaint under the Act, backed by a general outcry from Oxfordshire library users, did it seems have some effect. The council condescended to reduce the proposed number of library closures. Kennington was among those spared.

55

Ageism and Beardism

One of the few agreeable things about the numerous isms to which political correctness has subjected us is that each person can find at least one of them that applies to herself or himself (note the scrupulous correctness of that order of pronouns). As a pensioner of hoary standing I myself glory in the protectiveness of those such as Lord Janner of Braunstone who get anxious about ageism. On 5 March 2001 he asked Mr Blair's Cabinet Office Minister Lord Falconer whether the Blair Government would take steps to end age discrimination in the Civil Service. The reply was that the Government have already taken such steps. The Cabinet Office has issued age diversity guidance to all departments and agencies, and monitors implementation each year. It is also working with departments and agencies to review their policies in the light of the recommendations of the Performance and Innovation Unit's report, *Winning the Generation Game.*

How snappy with their titles the present lot are; so very different from the days when I was subject to Cabinet Office rule as one of the parliamentary counsel. Of course the range of choice has narrowed. It is now always necessary to be telly-orientated, so that the intended audience will catch the drift. All part of the dumbing-down process we are getting so used to. Perhaps Mr Bruce Forsyth is an honorary member of the Performance and Innovation Unit.

Lord Falconer added that the Cabinet Office is considering a scheme for the flexible deployment of senior civil servants aged over 50 aimed at offering a wide range of career and retirement options. These will include increased opportunities for some civil servants more easily to extend their careers beyond the age of 60. Departments and agencies are also considering the feasibility of change in their retirement policies for staff at more junior level. So the firm sands become more shifting. When I was a civil servant you retired at 60 and that was that. Everyone knew where they were, and could plan accordingly. Some people worked out their retirement plans when they were 30 or less.

After further questioning by Lord Janner it was revealed by Lord Falconer that the Government has signed up to an anti-age discrimination directive of the European Union and is working to try to make that a reality within the Civil Service. They are also considering a scheme whereby from 50 plus a Civil Service career path which does not necessarily end at 60 can be mapped out.

Then came the kind of totally irrelevant interjection for which the House of Lords is notorious (in that respect, nothing has changed).

Baroness Greengross: My Lords, is the Minister aware that there is age discrimination in professions other than the Civil Service, one of them being the Bar? Although there is no fixed retirement age in many parts of the legal profession, the Bar stands accused of age discriminatory practices. Is he aware that it is difficult to get a pupilage even if one is a mature student of about 35?

Lord Falconer easily side-stepped that one, whereupon the former Chingford polecat chipped in.

Lord Tebbit: My Lords, does the Minister think that it is a sign of increasing age that both questions and answers elongate?

Lord Falconer apologised for the length of his answers. Another peer then brought things back to the question before the House.

Lord Mackenzie of Framwellgate: My Lords, as regards discrimination in the Home Office, when I was a young detective inspector I sported a full beard when I was a member of the drugs squad. I applied for a job at the Home Office as a superintendent and I was required to shave it off. Will the Minister assure me that 'beardism' does not still exist in the Home Office?

Lord Falconer tiredly replied that the question was about age discrimination rather than facial hair discrimination. It seems that beardism has not yet become a PC fetish. There is still time for a revival of the game of beaver that flourished around a century ago (a little before my time, but my mother used to talk of it). Skittish young girls would rush up to a bearded man in the street and tug his beard, yelling 'Beaver!'. What satisfaction that gave them I am not sure.

I was glad to see, by the way, the recent case where a bearded chef, refused a job in the food department by Waitrose because beards harbour bacteria, lost his case before the employment tribunal. Thankfully, there are still some vestiges of common sense around.

Then came another irrelevant intervention.

Lord Mowbray and Stourton: My Lords, while being in complete agreement with the noble and learned Lord's answers, how will he deal with the many members of the clan Buggins?

Here Lord Falconer gave up, saying he was not sure what the question meant. Evidently this modernising young Cabinet Office minister has never even heard of what used to be a basic feature of our Civil Service: Buggins' turn.

56

A Candid Friend of Viscount Tonypandy

Of all plagues, good Heaven, thy wrath can send
Save, save, oh save me from the candid friend!

The late George Thomas MP, Speaker of the House of Commons and later Viscount Tonypandy, was my friend. So I was interested to see the Sunday Times piece about him on 18 March 2001 headlined 'The Speaker's Secret'. When reading on I found, as I had feared, that this was a disreputable secret. The purveyor of this disreputable secret to the public, Leo Abse, claims also to have been a friend of the late respected Viscount. Abse is a solicitor. Indeed this proud man claims to be the first solicitor in history to be granted audience in the High Court.

Mr Abse must know that as a solicitor he is bound by the duties of professional confidentiality. The late viscount confided his disreputable secret to Mr Abse, so he was bound to keep it hidden even unto death – and beyond. As a conscientious solicitor Mr Abse is sure to have studied my 1969 book *Professional Ethics: the Consultant Professions and their Code*, where at page 74 it says: 'The duty to maintain confidences does not of course end with the practitioner-client relationship. As Sir Thomas Lund put it, "The duration of the privilege is for ever".' Yet the venerable Mr Abse (he is now aged 86) does not seem to see it that way. Perhaps he would claim that George was not a client, but just a friend.

I first met George in the House of Commons in the 1950s. He was a chairman of committees, and I was a draftsman of Bills. In standing committee it was then the custom for the draftsman to sit next to the chairman and give him expert advice on the legal meaning of the Bill and relevant points of parliamentary procedure. I found George exceptionally warm and friendly, though always humble. We struck up a rapport, which in time extended beyond the confines of the House of Commons. George came to tea at my Georgian mansion on the North Downs in Surrey. He appeared fascinated when we explained that the old house was formerly the rectory for the manor of Farleigh, given in 1262 to endow Merton College Oxford on its foundation. George was absorbed when we explained that as the college were still lords of the manor they had to be joined in the conveyance of the house to us, and that the other parties were Her Majesty the Queen (by Order in Council) and Bertram, by divine permission Lord Bishop of Southwark.

George maintained his interest in our family, and we kept in touch. I recall that on one occasion in the lobby of the House of Commons George introduced me to a young man he described as a promising Labour MP, Mr Anthony Wedgwood-Benn. The promising young man shook my hand with an absent air.

Mr Abse, formerly a backbench Labour MP, published his autobiography in 1973. It was called *Private Member*, a clever punning title. In the House of Commons a back-bencher is called a private member. But Mr Abse was also identified with another sort of private member. He pioneered the 1967 Sexual Offences Act, which released British homosexuals from their long bondage. Mr Abse now dramatically reveals that Viscount Tonypandy was numbered among those thus freed.

In *Private Member* Mr Abse records that, when in 1972 George's 90-year old mother died, almost all the Welsh MPs defied a 3-line whip to travel to Wales for her funeral. That says something about how George was regarded by his colleagues. Yet now Mr Abse pours scorn on him as a mother-fixated closet queer continually needing help from Mr Abse to fend off blackmailing youths.

In the *Sunday Times* article Mr Abse asks: 'Am I now, belatedly, betraying my friend in telling of the shadows in which, away from the pomp and glory of the Palace of Westminster, and, indeed, of Buckingham Palace, he was humiliatingly forced to walk?' The short answer is yes. The matter is made worse by the fact that Mr Abse pats himself on the back for having protected the viscount from discovery. 'I take pride that I had been able to shield him a little, so that he was unbesmirched when his time came.' The time referred to was George's funeral in Westminster

Abbey, following his death from throat cancer. It was attended by the Prince of Wales, representing the Queen, and passed off as a great occasion unbesmirched as Mr Abse says.

Well, I don't know. By the way the verse at the head of this chapter was composed by George Canning MP. Famous for fighting a duel with Castlereagh in 1809, he too was the victim of disloyal friends – but that's another story.

57

A Filkin Filleting or Vazectomy

Why should a solicitor's firm whose true name is Bindman & Co be miscalled by Private Eye (23 March 2001) Blindman & Co? The obvious suggestion is that they had turned a blind eye to something they shouldn't have. This arose in connection with an investigation by the Parliamentary Commissioner for Standards, Ms Elizabeth Filkin, into Mr Blair's Minister for Europe the Asian MP Mr Keith Vaz. In this inquiry Mr Geoffrey Bindman acted as Mr Vaz's legal adviser. On reading Ms Filkin's report dated 9 March 2001 I felt her operation might appropriately be called a Vazectomy, since it left the public substance of Mr Vaz rather less complete than before. He has since faded from public view, having been dropped as a Minister by Mr Blair after the 2001 general election.

I will return to Ms Filkin's report, but first I would say as a lawyer that I am troubled by the *Private Eye* squib, following an attack by Mr Blair's Home Secretary on some defence solicitors. It used to be thought that, like Caesar's wife, a solicitor, who after all is an officer of the Supreme Court, should be above reproach. Is that no longer the standard offered? If so we should be very worried.

Before feminism and equal opportunities changed everything, the stern name of Sir Thomas Lund, Secretary General of the Law Society, made dodgy solicitors quake in their boots. In my 1969 book *Professional Ethics: The Consultant Professions and their Code* I quoted Sir Thomas as saying that only the very highest conduct is consistent with membership of the solicitors' profession. He said further that a solicitor should never do anything dishonest or dishonourable, even under pressure from his most valuable client.

The piece in *Private Eye* indicated that its attack on Mr Bindman had to do with his valuable client Mr Vaz. Those who wish to investigate the conduct of Mr Bindman in detail can study Ms Filkin's report of nearly 100 pages. All

I have space to do here is pick out one or two items.

Ms Filkin's report said that in dealing with her inquiries Mr Vaz relied extensively on his solicitor, Mr Bindman, 'whose dealings with us were courteous and efficient'. It then expressed a desire that MPs in such situations should communicate with her directly, rather than through an intermediary. I read that as a rebuke to Mr Bindman as an outsider intruding on an internal parliamentary matter.

Ms Filkin then said that after receiving letters from Bindmans stating that Mr Vaz did not wish to answer any further questions she decided to bring her inquiry to what she obviously felt was a premature conclusion.

I then came across something in her report that reminded me of what I wrote in chapter 20. It concerned Ms Filkin's previous report on a complaint that a Tory MP, Tony Baldry, received a loan of £5000 from Mr Sarosh Zaiwalla and then recommended his inclusion in the next Honours List. So there is an interesting link between the finaglings of the Tory MP Tony Baldry and those of the Labour Minister Keith Vaz. A flavour is given in the following extract from Ms Filkin's later report-

> In a letter to Bindmans dated 11 July 2000 I invited Mr Vaz to comment on the further information provided by Mr Zaiwalla from his cashbook records relating to two payments, one of £250 to Mr Vaz's office account in January 1993 and the other of £200 to a publisher, Wildberry, for a calendar linked to Mr Vaz. In response, Mr Vaz, in a letter from Bindmans dated 17 July, said: 'You refer to Mr Zaiwalla's "cash books", though you have not forwarded me a copy of the extract, nor have you given me a copy of the transcript of the comments made by Mr Zaiwalla. Mr Zaiwalla is responsible for his own accounts.
>
> I wrote again to Bindmans on 3 October 2000 to seek a clear answer from Mr Vaz as to whether he had received the £250 donation which Mr Zaiwalla said he had made to Mr Vaz's office account in January 1993. In response, in a letter dated 2 November 2000 Bindmans replied: "Mr Vaz made it quite clear to you in his letter of 16 February 2000 that he could well have encouraged Mr Zaiwalla to make

contributions to charities or events, but he is equally ada-
mant that he has never received any personal benefit in any
shape or form from Mr Zaiwalla".'

We then learnt that Ms Filkin had started yet another
investigation into the doings of Mr Vaz. Whether he had
Mr Bindman's assistance in this, in view of Ms Filkin's
rebuke, one does not know. I could find nothing in her
report dated 9 March 2001 that would justify the
suggestion that Mr Bindman's conduct was in any way
disreputable.

In February 2002, in relation to these matters, Mr Vaz
was censured by the House of Commons and suspended
from its service for a month. Some people, subjected to this
disgrace, would have resigned as an MP. Mr Vaz did not do
this, preferring to brazen it out. But his reputation has
gone.

58

The Commons at its Best

The House of Commons is at its best when the whips are off and it is debating a true House matter. That was the case on 22 March 2001, when it debated how the Speaker should in future be elected. The method of election of Speaker Martin (known as Gorbals Mick) on 23 October 2000, following the resignation of Betty Boothroyd, was felt by many MPs to be unsatisfactory. So a select committee chaired by Nicolas Winterton MP (Conservative) suggested improvements. Gordon Prentice MP (Labour), who had organised a hustings for the Martin election, said this –

> The report [of the Winterton Committee] touches on the hustings that I organised. There was a tremendous pressure for change. When the number of candidates ballooned from five to seven, eight, eleven and twelve, I asked myself why we were getting so many candidates. The Speakership brings instant celebrity, nationwide recognition, a nice house and probably quite a big salary, but something has happened recently. It might have something to do with the way in which Betty Boothroyd carried out her role as Speaker, but no one envisaged that so many candidates would compete for the Speakership. Within a few hours, down on the Terrace, I had more than 100 names of Members – more than one sixth of the membership of the House of Commons – calling for the system to be changed and for an opportunity to quiz the individual candidates.

The point was not that the wrong man had been elected, and this is one of the remarkable features of the whole business. Everyone agreed in that Commons debate that the right man was now Speaker and that the same man would also be elected under the new system. The man in question, Michael Martin, used to be a sheet metal worker in a factory. He is a Roman Catholic, born and bred in a Glasgow tenement in the Gorbals. His recreations are hill walking, local history and piping. He made his name as a shop steward and trade union organiser.

Speaker Martin seemed to have the gift of being popular. There was something magnificent about the way this unlikely man initially captured the hearts of MPs. At first he successfully exercised that most difficult function of controlling House of Commons debates with impartiality and authority. In his achievement one seemed to glimpse the reality of the British constitutional genius. Yet further events, recalled below, cast doubt on that.

The House of Commons has been called the best gentleman's club in Europe. Mr Gerald Kaufman (Manchester, Gorton) said in the debate on 22 March 2001 -

> If there is anything that I dislike about the House, it is the smug club atmosphere that is cultivated here – the notion that this place is a gentleman's club and that debates such as this one, as distinct from party political debates, are conducted within some sort of cosy consensus.

The House disagreed with him on that. The big issue was whether there should be a secret ballot for Speaker, or whether as universally happens with House of Commons votes, and has hitherto happened with the election of the Speaker, the names of those voting should be disclosed. The arguments are nicely balanced, and so was the vote. 92 voted for retaining the present system; 94 voted for a secret ballot. A feature of the debate was Tony Benn's farewell speech. MPs of all parties joined in praise of this fine orator and parliamentarian. Here are some extracts from his acclaimed address.

> Years ago, when I was canvassing in Bristol, I asked a woman to support me and she replied, 'Mr. Benn, the ballet is secret'. I thought of her dancing alone in the bedroom, where no candidate was allowed to know about it . . . [I]n the course of my life I have developed five little democratic questions. If one meets a powerful person – Adolf Hitler, Joe Stalin or Bill Gates – ask them five questions: 'What power have you got? Where did you get it from? In whose interests do you exercise it? To whom are you accountable? And how can we get rid of

you?' . . . [T]he establishment has seen Parliament as a means of management: if there is a Parliament, people will not cause trouble, whereas, of course, the people see it as a means of representation.'

That is all very well, but I regret the venerable, departing Mr Benn's crass way of glorying in illegality. In his final speech he told the Speaker at the start that he intended to wander far out of order, and expected this to be allowed. He ended his speech with a boast of his unlawful conduct in the House.

I have put up several plaques – quite illegally, without permission; I screwed them up myself. One was in the broom cupboard to commemorate Emily Wilding Davison, and another celebrated the people who fought for democracy and those who run the House.

I find it sad that a man who has spent his life as a legislator should have so little regard for the rule of law.

Since his election, Speaker Martin has slipped from grace. As I have said, his nickname now is Gorbals Mick. Mr Tony Benn says he is pleased that Gorbals Mick has broken with precedent by supping with back-benchers in the House of Commons tearoom. (Until now the Speaker, for good reason, has hung aloof from mixing socially with MPs). Others think Speaker Martin has shown petulance, and a failure to grasp the realities of his high office. Perhaps too much was expected of him. I am sure he does his best. But is it good enough? Only time will tell.

Following Prime Minister's Questions on 2 May 2001 Speaker Martin, who is still the Labour MP for Shettleston, Glasgow, had a bad press. In *The Daily Mail* Quentin Letts, who claims to have invented the nickname Gorbals Mick, said he lost it completely. 'Dooon't tell me hoo to do mah job', he shrieked at the Opposition benches. Letts was surprised at the way he 'so comprehensively lost his rag' and felt MPs on all sides were stunned by his incompetence. In The Times Matthew Parris said the Speaker 'blew his top'. In *The Daily Telegraph* Frank Johnson, in a reference to the anarchist riots on May Day 2001, reported that 'renewed anti-Speaker rioting' had broken out, while Benedict Brogan, political correspondent, said Mr Martin had lost the confidence of Conservative MPs. 'They see him as biased towards the Government and say he is not up to the job'.

It is a mystery how the unanimous goodwill to Mr Martin displayed only a month earlier in the debate on a new method of electing the Speaker seemed to have evaporated. The trouble on 2 May 2001 started when, instead of answering a question from Mr Hague on the Wembley Stadium fiasco, Mr Blair read out bits from an obscure Conservative candidate's leaflet attacking his own leader. As this was clearly out of order the Conservatives thought the Speaker should stop Mr Blair, which he failed to do. They showed their feelings with shouts of 'Order!' It is the Speaker's prerogative to keep order, so Mr Martin got annoyed at this outcry. When Mr Blair resumed by saying his Government had put a record amount of money into schools, hospitals, transport and police, adding 'and it is the Conservative party that would cut the money', Gerald Howarth MP (Conservative, Aldershot) yelled 'Disgraceful'.

Mr Speaker: Order. Mr. Howarth, I hope that you were not referring to me. I know how to conduct my affairs and I hope that you are not attacking the Chair.

Mr Howarth: I shall raise a point of order at the end of Prime Minister's questions.

Mr Speaker: You are perfectly entitled to raise a point of order, and I will not deny you that, but no one will shout at this Chair while these proceedings are going on.

Later, raising his point of order, Mr Howarth said that during the episode in question there were a great many cries of 'Disgraceful' from Conservative Members. They were aimed not at the Chair but at the conduct of the Prime Minister, who had been gratuitously abusive to Mr Howarth's Party leader Mr Hague. Such behaviour tended to bring the House into disrepute with the public. Mr Blair should be answering questions instead of trying to score cheap points off Mr Hague on matters that did not relate to Prime Ministerial responsibilities.

Mr Speaker: Certainly, Prime Minister's Question Time this afternoon was very lively; I think that we can both agree with that. At all times, I must be able to use my judgment. The Prime Minister does not change the rules of the House. The House changes the rules. I am the custodian of those rules. I heard many honourable Members shouting, 'Disgraceful.' I did feel that some of those remarks were directed at me. I accept the honourable Gentleman's explanation that they were not directed at me – that is fine – but some were telling me to intervene and to stop the Prime Minister. I will use my judgment at all times in the House. It is for me to use my judgment. Let me put it on the record that the worst thing that can happen is for honourable Members to tell me to intervene, because in doing so they are telling me how to do my job. Believe me: I will stay put and I will not intervene in those circumstances. I will use my judgment.

Thus did Gorbals Mick convict himself out of his own mouth. By 'staying put' and not intervening just because MPs had told him to intervene he would be behaving like a spoilt child and emphatically not using his judgment.

Mr John Bercow MP (Buckingham, Conservative) then added his two-penn'orth, raising as a further point of order, the fact that 'on several dozen occasions in recent months' MPs had been busily been chatting to the Speaker while he was presiding. He added –

It would be extremely helpful to the efficient dispatch of business and the retention of good order if they did not do that, because we wish, of course, to have the full benefit at all times of your personal attention and of your intellectual resources.

Mr Speaker: That is a bit like the kettle calling the pot black, as the honourable Gentleman is one of the chatterers.

Following the general election on 7 June 2001, the first business of the new House of Commons when it met on 13 June was to elect a Speaker. (The next business was to swear in the new MPs one by one, which takes a very, very long time.) I wrote above about the new procedure adopted for the contested election of a Speaker. This new procedure was not needed on 13 June 2001, since surprisingly the re-election of Mr Michael Martin was not contested. The grave doubts expressed about his suitability which I recorded above had mysteriously vanished; and everyone who now spoke was full of praise for the doughty Roman Catholic Glaswegian otherwise known as Gorbals Mick. Mr Robin Cook, new Leader of the House, said that during Mr Martin's lengthy service on the Chairmen's Panel (where future Speakers learn their trade) many an awkward moment had been defused by his trademark catchphrase 'It's no' nice'.

> Since you came to office, your voice has become familiar in households across our country. You spoke for all your Scottish compatriots in the Chamber when you magnificently brushed aside an impertinent question from the BBC on your accent with the retort, 'I don't have an accent; other people have an accent'. Yours is of course an accent which would normally lend authority to one of the traditional roles of the Speaker: the selection of a Scotch whisky for the Speaker's brand. For you, though, as a teetotaller, that selection presented some obvious difficulties. Your solution delighted the Members whom you invited on to an all-party committee to carry out extensive research and tasting on your behalf.

Mr Cook added that if ever in this, the fifty-third Parliament of the United Kingdom of Great Britain and Northern Ireland, the media Lobby dared criticise the Speaker it would be because as Chairman of the Administration Committee he had banned Lobby correspondents from the Terrace of the Commons unless personally supervised by an MP. 'You thereby liberated a grateful House to relax in privacy on the Terrace in these summer months.'

Mr William Hague, reminding Mr Martin that 'just as you are about to resume your duties, I am planning to relinquish mine as Leader of the Opposition', said the Speaker is expected to cut himself off from previous party affiliations. 'You have indeed cut yourself off from party affiliations and served this House impartially. It has been a tradition of Speakers that they do not visit the Tea Room and bars. You have created a new tradition by being available and visiting the Tea Room and bars, but not having a drink there. That may keep you happy, although it is incomprehensible to the rest of us . . .'

The election of Mr Martin was supervised by Tam Dalyell, new Father of the House in succession to Ted Heath. Tam, the MP for Linlithgow, appeared on crutches. For this he attracted the jeers of Alex Salmond, speaking both for the Scottish National Party and Plaid Cymru:

> I thought I had seen everything in ten successful, gruelling campaigns involving Mr Dalyell since the 1960s. However, the election tactic of being injured in the service of Linlithgow Rovers football club is breathtaking.

Thanking the House for having re-elected him, Mr Martin said that campaigning as a Speaker seeking re-election was no easy matter.

> There is no party banner, so we had to find a trademark, and it was agreed that the friends of Mr Speaker would put a photograph of me in my formal clothes on every leaflet that was issued. We thought that was a good idea until one of the electors said to me, "I hope you don't mind me asking, Mr. Martin, but were you ever a minister in the Church of Scotland?" One gentleman said to me, "I hope you get the job. It will give you something to do when you're down in London."

Mr Martin, who has presumed to abandon ancient tradition in the shape of wig, knee breeches and silk stockings, will have plenty to do if, as many hope, he upholds another tradition and fights for back-benchers against the ever-encroaching Executive. Mr Hague said he regretted the diminution of the House's importance and reputation, which had contributed to the disconnection between the public and Parliament that was shown by the low voter turnout in the recent general election. This was a suitable valediction from one who had once held high hopes of a political career, only to see them dashed.

59

Foot and Mouth

Britain, along with some other European countries, has recently been visited with the cattle plague or murrain known as foot and mouth disease (FMD). It therefore became necessary to postpone the county council elections appointed by Act of Parliament to be held on 3 May 2001. This required an amending Act, so the Elections Bill was introduced and rushed through both Houses using the guillotine. The point was a simple one. The political parties were more or less agreed that FMD imposed a need for postponement. It might therefore have been expected that the Bill would be nodded through without debate. Anyone who thought that would be the case stands convicted of abysmal ignorance of the way the British constitution works.

In fact there was a great deal of parliamentary debate on this Bill. I take the Lords committee stage, report stage and third reading, all on 9 April 2001. Why was there so much to discuss, when all that was being done was postponing county council elections by a month from May 3 to June 7? Surely this was simple enough? In fact the postponement was not simple at all, and a lot of loose ends needed tidying up. Here are some of them.

County councils have an annual meeting, which takes place just after an election. Decisions on service delivery are arrived at, following the establishment of a new council. If the previous council year is extended by a month this has budgetary and other effects. Everything is suddenly thrown into disarray. During an extra month various things may happen to councillors. Some will die; others will resign. The political balance of a council may change, resulting in a change of control. For the LibDems Baroness Hamwee called this 'a dribbling away of democracy'. Another peeress put the matter graphically.

Baroness Scott of Needham Market: I am aware of the immense practical difficulties in trying to run a council on a month-by-month basis. Not least is the great difficulty in relation to the 25 per cent of councillors who do not intend to stand again in May. They will gradually either drift off and not turn up to meetings or, quite possibly, hand in their resignations and then there are no provisions for by-elections. That will leave areas unrepresented, councils changing hands, and so on. Another difficulty is that people will have incurred expenditure which the postponement of the elections may render abortive, the printing of leaflets mentioning the original date being an example. Is the Government to compensate them for this, and if so in what way?

Another peer raised a more substantial electioneering difficulty.

Lord Monro of Langholm: It is desperately important for candidates to meet the people. Years ago, one had perhaps 60 or 70 meetings in village halls over a period of three or four weeks, but nowadays local government and parliamentary elections increasingly involve walk-abouts. That means meeting the people in the streets and villages. However, that is exactly what we do not want to be happening if FMD has not substantially diminished in a few weeks' time.

This reminded peers of the fear that if the pestilence did not abate it might well be no easier to conduct the election campaign in June than it would have been to conduct the original one in May, and then where was the point of the delay? For the Government Lord Bassam said there was no perfect solution, and for the sake of the tourist industry it was necessary to have certainty. Some date had to be chosen, and the Government had picked this one. He might have added that they had done so more or less arbitrarily, and at random. No one could know when this current scourge of FMD would end. The Bill was founded on guesswork.

Baroness Hanham put her finger on the point that was in the back of everyone's mind: 'I am concerned that in this Bill we are not talking about local elections but the general election'.

We all knew, because he made it clear, that Tony Blair always intended to call a general election for the same day as local government elections were scheduled to be held, namely 3 May 2001. FMD, a visitation from elsewhere, exposed the folly of such long-term plotting. It also exposed the folly of those who, like Baroness Gould of Potternewton, still say, as she did, 'I firmly believe in having fixed-term Parliaments, just as we have fixed dates for local elections'. When will these people learn the wisdom of the old saying that while man proposes God disposes?

This Bill produced something previously unheard of. The Minister circulated to peers an explanatory document which was constantly referred to in the debate as 'the compendium letter'. Would this strange illuminating screed be made public by being included in Hansard? No. Why not? Open government is said to be the aim of Blairism. Does this prove that aim false, or not?

60

Does Your Credit Need Repairing?

As the draftsman of the Consumer Credit Act 1974, I am naturally interested when anyone suggests the Act has defects. Considering that it laid down a wholly new system for regulating consumer credit and hire transactions of every kind, I modestly think the Act has stood up pretty well to over a quarter of a century's wear and tear. Prophetically, it has even been found to comply with later European Union requirements. It has needed very little amendment over the years.

So I raised an eyebrow when on 10 April 2001 David Amess, the Conservative MP for Southend West, sought leave to bring in a Bill to amend the 1974 Act. He wanted to impose on the Director General of Fair Trading a duty to establish a code of practice for traders who offer consumers debt management and credit repair. This concept of 'credit repair' is new to me. It was not around in 1974, even though the idea behind it was. Debt management and credit repair are what the 1974 Act calls debt counselling (advising the debtor on how to settle his debts) and debt adjusting (taking over and settling the debts in return for regular payments).

Mr Amess alleged that the 'largely unregulated way in which the current system works' allowed the most vulnerable sectors of society to be led astray by advertisements, particularly in tabloid newspapers. He said that if his Bill were to become law, traders would be obliged to comply with a code. The Director General would be given power to enforce this code by use of compliance orders, fines and compensation orders. The Bill would require him, before publishing the code, to consult representatives of consumers and traders.

The Amess Bill would prescribe the issues to be addressed in the code of practice, including the advertising and marketing of personal debt services; the terms on which they are provided; charges for them; standards of service; arrangements for the protection of client moneys and for ensuring the competence of the trader's staff; procedures for handling complaints; and other such matters.

In 2001 the National Association of Citizens Advice Bureaux published a report, entitled 'Daylight Robbery', that highlighted the fact that consumer credit borrowing has increased dramatically in the past 20 years. At August 2000, outstanding unsecured consumer credit in the United Kingdom amounted to £122 billion, equivalent to £3,425 for every adult in the United Kingdom aged between 18 and 65. Today's consumers have forgotten (if they ever knew) the wise injunction to cut one's coat according to one's cloth. Consumers' growing enthusiasm to buy now and pay later has been matched by credit companies' willingness to devise an ever greater range of credit products. In the past two years, citizens advice bureaux across the country had reported a 37 per cent. increase in the number of inquiries on consumer credit debts. The number of commercial companies offering services for a fee to those who are in debt had mushroomed.

Mr Amess gave the House an example. A debtor with one dependent child contacted a debt management company for help with debts of £25,000. The company told him that his creditors would accept offers of £1 per month, which was obviously absurd. When bailiffs began to call at his home, the client discovered that in fact no agreement had been reached with the creditors. If he had used his common sense he would have realised that must be the case. But then if he had used his common sense he would never have run up such a gigantic debt.

What Mr Amess did not tell the House was that the 1974 Act already covers such a situation. A credit adjuster such as this needs a licence issued by the Director General under the Act, which would be revoked for such misbehaviour.

Mr Amess made no attempt to spell out with any precision the ways in which the Act was alleged to be inadequate. Instead he cited the Sunday Express –

A journalist there called Rachel Baird has, for the last few weeks, written a series of articles headed "Debt

Parasites Spark Crusade'', in which she has reported the experiences of all sorts of people who – sadly – have got into debt, panicked and gone to some of the companies that I am describing, with very unfortunate effects.

Many advertisements suggest that, for a fee, companies advertising credit repair services can wipe the slate clean for those who have got into money difficulties in the past and had court judgments recorded against them. Mr Amess said that was nonsense. He concluded –

There is a real need for consumers to be protected from the services of debt management and credit repair companies. Those needing such protection are undoubtedly the poorest and most vulnerable members of society. I hope that the House will support the Bill.

The House did support the Bill, and its introduction was agreed to. That was just House of Commons flummery. Everyone knew the Bill would not pass into law. In this case that flummery mattered little, for as I have indicated the Bill was unnecessary. It failed, and passed into oblivion. I readily admit that Mr Blair cannot be blamed for any of that. He is not responsible for every one of our woes.

61

Our Armed Forces and the Modern World

An ancient quirk of the British constitution insists, for what once seemed good reasons (but are so no longer), that we must not have a standing army – or for that matter a standing navy or a standing air force. So Parliament is still required to validate our Armed Forces on an annual basis – as if we could at any time choose not to have them. In the last resort, we innocent citizens always need to be protected from the mob. The police are scarcely sufficient. The Army stand in reserve, as the ultimate protection. Not a lot of people know that.

Hence it is that the service discipline Acts are renewed by legislation quinquennially, with in-between affirmative annual continuation orders debated in both Houses of Parliament. On 23 April 2001 the House of Lords gave a second reading to the Armed Forces Bill, which on passing would become the latest quinquennial Act. It was all arranged by our rulers, on accustomed lines, so that we could go on sleeping comfortably in our beds. I for one am grateful. Very, very grateful (think about it).

The debate that day turned on the how far the condition of our Armed Forces should be modified by current developments readily accepted and welcomed in civilian life, though perhaps not by all. On the traditional side Lord Burnham, who helped run *The Daily Telegraph* for over 30 years, quoted a recent speech by Lady Thatcher –

> I notice trends which threaten the core of military culture and the whole ethos which sustains it. The values of a risk-averse civilian society are being imposed on a military community to which they are essentially unsuited. . . A refusal to understand the realities of service life leads to unrealistic ideas taking root about how armed forces should be organised.

How very true – yet how little recognised. Lord Burnham reinforced this trenchant Thatcherite wisdom in his own words.

Political correctness and soft beds are not what the Armed Forces are for. John Major recalls in his autobiography, which I am reading at the moment, that when he visited elements of the Army shortly before the land stage of the Gulf War started, they told him, "It is why we joined. It is our job". That is the Army.

Lord Roper echoed this.

I started my military career not in soft beds, but in a hammock on a mess deck in an aircraft carrier. . . We all served as ordinary seamen and we discovered at an early stage that military life is different. . . We need to decide how and in which ways military society and discipline will evolve as other ideas and thoughts change in society. How should we take into account attitudes towards gender balance and diversity that are part of society today?

The next speaker was Earl Attlee. He is the grandson of the doughty post-war Prime Minister Clement Attlee, author of the following immortal lines about himself –

Few thought he was even a starter
There were many who thought themselves smarter
But he ended PM
CH and OM
An earl and a Knight of the Garter.

Earl Attlee gave his personal definition of political correctness. It is marked by a typically progressive orthodoxy, often involving issues of race, gender, sexual orientation, ecology and the environment. When this is applied to the Armed Forces by those with no relevant experience, 'there is usually a failure to recognise the realities of warfare involving significant casualties and personal sacrifice'.

Lord Monro of Langholm, a former Conservative junior minister, pointed out that females cannot carry weights over the distances a serviceman must nowadays cover. Could women, he asked, really have been expected to carry heavy haversacks and weapons when yomping over the mountains of the Falklands? Those who wanted women to do everything were asking the impossible.

Replying for the Government, Baroness Symons said a tri-service factual report was produced on 15 March 2001. It presented the results of academic and other work that would contribute to an assessment of the impact on combat effectiveness of removing the present exclusion of women from the Royal Marine general service, the Household Cavalry, the Royal Armoured Corps, the Infantry and the RAF Regiment. Moreover the services were conducting a risk analysis. On political correctness she added this.

> Nothing should be allowed to compromise the operational effectiveness of the Armed Forces. However, there are matters of respect for other people. . . none of your Lordships would want to sneer at such respect being given where it is properly due.

Many of their Lordships must have wondered what respect was due to feminist women who stupidly think the weaker sex has the muscle to engage in equal combat with rough, tough, warlike men.

This necessary Bill made minor changes in other areas. Decisions at courts martial will no longer be subject to judicial review in the High Court (they were soon to fall foul of the Human Rights Act). The Armed Forces will be empowered to require breath or urine samples to test for drugs or alcohol. Wider powers are given to the Ministry of Defence (MoD) police. When that notorious mischief-maker the Earl of Onslow observed that MoD police officers were widely known as 'Mod Plods' Baroness Symons recoiled.

> I know that the nomenclature that the noble Earl, Lord Onslow, used has common currency but it does not go down terribly well with the Ministry of Defence Police. If the noble Earl can bear to do so, it would be a kindness to refrain from using it.

The noble earl greeted this feminine manifestation of tenderness and concern for rough hairy military policemen with his usual broad grin. Others felt it was one more sloppy indication of the plight we are in, when push comes to shove. If you doubt what I say consult such knowledge-able authorities as Saddam Hussein or Osima Bin Laden, always assuming you can get anywhere near them.

62

Ulster the Endless Problem

I

Following Blair's victorious 2001 general election, the Queen's Speech was delivered to a breathless world on 20 June. It opened the proceedings of the fifty-third Parliament of the United Kingdom of Great Britain and Northern Ireland. Much was said in the media about its contents, and the parliamentary debates that ensued. I concentrate on Peter Mandelson's speech to the House of Commons.

This strange, potent man started by saying a good government needs a half-decent party to oppose it, which he thought was not in sight. Then he issued the remarkable injunction that 'we need to improve broad band roll-out'. Who knew what that meant? As he was recently the Secretary of State for Northern Ireland, Mandelson's observations on the province, delivered from the back benches, are of interest.

Mandelson complained that the Ulster Unionists are irretrievably hooked on their demand for the decommissioning by the republicans of their arms, and that the republicans are using that demand effectively to hold the peace process to ransom, to get their way on everything else that is of concern to them. Mandelson said we had finally reached the impasse on arms decommissioning that everyone has seen coming for a very long time.

Many of us have tried repeatedly to head off this impasse, using different permutations and formulations in relation to arms decommissioning. One of the first things that I did when I went to Northern Ireland was to join Senator Mitchell in his review. We produced a way forward on decommissioning from that; we then produced another permutation to head off the threatened collapse of the new Government and institutions early in 2000; we then came forward with another formulation after the suspension had taken place; and we came back with a further permutation in the talks that gave rise to the Hillsborough agreement in May 2000.

Mr Mandelson said he thought we had now run out of ways of postponing the issue of decommissioning, of parking it, of sidetracking it, or disguising it. It is, he said, sitting there right in the middle of the road, and there is no way of getting round it. 'It is going to have to be addressed.' Of course it has for years been addressed, readdressed, stamped with official stamps all over, and then returned to sender. Still it is stuck there in the middle of whatever road we seek to travel. How can this be?

The IRA has huge dumps of lethal illegal weapons dotted about in various places in the Republic of Ireland. The Irish Government know where they are. Each one of them is marked down on an official Irish map. I repeat, how can this be?

Why, I ask again, are these dumps allowed to remain? Though illegal, indeed criminal, they are officially recognised to exist by the Irish Government. Arrangements are made by that Government for them to be gazed at (sorry inspected) by an international group of the great and the good who are supposed to detect any use of the weapons or other disturbance of the dumps. I say again, how can this be?

Take it from the beginning. The dumps belong to the so-called Irish Republican Army. Why does the proper Irish Army, officially organised and financed by the Irish democratic state, not move in, take over the dumps, and destroy them – as it easily could if its controlling Government wished? Obviously its controlling Government does not wish, and that has always been the root of the trouble. Its controlling Government connives at, if it does not actively support, the wicked doings of the wicked men who run the IRA. So the dumps are allowed to remain. Iniquitous is the mildest word I could choose. And Tony Blair slimily goes along with it.

The Republic of Ireland prides itself on adhering to the rule of law, invented by the British and prized in democratic countries as the badge of high civilisation.

Yet the Irish Government allows this gross and festering affront to the rule of law to continue unchecked in its midst. How, I say yet again, can this be?

Back to Mr Mandelson. 'Some people say. . . that we should simply ignore the issue of arms in Northern Ireland. They suggest that we forget about decommissioning and find another road. After all, if the ceasefire is holding, which by and large it is, and if the peace in Northern Ireland is secure, which by and large it is, if arms are not in the main actually being used, why make such a fuss about them? Why not just let them lie there?' To his credit, Mandelson said that was a tempting thought but also a profoundly wrong thought. We stand no chance, he said, of stabilising democracy in Northern Ireland while armed paramilitary organisations are running around threatening to second guess the democratically elected politicians so that they can then take over and start calling the shots again. 'We simply cannot live and flourish as a democracy and a decent civic society in Northern Ireland in those circumstances.'

Opening certain of its arms dumps to international inspection was a major confidence-building measure by the Provisional IRA, continued Mr Mandelson. (Note the word 'certain'). 'I do not think that it would now be a huge step for it to make those dumps that have been opened to inspection and reinspection by the two international inspectors permanently accessible'. Permanently accessible? How feeble that sounds, and is. 'Certain' arms dumps were supposed to have been opened, but what about the other arms dumps that were not opened. Is this some game we are playing? The answer of course is yes.

II

Western civilisation has long embraced the rule of law; indeed that is said to be its triumph. What do you do with that high concept when faced with insurrection? Blair's recent answer from Northern Ireland is: you water it down when you think you have to.

Another belief of western civilisation is that people are entitled to self-determination. The inhabitants of a country have a right to choose their rulers, and their form of government. All very well, but it invites the question what is a country? The inhabitants of Gibraltar, currently under extreme pressure to unite with Spain, think their particular territory is a country on its own – and has therefore earned self-determination. The Spaniards disagree.

An impartial observer might think the British Isles are a country. They share a common language, and are geographically a unit. Their populations, consisting of English, Scottish, Irish and Welsh, are interlinked by history, marriage, genetics and other powerful factors. Yet majorities of the Scottish, Irish and Welsh disagree. This is simply because the English have a vastly larger population. Under democracy, another prized concept of western civilisation, the English would therefore rule the roost if the British Isles were to be considered one country. The Scottish, Irish and Welsh, or at any rate a majority of them, are not having that. What happens when the rule of law collides with this sort of realpolitik? Here is a recent example.

In 2001 Blair's Secretary of State for Northern Ireland, Dr John Reid MP, twice misused his powers under the Northern Ireland Act 2000 by purporting to suspend the Northern Ireland Assembly one day and restoring it the next day. The first suspension was effected by the Northern Ireland Act 2000 (Suspension of Devolved Government) Order 2001, which took effect on 11 August 2001. It was ended by the Northern Ireland Act 2000 (Restoration of Devolved Government) Order 2001, which took effect on 12 August 2001. The second suspension was effected by the Northern Ireland Act 2000 (Suspension of Devolved Government) (No 2) Order 2000, which took effect on 22 September 2001. It was ended by the Northern Ireland Act 2000 (Restoration of Devolved Government) (No 2) Order 2001, which took effect on 23 September 2001. On 28 September 2001 I had the following letter published in *The Times* –

For the second time, the Secretary of State for Northern Ireland has misused his powers under the Northern Ireland Act 2000 by suspending the Assembly one day and restoring it the next day. The Act gives him no power to do any such thing.

The Act says that as soon as is reasonably practicable after he has suspended the Assembly the Secretary of State must initiate a review under the Belfast Agreement, which necessarily takes at least six weeks to accomplish.

The Act further says that before restoring the Assembly the Secretary of State must take into account the result of the review. Obviously this means he has no power to restore the Assembly until at least six weeks have passed. He certainly has no power to restore it overnight.

What this means is that any person sufficiently interested could ask the High Court to quash the recent restoration order. Whatever else that did, it would at least strike a blow for the rule of law.

The provision of the 2000 Act requiring the Secretary of State to initiate a review after suspension of the Assembly is section 2(1). The provision requiring him to consider the result of the review before restoring the Assembly is section 2 (3). Both provisions are crystal clear, leaving no room for argument. No doubt that is why Dr Reid did not answer my letter in *The Times*. There was no answer he could give, except to confess that he had acted illegally. It was a shameful position for a British Secretary of State to put himself in. I thought the Opposition might take up the cudgels, so I wrote to Mr Quentin Davies MP, the Shadow Secretary of State for Northern Ireland. He took over a month to reply, and when it did come his answer was not very satisfactory. He said –

> Thank you for your letter about the Northern Ireland Act 2000 which sets out a very persuasive case that the Government were acting illegally in suspending the Assembly.
>
> I think you make an extremely good legal case. I did not, however, feel at the time, and I do not feel now, that it would be politically very expedient to press this since the alternatives available to the Government for various reasons did not seem to me to be likely to be conducive to decommissioning, which of course is the essential element of the Belfast Agreement which is yet to be implemented.
>
> I do, however, very much feel that the ploy of suspending

and restoring the Assembly cannot be used indefinitely otherwise the whole system of devolved government will become a mockery. John Reid has said that he does not intend to use it again, and I certainly intend to hold him to that.

I really do appreciate your time and trouble in thinking through this and letting us have the benefit of your work on it. If the right opportunity offers for me to pursue the line you suggest I will not fail to make use of the arguments you so carefully set out.

This looks very like what the law calls *connivance* by Mr Quentin Davies. A distinguished American scholar, Dr Bryan A Garner, says that connivance is 'passively allowing another to act illegally or immorally – silence and neglect when one should be vocal and monitory'. I am reminded of a fourteenth-century English entry on the Statute Roll which required every man to keep the enrolled ordinances and statutes 'without addition, or fraud, by covin, evasion, art or contrivance'. Who would have expected such a requirement to be needed for one of Her Majesty's Principal Secretaries of State in the twenty-first century?

That there has indeed been 'covin, evasion, art or contrivance' by Dr Reid is made abundantly clear when one looks at the official Explanatory Notes appended to the Northern Ireland Act 2000. These say that section 2 'sets out the conditions that must be fulfilled before the Secretary of State can end the suspension of the Northern Ireland Assembly'. The notes go on to stress that under section 2(1) the Secretary of State has to initiate a 'Review' under the Validation, Implementation and Review section of the Belfast Agreement. The relevant text from the Agreement is as follows –

If difficulties arise which require remedial action across the range of institutions, or otherwise require amendment of the British-Irish Agreement or relevant legislation, the process of review will fall to the two Governments in consultation with the parties in the Assembly. Each Government will be responsible for action in its own jurisdiction.

The notes say that to end the suspension of the Assembly and institutions the Secretary of State can make an order (a Restoration Order) under section 2(2) that makes section 1 of the Act (dealing with the practicalities of suspension) cease to have effect. 'However, before he makes such an Order, he has to take into account the result of the Review that has been undertaken'. The law could not be plainer, but has been flouted. The result is that the Northern Ireland Assembly, as functioning at the time of writing (early April 2002), is plainly illegal and invalid. Can anyone be happy about that?

III

I now come to the depths of the argument on Northern Ireland. From the early 1920s, when Northern Ireland came into separate existence as one part of the United Kingdom, the province has been treated by successive British Governments as significantly different from the remaining part. Over this period, unavowed official policy has been directed to securing that ultimately Northern Ireland shall be united with the south in one republic. There are several reasons for this policy. Northern Ireland is expensive to service. The British Government prefer, if they cannot have an ally across the Irish Sea, to have a neutral rather than a hostile force, which is made more likely if the north is conceded. It has been essential to retain the support of the United States, first against the Germans and later against the Russians. Because of the strong Irish lobby across the Atlantic, this is aided if our Government connives at the idea of ultimate Irish union. For these reasons the British Government have never wholeheartedly endorsed the concept most Britons innocently believe to be our national aim, namely the complete integration of Northern Ireland with the rest of the United Kingdom.

In 1990 the British MP Ian Gow was assassinated at his Sussex home by the IRA. As a friend of his I expressed in the Times the hope (vain of course) that events would speedily show Gow did not die in vain. I said that, to ensure this was the case, the Government should implement Ian's own wise solution to the problem of Northern Ireland. I take the following summary from a letter he wrote to me shortly before he was murdered.

Ian believed that the IRA is fuelled by continuing uncertainty over Northern Ireland's constitutional position. This is exacerbated by the Anglo-Irish Agreement, over which Ian resigned from the Government when it was signed in 1985. Ian believed it was a mistake to confer on the Irish Government the right to represent the nationalist population of Northern Ireland when they have their own elected MPs at Westminster. Ian objected to the *McGimpsey* judgment of the Irish Supreme Court in 1990, when they held it was the duty of the Irish Government to make good the boast in their Constitution that Northern Ireland is truly part of the Republic. Ian believed the Northern Ireland Secretary Peter Brooke should press for steps to be taken to remove this obnoxious clause. Brooke failed to do this, though in the end it was watered down.

On Mr Brooke's initiative to restore Devolution by consent Gow objected that 'the same Government which is resisting an Assembly in Edinburgh, on the ground that such an Assembly would injure the Union, is advocating an Assembly, with the support of the Irish government, in Belfast'. Ian wisely pointed out there can be no permanent resting place between the policy of retaining Northern Ireland within the United Kingdom and that of transferring it to the Republic. When I last spoke to him on 28 June 1990 he stressed that there can be no half way house between the Union and the Republic. It is one or the other. Yet Peter Brooke's aim was to set up a series of meetings which would lead, and I quote his own words, to a system which 'gives a role for both sides of the community'. The only role the nationalist side seek is to work towards leading the territory into the Republic. The only role the unionist side seek is to keep it within, and make it a fully-operative part of, the United Kingdom. One or other of these you can have, but not both. It is a logical impossibility, and 'talks' aimed at a compromise are therefore useless. Moreover the vain prospect of them impedes the true solution.

In a further letter published in *The Times* on 1 August 1990 I complained that the shilly-shallying continued. In memory of Ian Gow I asked Mrs Thatcher and her Government immediately to abandon the unstated (but clearly signalled) belief that one day Northern Ireland will by general consent be handed over to the Republic. I said this flew in the face of all the evidence, and fatally kept the IRA's armed struggle alive. 'There is much talk of the oxygen of publicity, but covert Government signals give a more potent boost – they nourish the terrorist with the oxygen of expectation'. It was all no good of course. The iniquitous policy was not abandoned.

When Blair came along he not merely continued the old chicanery, but enthusiastically embraced and accentuated it (as one would expect of him). Admittedly he had the support of many British people. On 20 July 1996 I wrote to *The Times* a letter saying –

Three letters you published on 19 July 1996 about Northern Ireland show an understanding of the status of the province that as a constitutional lawyer I find gravely flawed. Sir David Goodall thinks nationalists there should be encouraged to achieve 'equal legitimacy' with unionists, including a share of political power as nationalists. Mr Collie believes the nationalists are right to put their trust in the terrorist IRA. Dr Matthew says that in engineering the shift by nationalists away from their former easy tolerance of Orange marches Sinn Fein had 'powerful material to work on', implying justification for their treacherous work. All three ignore the fact that these nationalists are in truth British subjects. What, one may ask, is 'nationalism'? The OED says it is devotion to one's nation, which seems a reasonable definition. On that basis it is the unionists who are truly nationalist. The nation to which the so-called nationalists devote themselves is not theirs, for as I have said they are British subjects. These nationalists are a small minority, for over a third of the Catholics in Ulster wish to stay British subjects. It is an error to suppose that the irredentist faction have any justified claim against their government to be nurtured and fed in their disloyalty. With any other country this notion would be dismissed for what it is, an absurdity. Your leader of 15 July 1996 rightly says that when there was no ambiguity over Northern Ireland's future there was no effective republican terrorist campaign. Starved of the oxygen of hope, as you put it, the IRA was moribund. It has been sustained over the past 25 years, you correctly say, by the uncertainty of Ulster's position within the UK.

IV

I return to Blair's Secretary of State for Northern Ireland, Dr John Reid MP. On 3 March 2002 he spelt out his Blair-inspired philosophy on television. The policy is to treat with scrupulous equality on the one hand the people of Northern Ireland who accept they are British citizens and are loyal to the Queen and on the other hand the people of Northern Ireland who resent that they are British citizens and are disloyal to the Queen. This stands everything that citizenship means on its head. Traitors are equated with loyalists, and officially treated with as much considera-tion. It is a constitutional obscenity.

And Blair rubs his hands together and furthers it.

63

Women-only Short Lists

The Queen's Speech on 20 June 2001 (written of course by Mr Blair) contained the following promise or threat, depending on your point of view: 'My Government will prepare legislation to allow political parties to make positive moves to increase the representation of women in public life'. This was a weasel way of informing the nation (if it bothered to listen) that Labour would amend the Sex Discrimination Act to permit constituency parties, when selecting a parliamentary candidate, to impose a women-only short list.

I here introduce Mr. Parmjit Dhanda, newly-elected Labour MP for the ancient English city of Gloucester, formerly the Roman city of Glevum. I respectfully salute Mr Dhanda for having achieved selection by his constituency Labour party despite having little if anything to do with ancient Glevum. I salute him because Mr Dhanda was not selected from any politically correct ethnic-only shortlist. No restraint had been imposed on the freedom of choice of his constituency Labour party. They chose Mr Dhanda because they believed he was the best person to represent Gloucester in our nation's Parliament at Westminster. If under Labour's new proposals a women-only short list is imposed on that ancient city where will Mr Dhanda be?

On 27 June 2001 Mr Dhanda made in the House of Commons a graceful maiden speech in the debate on the Address. As protocol required, he mentioned his predecessor in the seat, Tessa Kingham. He carefully explained how, after a mere four years in Parliament as a so-called 'Blair babe', this immature Tessa became huffy and frustrated by 'the pace of change or, as she would say, the slowness of change in institutions such as the House of Commons and some of the jousting that goes with it'. The indignant Blair babe Tessa poured out her resentful feelings to readers of *The Guardian*, not having learnt in four years that great British institutions can be resistant to

257

the current itch for instant and constant change. The more soundly based they are, the more they are likely to resist. That is what our constitution is about, Tessa might have learnt. But she didn't.

Mr Dhanda shocked the House of Commons by reading out comments made by his local paper, *The Citizen*, when he was first selected as the Labour candidate.

> Labour can kiss goodbye to this seat. They might as well hand it over to the Conservatives now. The Labour Party in Gloucester has made the same mistake as the Tories in Cheltenham when they chose a black barrister as candidate and handed the seat to the Liberal Democrats. Mr. Dhanda could withdraw to allow another candidate to be adopted. . .

Hon. Members: Shame.

Mr Dhanda: I am not making this up, honestly. *The Citizen* said –

> Things were so much easier when candidates were picked by a handful of party elders in a smoke filled room rather than the whole party membership of between 400 and 500 people. . . Sad to say, many of the voters of Gloucestershire have yet to reach the advanced state of consciousness to accept a foreigner as their local MP.

The people of Gloucester proved they are better than that, went on Mr Dhanda, and I stand here as the very proud Member of Parliament for Gloucester. 'The people of Gloucester', he added 'are its greatest asset, and I shall do my utmost to deliver for them a city that is fit for them – a modern, confident and dynamic city that is fit for the 21st century'. That seems a tad presumptuous, one might think. Who on earth is this Mr Dhanda to think he can deliver any such thing to the ancient English city of Gloucester?

Mr Dhanda also said in the debate: 'I very much welcome the part of the Queen's Speech that will enable more women to be elected to the House, and I hope that people from ethnic minority backgrounds will also be encouraged to stand'.

Clearly the estimable Mr Dhanda is missing the point. I will try to explain it, step by step. The Sex Discrimination Act is based upon the moral principle that it is wrong to discriminate against women because they are women, or against men because they are men. Sex (or gender as it is now often called) should make no difference when it comes to choosing someone for a particular position. Being a moral principle, this admits of no exceptions. What is right is right in all situations, and what is wrong, wrong.

The theory that the membership of the House of Commons should exactly reflect the position in the country falls foul of the principle that an MP represents his or her constituents, and democracy demands that they have an unfettered choice. That indeed is the basic principle of representative democracy. If you allow an exception for women then logically you must allow an exception for all other under-represented groups. In no time at all we shall have disabled-only shortlists, old-age pensioner short lists (I would qualify for that), fattist, thinnest and dim-wittist shortlists. And also, as I have said, ethnic-minority short-lists.

What shall we do when these short lists conflict? How shall we reconcile the right of a Mr Dhanda to demand an ethnic-only shortlist and the right of a Tessa Kingham to a women-only shortlist? These puzzles arise from the simple fact that those who are in charge of our affairs will not think out the consequences of what they are about.

The Tories are no better. They too propose to introduce women-only shortlists for parliamentary elections.

64

The Problem with Voting

Our democracy depends upon voting. King Demos (to whom we are all committed) works his wiles on the basis that in an election people will record their votes, and the biggest vote will decide the issue. That may raise problems about the protection of persecuted minorities, such as those devoted to the time-honoured sport of hunting with hounds. I am not now concerned with that aspect. What I am concerned with is a mundane problem connected with the mechanics of voting, often overlooked. How, when collecting and counting the votes, can you be sure they are genuine? If a vote is not genuine it should not count, but exactly how do you check up on this? Any system of voting must lay down voters' qualifications. If you are not qualified to vote, your purported vote should not count. The electoral system, for obvious reasons, must also disallow multiple voting. One person one vote is the principle. It is undermined if people get away with voting twice, thrice – or even more often. That does happen. The fact that it happens is demonstrated by the Electoral Fraud (Northern Ireland) Bill, which received a second reading in the House of Commons on 10 July 2001 (later passed into law as part of the Elections Act 2001). Vote today, vote often is an old chestnut about Ulster elections. This Bill confirms its underlying truth. Why should that be?

I studied closely the Hansard report of the debate on the second reading of this worthy Bill. It did not reveal the answer to my question. I never thought it would. Every speaker was behaving politely, which meant skating on the surface. Truth, which lies deeper, was not troubled.

The truth here is that dishonest voting in Northern Ireland elections, for long an object of scorn, is merely a minor product of the age-old tussle between the north and south of that island. People who, either in the name of holy Ireland or the defence of the union, think nothing of tossing a petrol bomb through an old lady's window, are not going to stall at electoral malpractice. To them it seems trivial, though in its small way useful. Obviously, given their moral principles, they will make use of it whenever opportunity serves.

The second reading of the Bill was moved by the Parliamentary Under-Secretary of State for Northern Ireland, Mr. Desmond Browne MP. He said that the turnout at elections had been historically higher in Northern Ireland than in the rest of the United Kingdom. 'That suggests that the electorate in Northern Ireland are more politically active and more politically conscious than elsewhere in the UK.' Of course they are. We knew that already, if we had any sense. We also knew the reasons. What do you take us for?

Mr Browne went on to criticise 'vote stealing' and said there had been growing concern about the perceived level of electoral malpractice in Northern Ireland, though he did not specify in which quarters this concern was felt. Mr Browne added that electoral abuse was an affront to democracy. He went on –

> If there is a high level of abuse, or even if people only fear that that is the case, the democratic process will be under threat. We do not want voters in Northern Ireland to become disillusioned with politics because they fear that elections are unfair.

Of course, as we all know, the answer to this electoral malpractice is a return to the wartime system of universal identity cards. If you are privileged to live in the world's best democracy, which refugees from all over Europe and elsewhere constantly risk their lives to reach, then you should be willing to place your identity on record. What, unless you are the sort of person no state would want, have you got to lose?

In this Bill, as always, the Government was too timid to advance this obviously right solution. Instead Mr Browne resorted to the usual waffle. It is, he said, proposed to introduce, for Northern Ireland only, a photographic electoral identity card. It will apply only to elections. Why should this be? Why not seize the opportunity and introduce what is obviously required, an all-purpose identity card?

Of course no one in this pedestrian debate raised that central point, so brainwashed are we all on such matters. Instead, Mr Browne waffled on.

We have given the chief electoral officer extra resources to provide additional staff in both his headquarters and his area electoral offices. We have also recently commissioned research to quantify with more certainty the scale of electoral fraud in Northern Ireland. The results of the research should be available in September 2002. They will enable us to be better informed about the level of abuse and the form that it takes.

Do let us be better informed. About what we are fully informed on already. What is needed is action not waffle.

65

Mrs Dunwoody Triumphs

In chapter 42 I praised the redoubtable backbench Old Labour MP Mrs Gwyneth Dunwoody for bravely standing, unsuccessfully, for Speaker – and bravely voting against her own party's iniquitous proposal (sponsored of course by Mr Blair the Leader) to defer Commons divisions until a distant midweek afternoon, when the heated debate would be long over and the voting would be formal and meaningless. Now I am glad to record the belated triumph of Mrs Dunwoody over these forces of darkness. It arose in this way.

It was Lord St John of Fawsley (then Norman St John Stevas) who first had the bright idea of setting up a select committee of the House of Commons to superintend each major government department, and make sure it behaved properly. This highly democratic check by the legislature on the executive, first implemented in the 1979-83 Parliament, has proved a conspicuous success – even though government whips dislike it and at all times seek to suppress it. The more successful it has been in calling the executive to account (its prime function), the more government whips quite naturally have disliked it. Government ministers have followed along on that line. The only hope for democracy has been persons on the wireless, persons on the television, and of course persons writing in the newspapers. In other words the media. How ironic that dogsbody reporters should end up saving our democracy! What does that say about universal suffrage, so long fought for?

Perversely it is the whips of the three main parties who respectively choose the members of these vital select committees, a fact about which backbenchers of all parties have become increasingly restive. The dam broke on 16 July 2001, when the House of Commons considered the recommendations made by the Committee of Selection for the membership of most of the select committees. The hapless chairman of that committee, Mr John McWilliam

MP, admitted, to howls of rage, that all they had done was rubber-stamp the whips' choices.

Partly this backbench anger was induced by the fact that two Labour MPs who before the general election chaired their respective committees had been sacked by their own whips. They were Donald Anderson, outspoken chair of the Foreign Affairs Select Committee, and Mrs Dunwoody, outspoken chair of the Transport Sub-Committee of the Transport, Local Government and the Regions Select Committee. It will be understood that 'outspoken' here is code for bolshy, bloody-minded, recalcitrant and unbiddable, in the opinion that is of New Labour whips. No wonder John Prescott calls her 'Vinegar Lil'.

Mrs Dunwoody said she was astonished by the decision to sack Mr Anderson and herself, even though she did not consider she was irreplaceable on the Transport Sub-Committee. She thought the current Parliament was widely perceived as not doing its job properly. The select committees were regarded by the public as a means of 'carefully examining, not only what Whitehall and the Government are doing, but what all the arms of government and their myriad agencies are doing'. She added that there was no other way of doing the job.

Mrs Dunwoody argued that although people do not always understand the intricacies of what Parliament does, they do ask it to fulfil the role that voters expect it to fulfil, and that is not simply to go along with everything the executive proposes. The House of Commons must never become a great morass of dim people doing what they are told not by the electorate, but by the executive. 'What I need is the right to question, to examine and to produce reports on what Her Majesty's Government are doing in the name of government'. To which one can only add Hear! Hear! Mr Blair did not agree.

The new Leader of the House (Mr. Robin Cook MP) appeared shell-shocked at all this. It was not what he expected on the first outing in his new post. Mr Cook has a whining delivery. Today he whined that the debate had turned out to be more controversial than he would have wished. Some comments, he thought, were 'a bit overdone'. Labour MPs would be granted a free, that is unwhipped, vote in deciding at the end of the debate on whether the whips' selections excluding Anderson and Dunwoody would be confirmed. He hoped this would apply to Opposition MPs (it did).

Mr Cook added that the decision about who goes on to a popular select committee could never be made easy. The previous week, with some committees, Labour had faced the challenge of choosing a dozen or fewer members from 50 or 60 applicants. There would always be more MPs who were disappointed than those who were satisfied. 'But the difficulty in making the choice increases the importance of ensuring that the process is seen to be transparent, fair and under the control of the House'. Hear, hear, again cried the Labour backbenchers.

In the division that followed the House made its views clear. The Labour whips' decision to sack Mr Anderson was rejected by 301 votes to 231. Their decision to sack Mrs Dunwoody was rejected by 308 votes to 221. Democracy had won. Earlier, Mr Cook had made it clear that the method of appointing members of select committees would be over-hauled so as to give more power to backbenchers.

The media hailed it all as a great triumph for democracy, and a huge black eye for the control freak Prime Minister Mr Tony Blair.

Unfortunately when, in 2002, Labour MPs were given a free vote on Mr Cook's proposals they were voted down. Old Labour reasserted itself.

66

More Word Hijacking – this time it's 'Investment'

In chapter 39 I wrote about Blair's hijacking of the word *discrimination*. Now my subject is his hijacking of the word *investment*. That you might think is a dull, boring term. If so you would be wrong. It is in truth a vitally important word, and Blair has hijacked it for his own dishonest ends. He wouldn't have troubled to do that if he didn't think it important.

The current edition of the Oxford English Dictionary, the most authoritative source, defines investment in this sense as the conversion of money or circulating capital into some species of property from which an income or profit is expected to be derived in the ordinary course of trade or business. So to 'invest' money is to create a capital asset from which in each of the ensuing years income will arise. That has long been considered virtuous.

The reason it is considered virtuous is that the alternative to investing money in this way is to spend it on current needs, after which it is gone for ever. The investor builds up assets for the future; the spender dissipates assets for present aims. If the spender does too much of this dissipating he is condemned with the epithet *spendthrift*. You see the difference. There is *thrift* (widely admired) and there is the *spendthrift* (widely condemned). Mr Blair, when acting as a spendthrift, as he often does, would prefer to be considered thrifty instead. It looks better. It sound better. He wants to achieve this transformation, and he does. Quite how does he manage that feat of legerdemain? Easily, as I shall show.

The trick Mr Blair has grasped is to do the one thing while calling it the other. So he spends unthriftily on current needs while calling that *investment*. What a low trick, you will say. But that is the essence of Blairism. Low tricks are what he thrives on.

I am grateful to Matthew Parris of *The Times* for drawing attention to this particular Blairite trick. He has been on about it in those august columns for some time. The latest effusion came on 6 April 2002. I shall now give you the gist.

Parris starts by complaining of the debauching by the Chancellor of the Exchequer and the Prime Minister of the word 'invest'. He goes on –

> I wrote about this three years ago, when some kind of (perhaps unspoken) directive seemed to have been put out among ministers to employ the words 'invest' or 'investment' for all public spending ('public investment').

Parris then says that on the railways, meeting the deficit of a loss-making passenger service should be called paying a subsidy. Yet Blair calls it 'investment'. Increasing the rate of welfare benefits or police salaries is, by all accepted accounting standards, a revenue payment. Blair calls it 'investment'. Parris continues –

> Gradually, 'investment' words have been gradually spreading like nettles across the whole public expenditure patch, and the situation has now become so serious that we are in danger of losing 'investment' altogether as a useful term in civic affairs and leaving ourselves bereft of any shorthand means of communicating the difference between public spending which is meant to secure a return – 'investment' – and public spending which is simply meant for consumption: 'payout' or 'subsidy'.

Parris calls this a 'deft fudge' by Blair, but it don't think it's all that deft. A child could see through it, if the child looked. But then not many of the electorate do really look with the child's unblinkered stare. So Mr Blair gets away with it, or seems to. Of course if he really gets away with it then more fool us – we the electorate get what we deserve.

Parris has not finished.

> Centuries of fastidious differentiation between capital and revenue are plundered [by Blair] for the cachet lent by the word 'invest': a cachet lent by a once-useful, part-technical term which the politicians will steal in pursuit

of votes, exhaust, discredit and discard. Wherever politicians and their publicists gather as a Budget looms, watch out for this word and when you hear it, spit.

Well spitting may contravene some byelaw, and I shall not do that. Instead I shall chalk up one more mark against the name of slippery dishonest Blair. He is intent on contradicting and debasing an important concept. Winston Churchill grasped its wider meaning when he said -

There is no finer investment for any community than putting milk into babies. Healthy citizens are the greatest asset any country can have.

Of course we could go even wider than that and cite Thoreau in *Walden* (1854) -

Goodness is the only investment that never fails.

67

Jo Moore the Merrier

Tony Blair has done may things to destroy our great British constitution, so painstakingly built up over centuries. In this penultimate chapter I single out a new constitutional disease that might be called Jo-Mooreism. This dread cancer of the body politic is named after an egregious young woman who was one of the many manipulating creatures Blair brought in to undermine carefully-built Whitehall impartiality. Blair calls them special advisers. More accurately they would be called political advisers. It would be even more true to call them party-political advisers. The media call them spin doctors. Democratically they are anathema.

The senior among this crew have been given power by Blair, misusing the royal prerogative, to dictate to top civil servants – an unheard of thing in our governmental arrangements. Blair more than doubled the number of these scurrying political creatures he found on his arrival at 10 Downing Street. He seeks to have more and more in the purlieus, or even the very heart, of his New Labour Government – in fact the more the merrier. One of them was Jo Moore.

Blair's spin doctor Jo Moore owes her unique infamy to the fact that on 11 September 2001, the day the Twin Towers fell in New York, she advised her Whitehall colleagues that this was a good day for burying bad news (meaning bad news emanating from Blair's Government). When caught out in this monstrous piece of skulduggery Jo Moore should by any decent standards have at once resigned or been sacked – and then slunk slobbering on all fours into the wastes of oblivion, where she clearly belongs. Moore did not do this, but desperately clung to her well-paid job – supported by her Blairite boss the Right Honourable Stephen Byers MP, head of Blair's Department of Transport, Local Government and the Regions (DTLR). Byers had personally brought Moore in, having had previous experience of her partisan talents. So she brazened it out, and Blair amiably lent his support. The more the merrier, he thought. But in the end it all came horribly unstuck.

Why do I make such a big thing of this? Let me explain. Having myself been for many years a senior civil servant in Whitehall, I am appalled by these goings on. In those immediate post-war years, the 1950s, 1960s and 1970s, the thing we were all taught (as if we needed to be taught it) was that the civil service exists to provide a first-class impartial back-up to Ministers of the Crown. A politician given the seals of office can do nothing in isolation. Comprehensive, able support is required – and that is the historic function of the civil service. We'd all been taught that at public school and Oxbridge, and of course we accepted it. It was part of the story of making Democracy tolerable.

Another part of that story was that this backup must be provided on a neutral basis, when it came to party-political aspects. Britain does not have (or did not have) the American pork-barrel or spoils system, under which each incoming political party brings in its own supporters to staff government offices at the top level – and kicks out existing employees who are on the other side in politics. We in Britain found it much more effective for the public good to build up a highly competent, politically neutral, civil service offering, to the high-flyers it needed to employ, a permanent, satisfying career. We thought it obviously inefficient to employ, on the contrary, a body of assistants who were devoted to a particular party and knew they would all be kicked out when the other lot gained power (as inevitably they very soon would).

Blair is well on the way to destroying this admirable system, achieved over centuries. His method is to install at the top of each government department a bevy of Jo Moores. Their job is to disseminate to the media news of what is going on in government. Their instructions from him run contrary to what the public needs, namely an accurate, impartial account. What the Jo Moores are employed to do is put a spin on reality, so that good or bad it always appears to favour Mr Blair. Jo Moores are there to manipulate the news, and bury anything the public might dislike, to the prejudice of government. They superintend the burial grounds wherein democracy is interred.

Naturally enough, the manipulating, spinning, politicised, parvenu Jo Moores raise the ire of the permanent, neutral civil servants who have laboriously passed their difficult examinations and are still imbued with the old honest philosophy of service. We saw the result in February 2002, when Martin Sixsmith, director of communications in the DTLR, said of Jo Moore's spinning behaviour: up with this he would not put. Bad news about rail figures needed to be disseminated by the DTLR. The question was on which date should this be done. In the good old days it would have been done on whatever date was normal and natural. Under Blair, spin doctors ponder such questions with a view to deluding the public. If it's bad news they want to bury it. Jo Moore is their patron saint.

But if the news is bad from the DTLR, or any other Government department, the public have a right to know at once. Blair's Jo Moores do not think so. What they think, and are paid to think, is that the public, who pay their wages and finance their pension schemes, should be denied this vital information. It should be 'buried', so that we all miss hearing about it and are thus deceived. That will rebound to the glory of Mr Blair, whose only aim is to get enough votes to be re-elected. Votes are what he is after, and he does not care in the slightest if they are dishonestly obtained. Yet he poses all the time as a holy Joe, a true observant Christian. Hypocritical or what?

Martin Sixsmith, the upright civil servant of the old school, feared that the bad news about rail figures was going to be released by the DTLR on the day of the funeral of HRH the Princess Margaret. He sent out an email, copied to Jo Moore, to warn Mr Byers of this. It said –

> You spoke about possibly making this announcement on Friday. We should **not** do it on Friday, as that is the day on which Princess Margaret is being buried. There are too many connotations to the word "buried" for us to do anything on that day.

It was the end of Martin Sixsmith's career in the civil

service. Mr Byers did not like being so instructed by an impartial civil servant of the old school. He preferred the cosy ministrations of Jo Moore, but did at last realise that so far as she was concerned the game was up. She had acquired a reputation for bullying civil servants of the old neutral school, and had constantly aroused their wrath. She had a long history of behaving like this, and so at last had to go. Mr Byers did not fancy sacking her, so she had to be persuaded to resign. Byers promised her that if she would condescend to resign the blameless Martin Sixsmith would be forced to go too. As Mr Sixsmith innocently emerged from a hospital appointment he heard a radio news bulletin announce that Byers had said he had resigned. This was a lie. He had not resigned.

I come to Prime Minister's questions on 13 February 2002. The Leader of the Opposition was on to another piece of Blairite chicanery.

Mr Iain Duncan Smith (Chingford and Woodford Green): May I join the Prime Minister in offering our condolences to Her Majesty the Queen, the Queen Mother and the royal family on their sad loss? The Prime Minister is right to say that Princess Margaret was a strong servant of her country, through war and peace. She will be mourned and much missed throughout the whole country. [Here the Leader of the Opposition and of the Conservative Party performed a rapid switch.] When the Prime Minister signed the letter to his Romanian counterpart on behalf of LNM on 23 July 2001, was he or his chief of staff [*Interruption.*] I repeat, was he or his chief of staff aware that the owner of that company, Mr Mittal, had at any time-I repeat, at any time-donated money to his party? [In fact Mr Mittal, a short time earlier, had donated £125,000 to New Labour.]

The Prime Minister: It is of course a matter of public record that Mr Mittal is a donor to the Labour party and a supporter of the Labour party. Why is that a matter of public record? It is because this Government introduced the open rules for political funding. For years and years, no one had any idea of how the Conservative party or any political party was funded. We introduced rules of transparency. As the right honourable Member for Chingford and Woodford Green (Mr Duncan Smith) probably knows, the letter that I signed mentioned not Mr Mittal but his company, LNM, of which I had no knowledge. However, having said that, had I known that Mr Mittal was a supporter of the Labour party, it would have made no difference whatever to the signing of the letter. That was entirely justified, as was the advice from the embassy. This is a complete load of nonsense from beginning to end. It is not Watergate, it is Garbagegate. It is the biggest load of garbage since the last load of garbage, which was Enron.

Mr Duncan Smith: It is very interesting that the Prime Minister now says that it is garbage to raise a concern that he, as the Prime Minister and on behalf of the whole country, should have written a letter in support of a company-by the way, it is a competitor to our main steel manufacturer-which turns out to have fewer than one tenth of 1 per cent. of its employees working in the United Kingdom. The company is registered in the Dutch Antilles. Will the Prime Minister tell us whether at any stage he or his chief of staff were aware, as he signed the letter, that it was in support of someone who had donated money to the Labour party?

The Prime Minister: I have already said that it was a matter of public record that Mr Mittal was a donor to the Labour party. However, what the right honourable Gentleman says about the letter is total nonsense. It was written at the instigation of the British embassy in Romania. It was written for the very simple reason that this was a reform, namely the selling off of an old state industry, which we supported strongly. I am delighted that a British-based company has succeeded. What is more, I am pleased that the embassy asked us to do this-it was the right thing to do. If the right honourable Gentleman is seriously saying that be-cause the company is owned by someone who is a supporter of the Labour party, we should not write such a letter, even though the British embassy requests it, that is totally contrary to the practice of previous Governments throughout the ages.

Mr Duncan Smith: The Prime Minister already knows that, apparently, in the draft letter the word 'friend' [of Mr Blair] was struck out before he even signed it. The real point is not whether the Prime Minister was right to sign on behalf of the company but how many of the companies that employ fewer than 100 employees in this country and are registered abroad he backs by letters to foreign countries in support of contracts? The Prime Minister seems to have missed the point. Until he is able to say that he knew specifically about the matter and discussed it with his chief of staff and then decided, despite that, to go ahead, we will never be the clearer and will always be left doubting whether the Prime Minister acted in the best interests of Britain. To clear this up, will the Prime Minister now tell us whether he will agree to a full public and independent inquiry into this affair?

The Prime Minister: I can certainly tell the right hon. Gentleman the answer to that – it is no. As I pointed out a moment ago, I signed the letter unchanged, [Later proved to be a lie.] and it made no mention of Mr Mittal. However, had it done so, it would still have been entirely the right thing to do. The right honourable Gentleman says that it was wrong to sign the letter. I will explain again to Conservative Members why I did so. The reason the embassy in Romania asked us to sign the letter is because it was an important contract. We fully supported the Romanian Government's policy of economic reform. We therefore wanted to celebrate the fact that the contract had been awarded to a British company and to celebrate the fact that the Romanian Government's programme of economic reform was right for Romania. If the right honourable Gentleman reads the comments of the Romanian Prime Minister today, plainly puzzled at the nonsense being raised by Conservative Members, he will see that the decision to award the contract was made before the letter was even written. Therefore, all we were doing was welcoming the fact that this process of economic reform was going forward.

It was clever wriggle (like many a wriggle effected by Mr Blair) but it was no good, and it wouldn't do. Despite the fact that Mr Blair wriggled like an athletic worm who had been doing press-ups in an Olympic training gym the stench of fœtid Blairism arose and was carried far and wide throughout the House of Commons and well beyond. The truth, as later appeared, was that Blair did not sign the letter unchanged (the reference to Blair's being a 'friend' of Mittal was removed). The company was not British, but was registered in the Antilles. It had very few British employees and was in competition with Corus, a true British company (previously known as British Steel).

This is the final scenario. Blair's slimy Minister, Stephen Byers, said in a television interview in February 2002 that he had not interfered on questions concerning the disciplining of two civil servants in his department, Jo Moore and Martin Sixsmith. Later he admitted in the House of Commons that this was untrue: he had interfered. Moreover he had shown himself to be the boss, and exerted his bossiness. Jo Moore, although on the civil service payroll, was a so-called special adviser employed to further the aims of the Labour Party. Martin Sixsmith was a regular civil servant employed to supervise the department's communications in the usual impassive way long associated with our civil service. As civil servants they should both have been impartial. They should not have been liable to dismissal at the whim of a party boss.

Up till that time, February 2002, it had been a basic government principle that if a Minister was caught out in a lie in a matter concerning his ministerial responsibilities he must at once resign. Many before Byers had acted on that correct principle. We can't have liars in charge of our affairs. Who would want that? So any reputable Prime Minister must insist that the principle is upheld.

But Blair turned his back on that healthy principle, of course not announcing he was doing this. Blair is a master (so he thinks) of deviousness, but we might if we try easily see through him. In an elaborate masquerade before the House of Commons on 27 February 2002 Blair pretended not to be doing any such thing as betraying our constitution. Can you see through that? To give you a chance I continue with some extracts from the House of Commons Hansard reports of the debate on that day. You need to read these reports with a sceptical, analytical approach. Take nothing for granted. At the end I will give some concluding comments.

In the House of Commons on 27 February 2002 the Labour MP Tony McWalter (Hemel Hempstead) addressed a question to his Prime Minister, Tony Blair.

Mr McWalter: My right honourable Friend is sometimes subject to rather unflattering or even malevolent descriptions of his motivation. Will he provide the House with a brief characterisation of the political philosophy that he espouses and which underlies his policies?

Honourable Members: Hear, hear.

The Prime Minister: First, I should thank my hon. Friend for his question, which has evinced such sympathy in all parts of the House, about the criticism of me. The best example I can give is the rebuilding of the National Health Service today under this Government – extra investment. [*Interruption.*] For example, there is the appointment today of Sir Magdi Yacoub to head up the fellowship scheme that will allow internationally acclaimed surgeons and consultants from around the world to work in this country. I can assure the House and the country that that extra investment in our NHS will continue under this Government. Of course, it would be taken out by the Conservative party.

Mr Iain Duncan Smith (Chingford and Woodford Green): Does it remain a principle of the Prime Minister to sack any Cabinet Minister who lies?

The Prime Minister: Yes, of course. I expect the highest standards of propriety.

Mr Duncan Smith: Yesterday, the Transport Secretary

[Stephen Byers MP] admitted to the House that he told the British people something that was fundamentally untrue. Before the Prime Minister came to power, he said: 'I would expect Ministers in a Government I lead to resign if they lie'. If that is so, why is the Transport Secretary today still in his job and sitting on the Bench next to him?

The Prime Minister: I do not accept what the right honourable Gentleman has said. My right honourable Friend came to the House yesterday and made an absolutely full statement, and he and his Department should now be allowed to get on with the issues that really matter to people – for example, issues to do with the botched privatisation of transport and the extra investment in our transport system that it needs. Of course, that is the last thing the right honourable Gentleman will ever ask me about.

Mr Duncan Smith: Now we know that the Prime Minister clearly is not going to stand by his word . . . Before the Prime Minister came to power he also said that under his Government there would be 'no more sleaze, no more lies, no more broken promises'. It is bad enough that such a Cabinet Minister does not resign, but last night the Prime Minister rolled out the red carpet at No. 10 and congratulated him. Is it any wonder that the public's trust in politicians has fallen so low when the Prime Minister is too weak to root out dishonesty?

The Prime Minister: I can tell the right honourable Gentleman exactly what the Transport Secretary will concentrate on: sorting out a privatisation that has wrecked the state of Britain's railways, ensuring that we get the largest ever investment into the London underground and appointing the right people to the Strategic Rail Authority, so that we get the extra rolling stock and investment that the transport system needs. Those are the issues, and there are two parallel agendas. One agenda – that of the Conservative party and parts of the media – is to do with scandal and gossip, day after day. The other agenda is about the economy, living standards, jobs, the NHS, education, crime, and the real issues of transport. He can concentrate on the first; we will concentrate on the second.

Mr Charles Kennedy (Ross, Skye and Inverness, West): In spite of the somewhat inadequate inquiries of a minute or two ago, will the Prime Minister explain to people out there in the country why exactly he retains confidence in his Transport Secretary?

The Prime Minister: For the very reason contained in the statement made by the Secretary of State yesterday, where he explained exactly what has happened, and because I believe that in the end the judgment that should be made, and indeed will be made, about this Secretary of State and this Government will be on the real issues to do with transport-the things that actually concern people in this country. I know that the Conservative party does not want to argue about them, but we do.

Mr Henry Bellingham (North-West Norfolk): Further to the question of my right honourable Friend the Leader of the Opposition, will the Prime Minister say whether it is acceptable for a Cabinet Minister to lie and remain in office? Will he guarantee that he will not move the Secretary of State for Transport, Local Government and the Regions in the next reshuffle?

The Prime Minister: I do not accept what the honourable Gentleman said about my right honourable Friend.

Mr Andrew MacKay (Bracknell): On a point of order, Mr Speaker. Will you confirm that it has been a long-standing convention of the House that, in the interests of good cross-examination of Ministers, statements are released to Opposition spokesmen well in advance? Are you aware that the Secretary of State for Transport, Local Government and the Regions yesterday released his statement only a matter of minutes before coming to the Dispatch Box? Would you – [*Interruption.*] I am not surprised that the Government Chief Whip does not want to hear this. [*Interruption.*]

Mr Speaker: Order. Let me hear the right honourable Member's point of order.

Mr MacKay: I am grateful, Mr. Speaker. Would you deprecate such short notice, and, if it happens again, ensure that the sitting is suspended so that Opposition spokesmen can properly consider what is in the statement? It was quite clear yesterday that the admission that the Secretary of State [Mr Byers] had misled the British public on the Dimbleby programme was not given to other spokesmen in advance so that they could properly cross-examine him.

Mr Speaker: It is not a rule of the House, but a courtesy, that Ministers give as much warning as possible of any statement that they are going to make. I encourage Ministers to do that. [*Interruption.*] Order. If there is any difficulty or short notice in future, I can use my discretion, but I would rather encourage Ministers to give out their statements well in advance.

Mr Andrew Turner (Isle of Wight): Further to that point of order, Mr. Speaker.

Mr Speaker: There is nothing further to that point of order. I have explained the situation exactly.

Mr Crispin Blunt (Reigate): On a point of order, Mr. Speaker. Yesterday, at column 575, during questions on the Transport Secretary's statement, I asked: 'Did he make Martin Sixsmith's resignation a condition of Jo Moore's resignation?' The Secretary of State [Mr Byers] said 'No'. On 'Newsnight' last night, contemporaneous notes were revealed of a conversation between Sir Richard Mottram and Martin Sixsmith on the afternoon of 18 February. I quote directly –

The bigger roadblock is Byers. He's invested so much face in this that his credibility is very much on the line. He has also made a firm promise to Jo that if she stepped down he would get your head to roll as well so it would be very hard for him to announce that you hadn't completely resigned after all.

That confirms stories in *The Sunday Times* of 24 February –

Mr Speaker: Order. The honourable Gentleman is trying to use points of order to put a case. He is aware of the rules of the House. There are ways in which he can pursue matters, including parliamentary questions or Adjournment debates. He is trying to draw the Chair into the argument that he is advancing. I do not have anything further to say on that matter.

Mr Blunt *rose* –

Mr Speaker: Order. I do not have anything further to say on that matter.

Mr Blunt *rose* –

Mr Speaker: Order. I do not think that the honourable Gentleman should pursue this matter. I think that he has finished.

Mr Blunt *rose* –

Mr Speaker: Order. The matter is finished.

Mr Andrew Turner: On a point of order, Mr. Speaker. Yesterday, the House of Lords Annunciators announced the proposed statement by the Secretary of State for Transport, Local Government and the Regions at about 12 o'clock, but the Annunciators in this place did not give such notice until at least half an hour later. Is there anything that you can do to assist us in knowing when such statements will be made?

Mr Speaker: I do not control affairs in the other place.

There are a lot of criticisms I could spell out concerning the above transcript of what on a certain day was said in the House of Commons. I will forbear, asking my readers instead to read it themselves with close attention. That attention needs to be devoted to each of the participants, and I do not exclude the Speaker himself.

There is one thing however to which I do venture to draw

attention. Mr McWalter asked Blair to provide the House with a brief characterisation of the political philosophy that he espouses and which underlies his policies. In other words he was asking from Blair himself a description of Blairism, the subject of this book. Did he receive what he asked for on the floor of the House of Commons? No, he did not. Either that means there is really no such thing as Blairism or it means that Blair is not telling. I suggest the latter is obviously the truth. Blair has an agenda but he leaves us to spell it out, if we can.

So low has Blair brought our public services. Such are the rotten fruits of Blairism.

68

Blair's Nemesis: Daft Mo

In Greek mythology the lady Nemesis was the goddess of proportion, and avenger of public arrogance. Her attributes were a measuring rod, a bridle, a sword, and a scourge. She rode in a chariot drawn by griffins, and savagely smote all who opposed her. However Nemesis never acted in her own person, but always through others chosen as suitable spirits for executing her divine desires. Happily she continues to be active. Mr Blair has lately discovered that Dr Mo Mowlam has in this way been chosen to be his own Nemesis, after the blight of Blairism blasted her own political career.

The demure Mo (an abbreviation of Marjorie) gained her doctorate at the University of Iowa, and then became a research assistant to Tony Benn MP. She was the Labour MP for Redcar in Cleveland (formerly part of Yorkshire) from 1987 to 2001. Blair made Mo his Secretary of State for Northern Ireland from 1997 to 1999. She gives her recreations as jigsaws, swimming and darts. She failed to complete the jigsaw, and drowned politically when trying to swim against the Blairite tide. She polished up her skill at darts however by making certain numbers on her dartboard in Northern Ireland stand for particularly virulent opponents. She tells us in her 2002 memoir *Momentum*, from which much in this chapter is taken: 'I became a whizz shot on certain numbers'.

Blairism springs from a concept of supremacy. Tony feels he has to be on top, and many acolytes (paid by the taxpayer) are employed to ensure this. They were dismayed at what happened when Blair, in the middle of his grandiose televised speech to the nation, ushered Mo Mowlam on to the platform at the Labour Party conference in 1998. The crowded hall erupted, though that had not been planned. Everyone stood up, which was an unscheduled embarrassment. There was unexpected cheering and whooping, which added to the confusion among Blair's horrified spin doctors. All this went on for a very long time, and noisily. Blair was put out, and showed it. It was not what he had planned or expected. Chagrin was what he felt and showed. Little Mo paid the price, but later fought back. She wrote her autobiographical book *Momentum* to show Blair up. The title she chose is a little odd, one feels. The book is about Mo, which accounts for the first two letters of the title - but what did the learned doctor intend by the remainder? The OED defines momentum as the effect of inertia in the continuance of motion after the impulse has ceased. With our Mo, that figures.

Cheerfully accepting her appointed role (she makes a point of being cheerful), Mo duly acted her part as Blair's Nemesis. We know that power-obsessed politicians will stop at nothing to retain what they hold: consider the black tripehound Mugabe of Zimbabwe (lately the ad-mired Southern Rhodesia). Blair is Britain's fiendishly white, more polished, and less blatant Mugabe – and has shown that he too will stop at nothing.

Poor Mo Mowlam developed a brain tumour. Blair used her illness against her, as if her physical weakness had affected her mind and rendered her unfit for public office. This was not true (she was unfit before), but Blair proceeded as if it were. When she declined Tony's suggestion that she should run as Mayor of London in 2000 this was, she says, the last straw for Blair and Alastair Campbell his Sultan of Spin (see chapter 35 above). She adds –

> Was it a coincidence that it was around this time that the most aggressive and vicious off-the-record briefing against me began? A story appeared quoting a 'senior Government aide' as saying my battle with a brain tumour some years earlier had left me without the intellectual rigour to do my job. 'The illness appears to have affected her, and she doesn't seem able to do the job in the same way', ran one quote. 'That deft touch has gone'.

Mo Mowlam tells how as Secretary of State for Northern Ireland she was frequently by-passed by the Prime Minister, her authority undermined.

I was being treated as a girlie – a popular female commodity who would be useful with the voters. I was no longer a comrade-in-arms fighting for the same causes. In fact, I was beginning to feel more like a bag of potatoes that they just wanted to dump somewhere so that Peter Mandelson could go to Northern Ireland.

One Northern Ireland politician told Mowlam he was better off talking to the organ grinder at 10 Downing Street (Blair's chief-of-staff Jonathan Powell) rather than to her, the monkey. Announcements were made without her being included, and at times with her not even being told. She ceased to put her views forward because she knew they would just be ignored. She tried to console herself that she was being treated no worse than others among Blair's ministers. 'There was not much inclusivity for anyone, to be honest, unless you happened to be Jack Straw, Derry Irvine or Gordon Brown'. She tells in vivid detail how ministerial meetings were conducted at 10 Downing Street.

Depending on the subject, it was usually either Gordon Brown or Derry in the chair telling us what was going to happen. There was the odd comment from the other Ministers, and that was it. Contributions from others round the table didn't seem to have any value – there was a distinct sense that decisions had already been taken. In the end, I felt it was easier and more efficient to stay away and read the minutes afterwards.

Such is Cabinet government, once the glory of the advanced democratic British constitution, under the pernicious rule of Blairism.

Reading on in the pages of *Momentum* one begins to wonder however. Was this learned doctor really fit to be a Minister of the Crown? She glories in the shoddy tricks she played as Her Majesty's Secretary of State for Northern Ireland on the Queen's dignified bed at royal Hillsborough Castle.

The Queen's bed is enormous – one of the biggest I've ever seen. One weekend, when we had lots of visitors – including broadcasters Jeremy Paxman and John

Humphrys, former Culture Secretary Chris Smith and my Mum Tina - we tried to see if we could all get on it. The most we managed was 18.

The Minister of the Crown and learned Doctor Mo Mowlam had not finished with historic Hillsborough Castle, seat of the monarchy in Northern Ireland.

Then there is the throne room – a very grand place with gorgeous curtains and carpets, complete with two genuine thrones for investitures. It was a fantastic place for my husband Jon's children to play in, although I had to make sure that their games did not involve footballs. I also had to put a stop to some go-karting in there one Christmas.

The learned Secretary of State gleefully goes on to recall how at Hillsborough Castle she stored the prize-winning specimen from each year's conker tournament in a priceless piece of china, on loan from the Victoria and Albert Museum. What would Queen Victoria (or for that matter Prince Albert) have made of that gross piece of lèse majesté?

There is much more degradation. One night the learned doctor Mo Mowlam, invested with brief authority as Her Majesty's Secretary of State, invited to Hillsborough Castle the cast of the Rocky Horror Show, who had been playing in Belfast.

I think they had all expected dry sherry and a stuffy atmosphere, but we soon got the musical director on the piano – and we danced and sang the night away. I still have this wonderful image as we waved goodbye to them all. The sun was just beginning to rise as two white stretch limos, with arms and legs sticking out of the windows, swept out of the gates of Hillsborough Castle. . .

Sickening as this is, can it be redeemed by superb statecraft on Mo's part? See what you think from what follows.

Mo tells us how she went to visit convicted murderers at the notorious Maze Prison. Before doing so she consulted her mother, then in her 70s. 'Her view was that there was no alternative, so that was that'. Mo tells us, regarding the two as equal, that she was going to visit Johnny 'Mad Dog' Adair and the man she describes as 'the mass killer Michael Stone, who shot mourners at an IRA funeral'. As an upholder of the rule of law, I can't condone what Michael Stone did. But the rule of law has conspicuously failed us in Northern Ireland. When that happens you tend to get primal justice. Maybe Michael Stone will ultimately go down as a just executioner, stepping in where the apparatus of the state failed. The crass bag of potatoes Mo Mowlam would not be impressed by that, having absolutely no sense of patriotism whatsoever.

'I felt no fear' Mo proudly tells us of her official visit to the Maze Prison. I doubt if she saw that remark for what it truly was – a tribute to the efficiency of the British armed forces who were deputed to guard her. Mo is not much gone on being British – even though she is, I gather, British herself. As I say, patriotism does not seem to be a word in her vocabulary.

There is more to the harm this wretched woman caused, or would have liked to have caused, during her brief political career. She is hot on decriminalising lethal drugs. Outlawing drug dealing she describes as humbug. She admits to having smoked cannabis as a student, and what is more inhaling. When asked about this, Mo dodged the question.

> I knew that sooner or later , as Cabinet Enforcer co-ordinating the Government's anti-drugs policy, I would eventually be asked outright. I was sticking to a policy agreed with No. 10 that basically meant not answering the question at all. I'd had it pointed out to me quite forcibly that it would not be helpful to my Cabinet colleagues if I admitted anything.

We should be profoundly thankful that this woman is no longer a Minister of the Crown, for on her own admission she is dangerous.

> It is my firm belief that the only way to sort the whole mess out is to legalise all drugs: not just cannabis, but heroin, cocaine, ecstasy, the lot.

Many lovers of cannabis (otherwise known as Indian hemp, bhang, ganja or hashish) are opening their mouths to urge its legalisation. My belief that cannabis is a dangerous drug was formed many years ago. As a constitutional adviser to the Jamaica Government I was provided with a chauffeur-driven car while I was on the island. The driver, a wise old Jamaican, continually spoke to me of his experiences of the harmful effects of ganja (as they call cannabis in Jamaica). He felt very strongly about it. He told me stories of his schooldays, when about a third of the boys in his class smoked ganja. He said it was well known to ruin any hope they had of learning anything in school, giving rise to their nickname among the sensible boys of 'dopeheads'. He told me they spent their lives in a constant drug-induced daze. When they left school they were unfit for work, and joined the ranks of the permanent unemployed. Some became violent. A few became murderers. The word assassin derives from the Arabic hashishin, or eater of hashish.

The final point is that Mo's effusions are founded in vanity. Educated to begin with at the humblest level, in the Coundon Court comprehensive school, this woman really thinks she is a sage. She tells us –

> I would like to set up a series of what have already been nicknamed Mo-Mo homes: halfway houses for ex-addicts next to holiday homes for disabled people.

Wanting to have anything named after you is known as an early sign of paranoia. As a person who is registered disabled, I shall take very good care to avoid staying in a holiday home which is located next door to a Mo-Mo home for former drug addicts.

All this reflects little credit on Mo Mowlam. It reflects even less credit on the politician who elevated her, and then found her to be his Nemesis. Political judgment is what we require in our Prime Ministers. What political judgment is Tony Blair shown to possess when his Deputy Prime Minister John Prescott calls one of his former senior ministers 'Daft Mo'?

69

Blairism Buried

Well I do so hope all those previous grim chapters giving chapter and verse have succeeded in burying Blairism once and for all, lifting his sickly blight from our wholesome beloved country England. Dream on, you might say.

Well I will dream on. When it comes to our English history, I think the essence of Blairism will be seen down future years as the destruction of vital elements in our splendid constitution. It was so difficult to build up, that constitution, over so many bloody, fraught centuries. It was so easy to destroy, in a few crass Blairite years. Is that process of destruction now almost complete?

Through many generations our constitution has been seen as a thing of checks and balances, delicately structured. Not any more. In his bloated pride, Mr Blair was not having that when he achieved power in 1997. The political chalice that had fallen into his grasp he was, like grubby Mr Mugabe, determined to retain. Was it healthy for the British nation to enjoy through periodic general elections a rotation of political power, as most believed? Mr Blair found it inconvenient to think so.

Like grubby Mr Mugabe, this educated British man wanted his pet political party to retain uninterrupted power for a century or more. Blair believed that made sense, and desired a one-party state, governed by his party and headed by him, the sainted Maestro, for as long as nature made possible. Tyrants all over Africa (especially in Sierra Leone, but not in Zimbabwe) enthusiastically waved their spears, danced and shimmied in their grass skirts, and shouted again and again for Maestro Blair. His supporters at home would have done much the same if they had had the energy, or the grass skirts.

Now I come to the climax of these in and out glimpses of the blight of our country known as Blairism. Politically, Tony Blair is dishonest. Though educated at a high-grade public school (Fettes) and then at a high-grade college

(University College Oxford), this supple man has betrayed his privileged upbringing. What he wants for himself is the political spoils and the power. Having successfully grabbed all that (rather to his surprise), he is determined to hold on very tightly, just like Huey Long or any other Tammany Hall boss. Blair will work the system for his own ends, always maintaining he does it for the benefit of others.

This Blair would not cheat on his taxi fare. He is kind to his family, and a good father. His adolescent children love him (so far as we can gather). He regularly trots submissively to church, and prays to his God. But in a strange, contrary, way Blair thinks politics is a different realm, in which anything goes that you can get away with. In this book I have tried to show that anything does not go in politics. In the preceding chapters I hope to have made plain (with practical examples) the truth of that. Politics is about people, and people matter. When we talk about democracy, we are talking about nothing else but people. This whole story concerns people. I am thinking of the people next door, the old people, those who look to us in a last desperate hope, the ones who need help with their shopping and are lost without their medication.

Some think politics excuses dishonesty; indeed that is a widespread misconception. With all his educational advantages, one might have hoped Blair would escape it, see through its falsity, and teach the public otherwise. Alas he did not, and does not. In this chapter I aim to rub that in. Blair has let us down, when he might have done so much better for himself and all of us.

What the ultimate fate of this lamentable political philosophy known as Blairism will be I cannot at this moment tell. I am not sanguine. It seems to me that the future historians of the British nation will wish to bury our Mr Blair, of Fettes and Oxford (not to mention working-class Sedgfield, whose MP he is). They will want to bury him six feet down, with Jo Moore beside him. What he does is not what we want done. What he hopes is not what we want hoped. Blair is destructive of our true civilisation. He is a let-down.

I would now like to turn a right-angled corner and mention a strange, inequitable feature of our society. It has little to do with Blair, but I would still like to mention it – if only because Blair seems impervious to its sometimes tragic effects. It concerns those who *resist* the temptation to do wicked things. It applies to many areas, for example a man's hapless condition of being forever sexually smitten (against his will) by the transient sexual charms of pubescent boys. When people give in to such impulses they commit a criminal offence, and may be convicted. I am not concerned with that. If such people break the law, they deserve what they get (or so one must assume).

The people I am concerned with are those on the opposite side. They *resist* such temptation, and with heroic restraint do not break the law in this way. They deserve support. Blair fails to recognise the importance of their heroism. Here, I have to admit, Blair is not alone. This neglect is a common feature of our society. We should salute the many who, being sorely tempted to transgress in one way or another, resist that temptation and go on behaving lawfully, as they know they should. We have a lot to say about those who do transgress, but withhold praise – or even recognition – from the heroes who spurn the devil and resist. Often people do not even realise that these heroes are among their midst. I tried to express these thoughts in the following poem entitled Crime Resisters, which is included in the recently published volume of my collected poems entitled *Poemotions*.

I

Jack is glad his newspaper is filled with exploits:
say a man in his sixties exploiting a girl of eleven.
Jack pays Murdoch hard cash to be exploited;
a man in his sixties permitting himself indirectly to indulge.

Indirectly Jack indulges bright yearning for young girls:
a man of 64, having no business directly to exploit,
Jack's waning lust is still directed at innocent children;
but for the few years left he intends to go on resisting.

II

Dear Alice would love the good life, knowledgeable as she is;
telling Rembrandt from Picasso, the Dordogne from the
    Auvergne.
Doris, her little sister, knows nothing of all this;
a simple soul, she nevertheless deserves a break.

Good-life yearning Alice, brighter than each one of her
    bosses,
spots a foolproof way of cheating, a surefire treat for Doris -
no office person would find out, so that must make it all right.
Alice shrugs, and goes back to her embroidery of Windsor
Castle.

III

Muther Glod is gruesome,
sweats his glaumy paws,
longs to clutch, gruesomely
what hangs in Billy's drawers.

Muther Glod holds honour
high above desire:
honours Billy's growing,
banks down his fire.

In the chapters of this book I have given glimpses of what Blairism means. Many more such chapters could have been written, but perhaps this is enough. Certainly it is enough for me, but I have not quite finished.

In this book I have had a good go at Tony Blair, but I am not such a fool as to think he is the only target, or even the main one. The rot set in years ago. All our political parties are infected by the disease, yet it is the glory of the present British parliamentary democracy that our people have politicians who as MPs represent and articulate their (often unspoken) views and values.

In one way I respect and appreciate that. In another way I detest it. Before I sign off and say goodbye I would like to try and explain what the problem is with me. It will have to be quick, because I have a train to catch. I know the train may be late, since Blairite trains often are. But you do need to be there on the platform.

Briefly, the problem is that I have lived my life through eight decades: the 1920s, the 1930s, the 1940s, the 1950s, the 1960s, the 1970s, the 1980s and the 1990s. I even made it into our wonderful new millennium and tottered on into the 2000s. What does that mean? Ask yourself. Think about it. Consider it in terms of your own life. Glance back through your decades. I am mainly talking here about values, which is a compendium word for a number of things. How people should behave. What we think is important, and unimportant. How we should view other people. How we should regard our country. How we should assess foreigners or aliens. And so on, and so on. It is a long, long list, when you start to talk about personal values. But remember that when it comes to values each decade is potent – and different. *And each person is stamped with the values of their formative years.*

My problem is that this truth does not now seem to be recognised. When you live in a decade you are expected to adhere to that decade's values. But when the next decade comes along, you must obediently switch over. Everyone tells you that's what you must do, so you try to do it. The present decade looks back with scorn at the values of previous decades. But that may be misguided.

Reviewing *An Edwardian War and Peace* by Hugh and Mirabel Cecil, John Carey (*Sunday Times* 17 March 2002) said the book showed 'how keenly, honestly and painfully past generations pursued aims that now seem to us wrong or disgraceful'. The unstated suggestion is that these past aims were wrong or disgraceful, just because leaders of thought in our decade think that is what they were. By coincidence the answer to Mr Carey is given a few pages on. Reviewing *Making a Living in the Middle Ages* by Christopher Dyer, Danny Danziger says the book starts with a plea that *we do not patronise the past.* Then I come across a quote from the preface to *The Making of the English Working Class* by E P Thompson (emphasis added) –

> I am seeking to rescue the poor stockinger, the Luddite cropper, the 'obsolete' hand-loom weaver, the 'utopian' artisan, and even the deluded follower of Joanna Southcott, from *the enormous condescension of posterity*.

Posterity now condescends enormously to the values I indicated in chapter 1, when I talked about being in the Harrow School Speech Room in the 1930s. More than that, posterity dismisses those values out of hand. Values like: being proud of the British Empire; living in a class system where people know their place; deference to one's superiors; a plentiful supply of uneducated menials; stern discipline, with which all must comply in their different ways as society ordered; no nonsense from anybody below you. In those days if things were hard you accepted it, for you did not expect things to be soft. You gritted your teeth, below a stiff upper lip.

I was a child or adolescent when I absorbed those values of the 1930s. I was at the impressionable age. The impression is there still. It is stamped on me. No one has come along to remove it, even if they could. So there it stays. In essence I am stamped and dyed as a 1930s person. That does not mean I believe the values of my decade were the best ever; far from it. I was born only five years after the Great War ended, and I bitterly regret the values that led to that war. Let me lift a corner on that.

While still Prince of Wales, the future King George V, on returning from a tour of his future realms in the British Empire, delivered a speech at London's Guildhall – a location pregnant with England's history. The date was 5 December 1901. The prince felt concerned for England, and wished to alert his future subjects to the dangers that he perceived lay ahead. How right he was to do so, but of course they took no notice.

The cultural and human catastrophe known as the Great War, or War to end all Wars, lay only a few years ahead. It began on 4 August 1914. Today we would think that our Secretary of State for Foreign Affairs, or Foreign Secretary, would be held to have some responsibility for such a horrible and disastrous event, which wiped out a noble culture and ultimately led to the blight we know as

Blairism. It was not so in 1914-18.

From 1905 to 1916 the British Foreign Secretary was a dilettante called Sir Edward Grey, Baronet. The chief publication to date of this classic amateur was a book entitled *Fly-Fishing*. Another consuming interest of his was ornithology. A well-known photograph shows Grey sitting on a garden seat with birds perched all round him. One even squats on his hat, making him look absurd. Grey admitted that this was the environment in which he was happiest. Foreign policy was an obnoxious, regrettable side of his life; he was after all a confessed amateur. If only the Germans under Kaiser Wilhelm would behave like the obedient birds he was used to and loved! But they didn't of course.

Did this well-meaning hapless baronet suffer any disgrace when his foreign policy was shown to have led our nation into quite the most disastrous of its many wars? On the contrary, two years into the Great War this clown was created Viscount Grey of Falloden. In *Who's Who* he boasted of owning 'about 2000 acres'. To his publications previously mentioned, he added *Charm of Birds*. And all that was what brought Europe into its culminating disaster, the Great War. A supreme culture fell victim to absurd amateurishness. I was born in the immediate aftermath.

As I said, my decade is the 1930s, which means I have a lot of difficulty with such Blairite terms as 'racism'. In 2001 *Daily The Telegraph's* Peter Simple wrote –

> For the hundredth time of asking: What is 'racism'? It is certainly a term which no sensible person should use except between inverted commas. Of recent coinage, it is now continually employed to infect the ordinary human awareness of racial differences and in this sense everybody on earth is a 'racist' – with dark stain of Nazi evil. It has been an immensely powerful instrument of thought control.

Earlier, in 1975, *The Daily Telegraph* said that racism, or racialism, or racial discrimination, covered everything from a vile form of monomania to the innocent preference of human beings for association with their own kind. That shows how confused is the meaning of this novel, potent, coinage.

Can the OED help? The current edition equates racism with racialism, which it defines as: belief in the superiority of a particular race leading to prejudice and antagonism towards people of other races, especially those in close proximity who may be felt as a threat to one's cultural and racial integrity or economic well-being. This is unsound, and leaves no room for such ordinary human characteristics as preference, liking, disliking, partisanship, patriotism and so forth. None of these necessarily involves a heartfelt claim of superiority: think of the football supporter. One of the detestable features of the Blairite tendency to damn so many people with the sticky brand 'racism' is its widely indeterminite meaning.

What this tendency has come to is illustrated by the following extract from the *Commons Hansard* for 16 July 1999. The initial speaker was Mr John Greenway, Tory Shadow Home Affairs spokesman. It was a debate on London policing.

> Two weeks ago tomorrow my daughter, Louise, was married in the House of Commons. We had a wonderful day. At 2 o'clock I went to my front door in Gilbert Road, Kennington, to see whether the vintage taxi that we had hired for the occasion had arrived. Indeed it had. Parked alongside it was a police car with a blue flashing light. While the gentleman who drove the taxi had been waiting for the appropriate time to knock on my door to say, 'I have arrived, Mr. Greenway, to take you and your daughter to the House of Commons,' three young black boys aged 15 or 16 on mountain bikes jumped into his cab and robbed him of his bag, his wallet and his driving licence. We could have a debate about what we should be doing to protect cab drivers. However, I have related an experience that occurs all too frequently. I found it astonishing that, in broad daylight-
>
> **Ms Oona King (Bethnal Green and Bow):** Will the honourable Gentleman give way?
>
> **Mr Greenway:** I shall finish the story. I am quite

happy to give way to the honourable Lady. [*Interruption.*] The incident took place in the constituency of the Under-Secretary. I found it astonishing that, in broad daylight in a London street at 2 o'clock in the afternoon such an incident should occur. I have the highest regard for the police officers for the speed with which they came to the incident. They were clearly of the view that such incidents occurred all too frequently. I make no point other than that it is such incidents – everyone knows somebody who has such an experience – that give rise to the fear of crime. That is why it is crucial that the police continue to be able to police in London without fear or favour, notwithstanding what was in the Macpherson report.

Ms King: Has the honourable Gentleman ever mentioned in the House the skin colour of people involved in such incidents when they are white? Is he able to recognise the anger with which his remarks are received? I do not describe Opposition Members as white Members. They are MPs. Will the honourable Gentleman please recognise the anger that he causes when he does this? It is quite disgraceful.

Mr. Greenway: I find the honourable Lady's comment quite disgraceful. I am making no point other than relating to the House an incident that occurred within a mile of the House that is typical of other incidents. The police know – it does no one any good to try to hide this point –

Mr. McNulty: What point?

Mr. Greenway: I have made the point that three 16-year-old coloured boys [*Interruption*] Black boys. The fact that the police know who these people are adds to the situation that we have to face. [*Interruption.*]

Mr. Deputy Speaker (Sir Alan Haselhurst): Order. Perhaps the House should calm down. We will not have shouting from a sedentary position.

Mr. Greenway: I am amazed at the reaction of Labour Members –

Mr. Iain Coleman (Hammersmith and Fulham): Will the honourable Gentleman give way?

Mr. Greenway: No. It is time to wind up, and I have one or two more things to say.

Mr. John Wilkinson (Ruislip-Northwood): Will my honourable Friend allow me?

Mr. Greenway: I give way to my honourable Friend.

Mr. Wilkinson: It is entirely appropriate, is it not, Mr. Deputy Speaker, for an honourable Member, whether from the Front Bench or the Back Benches, to describe the characteristics – [Honourable Members: No, it is not.] – of any suspected criminal, be that person black, white, brown, yellow, long-haired, short-haired or anything else? My honourable Friend was merely describing the participants, as he thought them to be, in an act of violent crime. In that, he is making no other judgment at all.

Mr. Greenway: I am grateful to my honourable Friend. He sums up entirely the point that I am making.

The reference to the Macpherson report betokened a shameful use of the term 'racism' by one who should certainly have known better. He was the Honourable Sir William Macpherson of Cluny, a former High Court judge. His report on a notorious London murder found that the Metropolitan Police were 'institutionally racist'. This slur, adding one very imprecise term to another, thereafter deterred police officers in London from stopping and searching black youths. This led to an increase in street crime, and vividly illustrates the dangers of Blairism.

A Gallup survey in April 2000, limited to people who call themselves English, found that 73 percent said we English are suspicious of foreigners, and 71 per cent believed the English are reserved and like to 'keep themselves to themselves'. That pretty well says it all about allegations of so-called 'racism'. The Macpherson Report is but the latest example of how this nation is losing its marbles over that topic. Evil is equally wrong whether there are so-called racist elements or not. Nearly always there are not.

Zealots can find racism anywhere if they want to. In 1998 the Home Office carried out an internal inquiry and reported many of its own highly respectable staff had 'racist attitudes'. Yet in 1992 a government grant of £71,000 had been paid to encourage the 'immersion' method of teaching English-speaking children Welsh as a second language. Was this not 'racist'? They would have been far better off in the jobs market having learnt French as a second language.

In 1994 the Sunday Times reported that no theatre in Britain will nowadays stage *Othello* without a black actor in the leading role of the moor of Venice. To reserve a part for actors of one ethnic group is a clear form of racism (apart from the fact that according to my 1911 edition of the *Encyclopedia Britannica* moors are essentially a white, not a black, race). In 1995 a *Sunday Times* reporter accused British Airways of being 'racist' because their promotional film showed the airline to be managed and staffed by typical Britons. It would make as much sense to attack Lufthansa because it is run by Germans, or Air India because it is run by Indians, or Aer Lingus because it is run by Irish, or Cyprus Airways because it is run by Cypriots. This is not racism but realism.

When one surveys the whole globe, covering Europe, Asia, Africa, America and Australasia, it is absurd to suppose there are not profound racial-ethnic-cultural differences between peoples from different areas. These are bound to affect our expectations of how a person will behave in varied circumstances. It is but human to prefer to mix with people of one's own racial-ethnic-cultural grouping, simply because one knows in advance what their mindset will be. Before the 1960s it was common to speak of racial prejudice as something faintly regrettable that nevertheless most of us share, like lust, jealousy or ambition. It was accepted as an essential component of human nature. It is still that, but now the understanding has been arbitrarily withdrawn. Ninety-five per cent of the people of England, Scotland, Wales and Northern Ireland are still much the same amalgam of Angles, Saxons, Jutes, Picts, Celts, Gaels and Scandinavians they have been for a thousand years and more. Over the centuries, each element has been treated by the others with 'racism'. We had grown used to it. It was part of life. We accepted it in a grown-up way. Then came political correctness.

I mentioned 'racial-ethnic-cultural grouping'. The essence here is 'culture'. Essentially it is a person's culture that matters to people, not his or her race. That brings us to another of the multitude of Blairite follies, multiculturalism, which I discussed in chapter 29. It is false to human nature because humans have a strong need to support, and be supported by, their own individual culture. Thus Blairism is false to human nature.

I just mentioned another perverse doctrine, which I believe underlies and sums up Blairism – namely political correctness. In 1992 Rob Scriven of the Oxford University Press (OUP) expressed the wish of his masters the Delegates of the Press (all of them Oxford dons) to publish my book entitled *A Dictionary of Political Correctness,* upon which I had bestowed much labour. The book said that the term political correctness has two meanings: a movement or an orthodoxy. For the first meaning I offered the following –

> A reactive linguistic, academic and social movement opposing in combination certain value systems, such as racism, sexism or ageism, which are perceived to be oppressive because based on the stereotyping of some groups as inferior, with consequent discrimination against them.

The orthodoxy was simply an intellectual structure set up and maintained by supporters of the said movement.

My elaborate book gave chapter and verse for all aspects of this strange yet potent philosophy known as political correctness. We were nearing publication, and the presses were humming, when Rob broke the news. The Delegates of the Press did not after all think, having regard to the United States market, that it would be politically correct for the OUP to publish my book. That is what comes of having as one's publisher a world-wide academic organisation. There was nothing more I could say, but there was no harm done. The OUP did not hold it against me, and published another of my books in 2001. But it does make

one wonder about Blairism. I really am worried about
Blairism. I do wish it would go away. But I fear it won't.

As I pen the final words of this chapter the news is
announced of the death, at the age of 101, of Queen
Elizabeth the Queen Mother. I end with the following poem
on that event (also included in my book of collected poems
entitled *Poemotions*).

Dead Queen Mum

*Written on the eve of the funeral of Queen Elizabeth the
Queen Mother at Westminster Abbey, 9 April 2002.*

I

I was born in the year you were married:
I have lived all my time in your life.
So at last you are dead, Queen Mother,
and that is the end of your strife.

A Glamis girl, always a Glamis girl,
you needed a castle for life.
The Castle of Mey you called it:
cutting out the old name with your knife.

By right: you'd changed your own name
when kindly marrying Bert.
The Prince was besotted – who would not be,
at the gifts you could assert.

We have all celebrated those wonders,
and now weep at your funeral gates.
Thousands upon thousands weep for you
and I do too.

We weep for what you meant to us
throughout the century past.
A devilish century it was to be sure -
but you always stood up to the blast.

We cry and cry, all your subjects cry,
at the loss we feel in our skin.
Thank you, oh thank you, for staying so long -
a centre of quiet in the din.

II

Now I must really concentrate,
attempting, before it's all too late,
to sum up what you meant to us
Queen Mum.

You meant the old values,
though you would never have dreamt of saying it.
That's not the way they worked -
the signals in your special eyes.

The old values are no values
in your old subject's eyes of today.
But some of us still remember
what those values had to say.

We won't bury them with you, dear Ma'am,
as tomorrow you sink in the vault.
We have more regard for you than that
and shriek Hallelujah! hail Mary!

You are the best we ever knew.
We look to you to see us through,
even after tomorrow's brew,
in Windsor's civilised vault.

They will pray and pray, and sing away,
and what is wrong with that anyway?
They will sing away all you have to say -
There's a great deal wrong with that.

III

The nitty gritty is not so pretty -
and when it comes down to that:
I'm not a happy chappy, now you Queen Mum have gone.
You walked with me all my days, and I'm sad.

My days will be lonely, now that you've gone.
Who will stand by my values now?
Who will care, anywhere, now that you've gone?
Oh, Oh, I'm the deserted one.

Good-bye Queen Mother, we love you so.
Your crooked smile, the silly hat,
told us all where it's at.
We'll miss you badly, and that's a fact.

IV

One final thought, as I go on my way,
bereft and listless without you:
one final thought, you'll relish I think,
indeed know – I would never doubt you.

This final thought I hug to myself;
it's about your last achievement.
As you sailed away, having done your best,
as you sailed away to Heaven,

Ma'am you spun a jest – and what a jest!
I spotted it here in Devon -
the land where Drake and Raleigh lived,
and the Pilgrim Fathers set sail.

England, Devon means England,
and that is the joy of this jest,
Guardian folk thought England was gone
and so put you Ma'am to rest.

The stupid, slimy *Guardian* folk
rejoiced that you were dead.
'Day five: Queen Mother still dead' they wrote
and their stupid readers believed.

There'll be no one there, no one will come
wrote the stupid Guardian folk:
you conquered Ma'am, they came in bulk;
and that was your crowning stroke.

That was your crowning stroke, hurrah!
over stupid Guardian folk.
That was your crowning stroke, dear Ma'am,
and your very last joke.

70

What *is* Blairism?

Coupled with the detailed Index, the preceding chapters give a pretty full idea of what Blairism is, and the blight it casts. As a final aid to the reader I now set out summaries of some of the key points. Not all of these have been mentioned in the foregoing.

Treachery of the intelligentsia
Blairism is a virulent offshoot of the movement described in Julien Benda's 1927 book *La Trahison des Clercs* (translated by Richard Aldington as *The Betrayal of* [it should be 'by'] *the Intellectuals*), which attacked treachery by the intelligentsia towards the values in which they were reared – otherwise known as fouling one's own nest. In particular the intellectual value betrayed is disinterested scholarship - shockingly undermined by the thought-police monstrosity known as political correctness.

Falsifying of words
Blairism unhesitatingly adopts the technique of falsifying the meaning of words, when that suits it. For example Blairism calls ordinary government spending *investment*, because that sounds thrifty and therefore more prudent.

Feelings
Though it likes to be thought 'touchy-feely', Blairism is not really interested in people's feelings. Whatever a person's actual likes, dislikes, foibles and preferences may be (and we all have them), he or she must toe the line when it comes to Blairite *diktats* over things like racism, homophobia and sexism.

Formative years
Childhood and adolescence are the formative years when the values then current in your society are stamped on your soul or psyche indelibly. Those whose formative years occurred long before the values of Blairism came into

fashion have a very thin time - for which Blairism cares nothing.

Control freakery

Blairism loves to be in control. In other words Blairites are control freaks, not happy when anything is left to individual decision. In particular they love to control and manipulate news of what the Government is doing. Burying Government bad news is their particular forte.

England

The country that gave them birth holds a special position for Blairites – a little below that of every other country in the world.

English accents

The best accent is the one most clearly understood (thankfully BBC newsreaders still retain this characteristic). Blairism is uncomfortable with good accents, which are felt to convey unwelcome messages about the speaker's breeding, good manners, education, and so forth. Blairites prefer to promote people with bad accents such as the present Speaker of the House of Commons (who hails from the Glasgow Gorbals) because they are a walking demonstration of the Blairite philosophy that you don't need elocution lessons to succeed; rather the reverse. To show he believes this, Blair sometimes adopts a bad accent himself when he thinks it will appeal to those he is with.

Patriotism

Patriotism celebrates the indigenous culture. Since Blairism believes that the indigenous British culture has no more validity than any new culture currently represented (however exiguously) in Britain, Blairism has no use for patriotism.

The Queen

In view of her immense popularity with the people, Blairites are cautious how they display their inevitable opposition to Her Majesty. Blair's wife refuses to curtsey to the Queen, as she is supposed to. Blair confines himself to petty gestures like rudely sitting down at an audience *á deux* before the Queen herself does and trying to muscle in on the Queen Mother's funeral.

Honours system
The days of Lloyd George and Maundy Gregory have returned under Blairism, though this time there has to be more subtlety. Nevertheless if you have interests of your own to serve, the honour you get from Blair will be roughly proportionate to the size of your donation to his party.

Quangos
Blairism loves to set up a faceless Quango do what a Government department answerable to the electorate ought to be doing.

Europe
Everyone is uncertain what Britain's place in Europe should be, and whether or not we should join the Euro. True to their claim to excel, Blairites excel in promoting this uncertainty.

Rewriting history
Blairism has such a colossal ego it thinks it can rewrite history. Being also masochistic, it is eager to shoulder blame for supposed wrongs committed by Britons long before any of us were born. It then takes delight in issuing nauseating 'apologies' for these. If not restrained, it will even go on to pay compensation for them - of course out of money that belongs not to Blairites but to the taxpayer.

'Modernising'
Disregarding the salutary maxim if it ain't broke don't fix it, Blairism is determined to 'modernize' everything in sight, thus scrapping the wisdom of the old in favour of the untried, half-baked wheezes of bright-eyed Blairite whizz-kids.

Islam
Muslims have been in a state of war with Christians and Jews since the foundation of Islam in the seventh century,

and now present a greater danger to us than for a long time. Blairism here uses its technique of gaze aversion (look away and pretend it's not so). This has also been found useful in Northern Ireland.

Multifaithism
Blairism believes that all religions should be given equal respect. This is obviously untrue, particularly if you are an adherent of a particular faith. The rot has even spread to our next ruler, Prince Charles, as the following interchange shows.
Francis Bennion to HRH Prince Charles (14 April 2002)
As a constitutional lawyer and former Anglican churchwarden (though presently, for reasons that will appear, an agnostic) I write to express my grave misgivings about the item concerning Your Royal Highness on the front page of today's *Sunday Times*. It is headed 'Charles takes on multifaith role', which immediately raises questions in view of your prospective position as Governor of the Church of England and Head of the Anglican Communion. I will not attempt to summarise the item here, since it is on record.

It seems your multi-faith campaign is to proceed under the name 'Respect'. You indicated in 1994 your intention to reign as 'Defender of Faiths' rather than under your correct title, 'Defender of the Faith'. I protested at the time, and have continued to protest, at this. I repeat my protest now. It is particularly regrettable that 'Respect' is apparently to be launched on the day before Her Majesty addresses Parliament on the occasion of her Golden Jubilee. Many people I have spoken to are incensed about that. It will cause grave offence among British people.

The name 'Respect' apparently indicates that those promoting it think all religious faiths are equally worthy of respect. This is directly contrary to the teaching of Christianity, based on Christ's own words. He said that it was only through Him that sinners could be redeemed and gain access to the presence of God. On that basis Christians endeavoured to convert the heathen through many centuries. I myself worked assiduously for the Church's Mission to the Jews. I have faltered in recent years (now being reduced to calling myself an agnostic) only because the leaders of my Church have wandered from the path I was taught to be true.

The founding of 'Respect' is in line with recent legislation making certain offences more heavily punishable if there is a religious element. This is defined by reference to religious belief or lack of religious belief. On 19 November 2001 the Times published the following from me as its lead letter –

> The Government's Anti-Terrorism, Crime and Security Bill, introduced on November 12, punishes religious hatred. This it describes as hatred against a group of persons 'defined by reference to religious belief or lack of religious belief'.
>
> The Bill does not define 'hatred' or 'religious belief', which are both notoriously inexact. It will be punishable 'religious hatred' to criticise a bunch of atheists. Is this really what we want our laws to do?
>
> The penalty for this newly-invented thought crime will be imprisonment for up to seven years. That might be inflicted on a comic who jeers at so-called religions that chop off a thief's hand or stone to death a woman caught in adultery. Is this really what we want?
>
> Or an earnest do-gooder might be imprisoned for criticising so-called religions that prevent a desperately ill child being given a blood transfusion. Again, is that what we want?
>
> I myself am an agnostic, with no desire to defend atheists who presume to have greater knowledge of the Universe than is given to mankind. I claim the right to criticise them. Do I really deserve to be locked up?
>
> The same goes for the multitude of people who endlessly debate faith, and argue for ever about our place in the cosmos. It is what humans have done from time immemorial.
>
> Will Mr Blair kindly get off our backs?

That letter gives some reasons why a particular religion may not be worthy of respect, indeed may need to be combated. I could cite many more. There are religions that impose female circumcision. There are those that justify forcible arranged marriages. There are those that believe in sun worship, or kneel before the spirits of the trees. There are those founded by charismatic men wholly to channel financial, sexual or other benefits in their own direction. There are cults, and brainwashing. Many so-called religions are fraudulent, and need to be combated not 'respected'. Many pose acute dangers to the body politic.

Some activists will dish up, as an answer to these objections, that we can easily distinguish between false or fraudulent religions and those that are well-established and respectable. That is not so. Some long-established religions advocate practices we British regard as cruel and unciv- ilised. The Muslim Taliban forbade music, whereas music is an icon of our western civilisation. Many Muslim coun- tries, for example Nigeria, believe even today that a woman caught in adultery should be stoned to death. Some Muslim countries are even increasing the severity of their punish- ments for religious transgression. The Hindus believe in a caste system with so-called untouchables at its base.

I hope I have said enough to convince Your Royal Highness that the course you are reported as being embarked upon would be most unwise, and should be changed.

HRH Prince Charles to Francis Bennion (6 June 2002)
The Prince of Wales has asked me to thank you for your letter of 14 April in connection with the new initiative, Respect, and to apologise for the time it has taken to reply. This is due, as I am sure you will appreciate, to the tremendous number of letters His Royal Highness has received following the death of Queen Elizabeth the Queen Mother.

The Prince of Wales is grateful to you for taking the trouble to write as you did and for outlining your concerns. His Royal Highness believes very strongly that the world in which we live can only become a safer and more united place if we all make the effort to tolerate, accept and understand cultures, beliefs and faiths different from our own. The recent terrible events have only served to emphasise one of the eternal and painful lessons of human history – that hatred breeds hatred, and violence breeds violence.

Respect is meant, above all, to be a <u>practical</u> way of supporting and helping the community we all serve through the mobilisation of faith, and encouraging others to do the same. Reflection, tolerance, respect and a readiness to listen to and help our fellow man are - as they always have been – basic and universal requisites of a civilised society. For all those reasons, the more who can be involved in *respect* in a practical way, from all faiths and none, the better.

This comes with The Prince of Wales's prayers and best wishes.

Francis Bennion to HRH Prince Charles (14 April 2002) I am dismayed at your reply, which ignores all my arguments. One cannot have respect for faith just because it is faith. Hitler had faith in National Socialism, and I spent five years of my young life as an RAF pilot fighting that, along with many others. Nor must one tolerate the intolerable.

Finally - Blair's political philosophy
If you think I have had difficulty in spelling out in this book just what the Blairite philosophy is, don't be surprised. Tony Blair himself can't do it. When in 2002 he was directly asked in the House of Commons by one of his own MPs to 'provide the House with a brief characterisation of the political philosophy that he espouses' all he could manage was a few lame words about extra 'investment' in the National Health Service (see pages 276 and 281).

Footnote
Please don't write in and say that some of the above characteristics are occasionally found in the doctrines of other political parties. Regrettably, that is so. But it is with Blair's New Labour party that they flourish in their most concentrated and virulent form. Blairism springs out in so many ways that this book has been able to present only a selection of its manifestations. Every day there are new instances; and I have been quite unable to keep up with them all.

INDEX

abortion. 127
Abse, Leo. 224-226
accents 304
Act of Parliament 28, 81-83
– *and see* bills, parliamentary; statutory interpretation
Adams, Gerry 14-15, 62, 176
'ageism' 27, 66, 126, 221-223
air travel 152
alcohol. 120-121
Allenby, Field-Marshal Viscount 15
Amess, David. 151-152, 240-242
Amin, Idi 159
Amnesty International 175
Anderson, Donald. 264-265
animals 28, 34, 35-37, 125-127
– *and see* direct action; foxhunting; fur-farming
Archer, Jeffrey 36
aristocracy 17, 22
– *and see* House of Lords
Armed Forces, the. 243-246
Ashdown, Paddy 188
asylum seekers 148
Attlee, Clement. 31, 215, 244
Attlee, Earl 244
Attorney General 129-134
Australia 185

Baker, Ken 135, 137
Baldry, Tony 91-94, 228
Banks, Tony 100
Bar of England and Wales 215-217, 222
Barnett, Isobel 49
Barrow, George. 164
Bassam of Brighton, Lord. 54, 83, 238
'beardism' 222-223
Beaumont of Whitley, Lord 53
Begg, Anne 188
Bellingham, Henry 278
Benn, Tony 225, 231-232, 282
Bennion, Thomas Roscoe 212
Bentley, Derek 72-77, 80
Bercow, John 90, 133, 202, 234

Bermingham, Gerald............................. 69-70
Bevan, Aneurin..................................... 14
Beveridge, Sir William 26
bills, parliamentary....... 33-34, 38-39, 41, 53, 58, 59, 102-103
Bindman, Geoffrey 227-229
Bing, Geoffrey.................................... 183
Bingham of Cornhill, Lord 37, 48, 72, 75-76
Blair babes 67, 69-70, 187, 257
Blairism.................. 9-10, 13-18, 27, 28, 50, 76-77, 80,
               88, 91, 93, 119, 129, 133, 147-149, 164-166,
           170, 208, 266-268, 275, 276, 284, 288-300, 304-307
   – and see 'modernising'
Blackstone, Tessa 136-137
Blatch, Baroness.................................. 136
Blunt, Crispin 279
Boateng, Paul 90
Body, Richard 150
Boothroyd, Betty.............. 19, 98-100, 116, 147-149, 230
Bossom, Alfred 54
Bowman, Andrew 162-163
Bridge, Lord 81
British Empire, the................. 7, 32, 176, 184, 190, 293
British Isles..................................... 250
Brittan, Leon.................................... 141
Brogan, Benedict 233
Brown, Chris.............................. 172, 200
Brown, Gordon 19, 135-137, 200, 213, 267, 284
Browne, Desmond 261-262
Browne-Wilkinson, Lord.......................... 219
Bruce, Ian 71
Buchan, Norman.............................. 168-169
Buggins' turn 223
Burford, Earl of................................. 19
Burke, Edmund................................... 26
Burnett, John 130-132, 197-198
Burnham, Lord 243-244
Burns, Lord..................................... 100
Burton, Air Vice Marshal......................... 146
Byers, Stephen 10, 269-281
Byford, Baroness................................ 141

CAFCASS 90
Cairns, David 207-208
Campaign for Real Ale (CAMRA) 145

Campbell, Alastair 147-149, 283
Campbell, Anne. 199
Cannadine, David 11, 13
Canning, George 226
Carey. John. 292
Cecil, Hugh. 292
Cecil, Mirabel 292
Chapman, Ben. 144-145
Charles, Prince of Wales 226
Chesterton, G K 8, 207
Churchill, Winston 9, 54, 268
civil service. 270
Clarke, Charles. 203
Clarke, Ken. 196-197
Clarke, Lord Justice 78-79
class. 11-13, 123-124, 135-137, 184, 293
    – and see – aristocracy
Clifton-Brown, Geoffrey 145
Clyde, Lord 58
Cobbett, William. 138
Coleman, Iain 297
colour prejudice 16-17, 124, 125, 159-163, 166-167, 257-259
Colvin, Michael. 187
Commission for Racial Equality. 125, 130
Commonwealth Parliamentary Association 150
Cook, Robin 235, 264-265
consumer credit. 240-242
control freakery 304
Cope of Berkeley, Lord. 45
Cormack, Patrick 97
Council of Europe. 108-110
countryside, the
    – see animals; foot and mouth disease; foxhunting; fur-
    farming; roam, right to
Cox, Tom. 108-110, 150-151
Craig, Christopher 74
Cranborne, Viscount. 54
Cranston, Ross 102-103, 130, 131, 133
criminal justice –
    conspiracy. 169-173, 199-203
    corporate homicide. 104-107
    Criminal Cases Review Commission 74
    Crown Prosecution Service 129-134, 171
    fair trial, right to 101-102

International Criminal Court............... 34, 174-176
jury system 32-33, 44-49, 75, 133
Probation Service 88-90
– *and see* human rights; police; treason
Cryer, Ann 121
culture......................... 12, 17, 126, 159-167, 299
Cyprus problem.......................... 108-110, 150-151

Dalyell, Tam 203, 236
Danziger, Danny...................................... 292
Davidson, Viscount......................... 22, 31
Davies, Gavyn................................... 16
Davies, Quentin 251-252
Davis, David 177
Davison, Emily Wilding 232
Day, Michael.................................... 125
Day, Stephen.................................... 121
deference.................................... 293
Democracy........................ 9-10, 17, 20, 31, 43, 51,
                86, 94, 98, 172-173, 250, 260-263, 270
Denham, Lord................................ 142-143
Denham, Thomas 32
Denktash, Ralf 150
Denman, Sylvia.................................. 130
Desai, Lord 137
Dewar, Donald 187
Dhanda, Parmjit 257-259
direct action –
    animal rights protests.................... 172, 199-203
    fuel protests 169-173, 200
    'guerrilla gardening'.................... 172, 200
    hunt saboteurs 170
    sport disruption........................... 170
disabled, the 26-28, 125, 126, 287
discipline.................................... 293
discrimination............... 124-128, 130, 164-167, 257-259
    – *and see* religious discrimination
Dismore, Andrew 98, 104-107
Dixon-Smith, Lord........................... 60
domestic sanctuary, principle of................... 193
Donaldson of Lymington, Lord.................. 180-182
Douglas-Mann, Bruce........................... 84-85
drugs..................................... 286-287
Duncan Smith, Iain......................... 98, 272-277

Dunwoody, Gwyneth ('Vinegar Lil') 177-179, 263-265
Durham, Bishop of 115
Dyer, Christopher 292
Dyke, Greg 16

education –
    citizenship, in 10-11
    English literature, in 15-16
    General Teaching Council (GTC) 111-113
    higher 135-137
    information technology (IT) 38
    libraries 218-220
    multicultural 123-124
    Professional Association of Teachers (PAT) 113
    Sarah Bonnell School 95-97
    school terms 53
    specialist schools 95-97
    teachers 11, 95-97, 111-113, 151, 154, 188
    – and see England
Edwards, Huw 175
elections 33, 50-55, 81-83, 159-163, 237-239, 257-262
Élitism 8, 10, 17, 20, 126, 185-186
Elton, Lord 59
England –
    history of 9, 11-12, 46, 88, 131, 158, 165-166, 182, 305
    regional assemblies 189
    undermining of 7, 9, 18, 165, 304
Equitable Life 133-134
Euro 212-214
European Union 13, 165, 190-192, 240, 305
Falconer, Lord 221-222
Farm Animal Welfare Council 118
feelings, personal 294-295, 304
Feldman, Lord 93
Fettes College 8
Filkin, Elizabeth 91-94, 227-229
Fitzpatrick, Jim 133
foot and mouth disease (FMD) 237-239
formative years 292-294, 304
Forth, Eric 186, 208, 209
foxhunting 57, 98-100, 260
    – and see direct action
Freedom Under Law 170
Freemasons 212

fuel protests – *see* direct action
fur farming 35-37, 117-119

Galbraith, Sam 27
Garner, Bryan A 252
Garnier, Edward 103, 130-131, 133
George V, King 293
Ghana 124, 183-184
Gibraltar 250
Gibson, Ian 201-202
Gillis, Judge 170
Glidewell, Lord Justice 130-131
Goddard, Lord 74-75
Goering, Hermann 44
Goodall, David 255
Goodhart, Lord 82-83
Gould of Potternewton, Baroness 239
Gow, Ian 253-255
Granby, Marquess of 146
Gray, James 100, 119
Great War 293-294
Greengross, Baroness 222
Greenway, John 295-297
Gregory, Maundy 22, 91, 184
Grey of Falloden, Viscount 293-294
Grieve, Dominic 69, 152, 179
Griffiths, Nigel 67
Hague, William 19, 67-68, 92, 93,
                    187-189, 191-192, 213, 235-236
Hailsham of St Marylebone, Lord 215
Hain, Peter 170, 174-176
  – *and see* direct action
Hale, Leslie 46-47
Hamilton, Neil 208
Hamwee, Baroness 59-60
Hanham, Baroness 238
Harries, Richard 58
Harris, Evan 153-154, 160
Harte, Bret 29
Hartley, L P 76
Haselhurst, Alan 296
Hawkins, Nick 70
Hayes, John 78
Heald, Oliver 139, 140

Healey, Denis 12, 197
Heap, Desmond 196
Herald of Free Enterprise disaster 104-105
Herbert, A P 175
Heritage, Frank 183
Hewart, Lord. 216
Hewitt, Patricia 38
High Court of Chivalry. 217
history - *see* England
Hogg, Douglas. 63, 99-100
Home of the Hirsel, Lord 114
'homophobia'........ 56-61, 125, 126, 154-155, 180-182, 224-226
Honours system –
    abuse of............................. 91-94, 183-186
    Political Honours Scrutiny Committee 24
    reform of 183-186
    workings of 91-94, 183-186, 305
    – *and see* Gregory, Maundy; Lloyd George, David
Hood, Jimmy. 168-173
House of Commons –
    adjournment debates. 120-122, 150-152
    character of. 26
    clergy disqualification. 207-211
    divisions 178-179
    Irish MPs allowed to be Members of 62-65
    jokes 187-189
    mobile phones 99-100
    oath, refusal to take 62-63, 65
    official box. 46
    pre-eminent chamber, as. 20
    select committees of 39, 106, 263
    Speaker, The. 230-236
    – *and see* Boothroyd, Betty; Dunwoody, Gwyneth; Martin, Michael; Tonypandy, Viscount
    turncoat MPs 84-87
    workings of. 116, 121-122
    – *and see* Filkin, Elizabeth; Parliament
House of Lords –
    bishops 211
    Bishops' Bar 114
    'reform' of 17, 19-25, 27, 29-31
    workings of 114-116
house sales 193-195
Howard, David 166-167

Howarth, George. 81
Howarth, Gerald. 64, 85-87, 200-201, 208, 233
Howe of Aberavon, Lord 197, 217
human rights. 41-43, 69-70, 101-103, 108-110,
126-128, 133, 143, 155, 174, 191-192, 245
 – *and see* speech, freedom of
Hunt, Lord 204
Hutber, Patrick. 12

identity cards 261-262
information technology (IT). 38-40, 91, 151
inspectorates, statutory 131, 134
intelligentsia, the 86, 304
International Criminal Court – *see* criminal justice
'investment'. 266-268
Ireland, Republic of 62-65, 122, 184-185, 248-249
Irvine, Derry. 43, 69, 70, 215-217, 284
Islam 11, 86, 153-154, 159-163, 305
 – *and see* Rushdie, Salman
Israel. 161
Jack, Michael 197-198
Jackson, Glenda 100
Jamaica. 287
James, Lord Justice 170-171
James, P D 136
Janner of Braunstone, Lord 221-222
Jay, Baroness 114-115, 135-137
Jenkins, Roy 47, 135-136, 217
Joad, C E M 49
Johnson, Frank. 232-233
Johst, Hans. 44
Jones, Janet 41, 43
Jowitt, William 215
judiciary 129-131

Kaufman, Gerald. 231
Kemp, Fraser. 184-186
Kennedy, Charles 66, 278
Kennedy, Jane 69-71, 101-102
Kennel Club 151-152
Kennington (Oxfordshire). 219-220
Key, Robert. 208
Khamisa, Mohammed 159-163
Kidney, David. 70-71

King, Oona 295-297
Kingham, Tessa............................... 257-258
King's Cross fire 104
Kinsey, Alfred................................. 201-202
Kumar, Ashok................................... 122

La Trahison des Clercs 304
Latin 72-73, 123
law............................ 42, 72-73, 97, 127, 183,
                        191-192, 196-198, 215-216, 249
– and *see* tax law, improving
Law Commission............................. 105, 171
Lawrence, Stephen 85
Learned Hand, Judge 32-33
Leigh, Edward................................ 153-154
Lester of Herne Hill, Lord 41, 42
Letts, Quentin.................................... 232
Lewis, Julian.............................. 86, 174-176
libraries – *see* education
Lilley, Peter 198
Livingstone, Ken..................... 36, 98-100, 149
Lloyd George, David............................. 22
Lloyd-Hughes, Trevor............................ 148
local government 56-57, 82, 219, 237-239
London –
    Greater London Authority 36, 139
    Lord Mayor of................................. 37
    Mayor of 36-37, 282 ....
    – *and see* Livingstone, Ken
    policing of................................. 138-140
Long, Huey 289
Longford, Lord 205
Lord Chancellor 69-71
    – *and see* Irvine, Derry
Love, Andrew 150
Lund, Thomas.............................. 224, 227
Lyell, Nicholas 48, 131

McDonagh, Margaret............................. 53
McDonagh, Siobhain 211
McGuinness, Martin.............................. 176
MacKay, Andrew 278-279
Mackay of Ardbrecknish, Lord 54
Mackay of Clashfern, Lord........................ 215

Mackenzie of Framwellgate, Lord 222
Mackinlay, Andrew 102
McLoughlin, Patrick. 79-80
MacManaway, James 210
Macpherson, William (of Cluny) 297
Mactaggart, Fiona 202
McWalter, Tony 276, 281
McWilliam, John 263-264
Maginnis, Ken 64
Major, John 11, 91
Mandelson, Peter 247-249, 284
Marchioness disaster. 78-80
Margaret, HRH Princess 271-272
Marti, José 172-173
Martin, Michael ('Gorbals Mick') . . . 188-189, 230-236, 279-281
Mates, Michael 64-65
Maurois, André. 220
Maxwell-Fyfe, David. 78
May, Lord Justice. 73
media, the 263
Media Monitoring Unit 148
Megarry, Robert 48
Metric Martyrs 83
Michael, Alun. 68
millennium, the. 32
Miller, Andrew 169
Milne, A 91-94
Milton, John 45
'modernising'. 15, 22-23, 32, 33-34, 39-40,
                                        56, 59, 67, 139, 178-179, 305
moneylending *see* consumer credit
Monro of Langholm, Lord 238, 244-245
Moore, Jo 269-281, 289
Moran, Lord 142
Morgan, Rhodri. 68
Morley, Elliott 35, 117-119
morning-after pill 204-206
Morris, Estelle 95-97
Morris, John 187
Morris, Lord 137
Mortimer, John. 152
Mowbray and Stourton, Lord. 223
Mowlam, Mo ('Daft Mo') 177-178, 282-287
Mugabe, Robert 7, 10, 14, 124, 283, 288

'multiculturism'. 46, 85-86, 122-128, 151, 162, 299
Muslims
  – *see* Islam

National Health Service.   14
Neill of Bladen, Lord   51
New Zealand.   193
Nkrumah, Kwame.   183-184
Nolan, Lord. 51, 172, 200-201
Norfolk, Duke of.   57-58
Northern Ireland. 13, 14, 109-110, 122, 176,
                    178, 247-256, 260-262, 282-287, 305
Oaten, Mark   121-122
O'Brien, Mike 100, 208
O'Connell, Daniel   32
O'Neill, Onora.   134
Onslow, Earl of.   245
open government.   239
Opik, Lembit   100
Oxford University 8-9, 135-137, 144

Palmer, Nick.   28
Parekh of Runneymede, Lord   54
parish councils   61
Parliament –
  ceremonial of.   32
  impeachment of magnates   216
  Queen's Speech 32-34, 187-189, 247
  women in.   257-259
  – *and see* Act of Parliament; bills, parliamentary;
  House of Commons; House of Lords
Parliament Acts 20, 180-182
Parliamentary Counsel 34, 39, 59, 183, 221
Parris, Matthew 232, 266-268
patriotism 286, 305
Peel, Robert. 138, 139
pensions. 26-28, 66-67
Performance and Innovation Unit   221
Peston, Maurice   114-115
Peyton, Lord   58-60
Phillips, Morgan.   177
Philpot, Oliver   145-146
Pierrepoint, Albert   74
Pindar, Peter.   84

police. 138-140, 199-203, 295-297
political correctness –
    Armed Forces, and 243-246
    general 14, 125-126, 165, 167, 221, 299-300
    jury trial 48
    Parliament. 257
    – *and see* 'ageism'; 'beardism'; colour prejudice; disabled, the; discrimination; 'multiculturism'; 'racism'; religious discrimination; 'sexism'
political parties –
    candidates, selection of. 159-163
    control of. 50-55
    financing of. 52-55, 272-275
politics. 289
Powell, Jonathan 284
Prentice, Gordon. 23-24, 70, 96, 230
Prescott, John. 78-79, 188, 287
Prime Minister's Questions 66-68
Primarolo, Dawn. 197
professionalism 71, 111, 115, 133, 224, 227
pub names. 144-146
Putin, Vladimir. 14

Quangos –
    Appointments Commission. 22-25
    Crown Prosecution Service Inspectorate. 129-134
    general 22, 129, 305
    Metropolitan Police Authority (MPA). 139
    university 137
Queen Elizabeth the Queen Mother. 300-303
Queen Elizabeth II 13, 22, 31, 32-34,
                           176, 215, 225, 284-285, 305
    – *and see* Parliament; royal prerogative

'racism' 85, 125, 126, 130, 148, 162, 294-299
    – *and see* colour prejudice
railways. 121, 267, 277
Raynsford, Nick 194
redistribution 12
Redwood, John 198, 209
Rees-Mogg, Lord. 30-31, 212-214
referendums. 50-55, 213
Reid, John. 250-253, 256
religious discrimination 153-158, 165-166, 305-307

Renton Committee 196
Renton, Lord.................................. 216
Richard, Ivor................................. 41
roam, right to 141-143
Rodgers of Quarry Bank, Lord................. 115
Rolfe, F W (Baron Corvo)..................... 16
Romania 272-275
Roper, Lord.................................. 244
Rowe, Andrew................................ 151
royal prerogative 23, 269
Ruddock, Joan 78
Ruffley, David 196
Rushdie, Salman............................ 154, 156-158

St Albans, Bishop of......................... 205-206
St John of Fawsley, Lord 263
Salmond, Alex............................... 236
Salter, Martin.............................. 150
Sanctuary Housing Association............... 159
Sayer, John................................ 113
Scarman, Lord.............................. 81
Scotland –
    monoculture 122
    Parliament.............................. 101, 254
Scott, C P 148
Scott of Needham Market, Baroness 237-238
Scriven, Rob 299
Scrivener, Anthony......................... 72
Seafield, Earl of 29
Seccombe, Baroness 57
'section 28'............................... 56-61
Sex Discrimination Act.................... 42, 125
'sexism' 125, 126, 243-246
    – and see Parliament
sexual ethics 158, 180-182, 204-206
Shakespeare, William..................... 15
Sheen, Mr Justice........................ 104-105
Shersby, Michael 163
Shrimpton, Michael 83
Singer, Mr Justice 86
Sixsmith, Martin......................... 271-272, 275, 279-280
Skegness 150
Skidelsky, Lord.......................... 135, 137
Skinner, Dennis 133-134

Smith, Chris 144-145, 218-220, 285
Smith, F E. 207
Smyth, Glen. 140
Society of Public Teachers of Law (SPTL). 171
solicitors 70-71, 195, 224-229
Southwark, Bishop of 205, 225
speech, freedom of. 155-158
special advisers. 149
 – and see Moore, Jo
Spence, Laura 135-137
spin doctors. 147-149
 – and see special advisers
Standards in Public Life, Committee on 51-52
Statute Law Society 196, 216
statutory interpretation 41-42, 59, 181
Steiner, Peter 125
Stevens, John 139-140
Stone, Michael 286
Strategic Communications Unit. 148
Strathclyde, Lord 114-115
Straw, Jack 45-48, 51-52, 89, 138-140, 199-203, 284
Surtees, Robert Smith. 98
Symons, Baroness 245

Taverne, Lord 84-85
tax law, improving 196-198
Taylor, Ian 203
Tebbit, Lord 222
temptation. 290-291
Tennyson, Alfred Lord 165, 184
terrorism 19, 33
Thatcher, Margaret 11, 101, 243
Thomas, Gareth. 120
Thomas of Gresford, Lord. 46
Thompson, E P 292-293
Thoreau, Henry David 268
Tipping, Paddy 24-25, 151
Tonypandy, Viscount 224-226
Tooley, Cauthar Maryam Latif. 95
treason 256
Turner, Andrew. 279-280
Tyler, Paul 152

United States 123, 153-154, 157, 175, 190, 270

values, personal 292-293
Vaz, Keith................................. 55, 227-229
Vis, Rudi 150-151

Waddington, Lord............................. 116
Wakeham, Lord................................ 23
Walmsley, Baroness 206
Waterson, Nigel 195
Welsh Assembly 68
Whitty, Lord 56-60, 141
Widdecombe, Anne ('Doris Karloff')............ 199, 208-209
Wilkinson, John 297
Williams of Mostyn, Lord..................... 45
Willis, Phil 97
Windham, William 84
Winnick, David.............................. 52, 209
Winterton, Ann.............................. 145
Winterton, Nicolas 230
Woodward, Shaun............................. 84-87
word hijacking 164-166, 266-268, 304
world government............................. 13-14
World of Property Housing Trust 159

Yacoub, Magdi 276
Young, Baroness......................... 136, 137, 204-206
Young, George 24, 52
Young, Lord 206
Young, Robin 145

Zaiwalla, Sarosh 91-94, 228-229